THE FABRIC OF OUR LIVES

THE
FABRIC
OF OUR LIVES

THE STORY OF
fabindia

RADHIKA SINGH

PENGUIN
VIKING

VIKING

Published by the Penguin Group

Penguin Books India Pvt. Ltd, 11 Community Centre, Panchsheel Park,
New Delhi 110 017, India

Penguin Group (USA) Inc., 375 Hudson Street, New York, New York 10014, USA

Penguin Group (Canada), 90 Eglinton Avenue East, Suite 700, Toronto,
Ontario, M4P 2Y3, Canada (a division of Pearson Penguin Canada Inc.)

Penguin Books Ltd, 80 Strand, London WC2R 0RL, England

Penguin Ireland, 25 St Stephen's Green, Dublin 2, Ireland
(a division of Penguin Books Ltd)

Penguin Group (Australia), 250 Camberwell Road, Camberwell,
Victoria 3124, Australia (a division of Pearson Australia Group Pty Ltd)

Penguin Group (NZ), 67 Apollo Drive, Rosedale, North Shore 0632,
New Zealand (a division of Pearson New Zealand Ltd)

Penguin Group (South Africa) (Pty) Ltd, 24 Sturdee Avenue, Rosebank,
Johannesburg 2196, South Africa

Penguin Books Ltd, Registered Offices: 80 Strand, London WC2R 0RL, England

First published in Viking by Penguin Books India 2010

Copyright © Fabindia 2010

10 9 8 7 6 5 4 3 2 1

ISBN 9780670084340

Typeset in Goudy Old Style by SŪRYA, New Delhi
Printed at Manipal Press Ltd, Manipal

For the craftspersons who constitute the 'heart' of India

Contents

Foreword

Fabindia was founded out of the passion my father had for the incredible craft traditions of India. He believed that they needed a market so that the producers could make a decent living practising their craft.

Fifty years later Fabindia is doing the same thing. *The Fabric of Our Lives* is the story of that journey spanning half a century.

Books on businesses usually follow a narrative of moving from one big event to another. In our story Radhika has focused on the people, on the everyday work and decisions that built, what is today, one of India's best-loved brands. At the end of the day any business is about its people, their motivations and the way they deal with the different situations that give a company its character.

One of the strange things about companies is that their characters communicate themselves to their customers. If you remain true to your ideals over time, word gets out. Remaining true to one's principles is hard in our fast-changing, fad-obsessed world and this is the story of how we have done just that.

If you are looking for management theories you won't find them here. What you will find instead is a human-scale story and that I believe is why we are who we are.

William Bissell

Author's Note

One evening in July 2006 I crossed William Bissell in a park in south Delhi. Chatting easily about the wonderful old trees of Delhi we decided to walk together. Along the way he casually asked me if I had any ideas about a special product to celebrate Fabindia's fiftieth anniversary coming up in 2010.

Equally casually I responded with as many ideas as poured out of my mouth regarding one of my favourite retail companies. 'I could do so many exciting things with Fabindia,' I said, as a peacock call ended my stream-of-consciousness volubility. 'So send me a concept note,' said William as we parted company. 'Was he being serious?' I wondered, but decided to work on a concept while deep, warm thoughts stirred my memory. Writing my first proposal for Fabindia's fiftieth birthday I relived part of my history.

Fifty Years of Fabindia: A Family Album

The legend of John Bissell

I first met Santa Claus in 1960, when I was six years old. He was tall and jolly, and visited us every year after the nativity play performance on Christmas day. Once he rode a camel and distributed sweets from a large red bag which was held high above our heads. At least that's the way I remember it.

This was at Playhouse, a nursery school established by Bim Bissell. Bim was my first teacher and 'Santa Claus' was her husband, John Bissell. Since then, I have never been able to disassociate John from Santa Claus in my mind.

Sixteen years later in 1976, I walked into a newly opened store in Delhi and bought my first kurta, establishing my identity with hundreds of other Delhi University students as the '70s flower-power generation. We wore jeans and kurtas, chappals and jholas, and 'made love not war'! Since then, I have worn a white kurta–pyjama (men's section!) every night. For thirty-four years.

That store was Fabindia, John Bissell's first retail outlet in Delhi, in Greater Kailash's hitherto unknown N-block market. As Fabindia evolved into India's most iconic garments and home furnishings company, the legend of John Bissell was born. N-block market became synonymous with Fabindia. All the other shops were either next to, opposite, behind, before, or between Fabindia.

Now it is referred to as the GK-1 Fabindia market.

In 1983 I moved to the high-altitude Kinnaur valley in Himachal Pradesh with my first husband, Vivek, who had been posted there as deputy commissioner. The DC's residence was a beautiful house in the village of Kalpa, situated at a height of 10,000 ft, with the awesome 20,000 ft Kinner Kailash ridge in our faces. While discussing the logistics of furnishing our home from that remote, phone-less, 500 km-from-Delhi mountain paradise, we discovered a letter in the office files written by the first collector,

Nalini Jayal, in the late '60s, to her friend John Bissell in New Delhi. The letter contained precise measurements and drawings of the windows, doors and the furniture in the DC's house, all of which were still entirely valid, twenty years later. John Bissell's reply, also filed, had some sample swatches attached with detailed notes describing how to use the material.

Vivek and I photocopied that letter, attached the swatches we wanted, and wrote a letter to John Bissell asking him to repeat the same exercise for us. We suggested delivery by the Delhi–Kalpa bus which left Delhi every night at 10 p.m., and took seventeen hours to complete the journey. A week later we received his reply. John Bissell had not forgotten that house, the furnishings, or his friend, Nalini Jayal! He was delighted with the coincidence, and the chance to refurnish the DC's residence in Kalpa. Six weeks later a large packet arrived by bus, with curtain and upholstery material. We had also sent a copy of that letter to Nalini Jayal. One year later, in the summer of 1984, Nalini Jayal drove up to Kalpa and stayed with us for a few days, with his family. My daughter was a few months old. He wept because the house looked exactly the same as it did when he had set it up in 1969. His son Rupin had grown up in that house.

Twenty years on, my flat in New Delhi is a Fabindia home. John Bissell is no more but 'Santa Claus' lives in my furnishings, furniture and crockery. I still sleep in a white kurta-pyjama (men's section). My daughter Ishita is wearing Fabindia (short) kurtas. A few months ago, my oldest and most beloved teacher, Bim, came over for dinner. Surrounded by the colours of Fabindia, she exclaimed, 'My God, do we make ALL this?!!'

So you see, the legend of John Bissell is woven into the warp and weft of my life.

Radhika Singh
First student, Playhouse School
Lifelong customer, Fabindia
New Delhi
30 July 2006

I suggested that the company produce a book to commemorate the fifty years defining its history and narrate personal stories from all the protagonists in the Fabindia saga. In my mind it was already a 'family album'. The proposal was emailed to William in August 2006 and I forgot about it. One year later, in the same park, William asked me if I was ready to start the project. And so I did.

July 2010 **Radhika Singh**

·1·

A BIOGRAPHY OF THE BEGINNING
1890-1960

One morning a young woman was just settling into her desk at the Cottage Industries Emporium in New Delhi. The office was on the second floor of the World War II barracks that housed both the Cottage Industries and the Handloom and Handicrafts Board. The day before had been a holiday, celebrating eleven years of India's independence from British rule, and national optimism was invigorating the team at the office. Her boss walked in and informed her that an American was expected to work as a consultant to the team. He had been brought in on a Ford Foundation grant to advise the government on reworking the design and marketing skills of the people working in the handloom sector in India, so that their products could compete in the international market. Remarking on the paucity of space in the office building, the boss requested Bim to give up her room to the consultant. 'He won't last long', he said to her reassuringly and said she could return to her desk when he left. 'And when will this young man arrive?' asked Bim, hoping to clear some of her work in the next few weeks. 'Oh, he'll be coming in today,' said the boss casually as he left the room. As Bim gazed at her boss's departing back in disbelief, someone came bounding up the wooden staircase leading to the second floor of the building. The staircase was a temporary structure and most other people climbed it gingerly. A short while later a young man, wearing a wide grin under a crew-cut head of hair, a seersucker suit and penny loafers, strode into her room. 'Hi,' he said, 'I'm John.'

The date was 16 August 1958, and the boss, Lakshmi Jain, was to be proved wrong. John Bissell stayed on. In fact, he never left. Two years later he started a company called Fabindia which slowly became synonymous with the revival of handloom in India. Fifty years on it is a household name in India with shops in every city supplying furnishings, floor coverings, bed and kitchen linen, furniture, organic food and beauty products, jewellery and a large range of apparel for men, women and children. This is its story.

To follow the history of John Bissell's tryst with India, we have to go back about a century. The Bissells, an old New England family, had traces of India running through three generations down to John Bissell. This was an unusual coincidence for an American family of the time. How strongly these connections affected John Bissell is conjecture, but it is a thread worth following because it ultimately led him to India.

John's grandfather, Richard Mervin Bissell, moved from Chicago to Hartford, Connecticut, in the 1890s. Having started as an insurance agent, he worked his way up the ladder rapidly, soon becoming president of the Hartford Fire Insurance Company, one of the largest insurance firms in the US. He grew his business successfully, and built an imposing office building in Hartford that bears testimony to his name. It follows therefore that Richard M. Bissell became a very wealthy man who then married Marie Truesdale a little later in his career. Looking for a suitable home for his family, Richard bought a large, eclectically designed mansion in Hartford from a man named Samuel Clemens in 1903. Samuel Clemens, or Mark Twain as he was later known to the world, had hired a well-known architect to design the house for him in 1873. It was built in a style both 'whimsically idiosyncratic' and modern, with the interiors interestingly inspired by the East, as described by the Mark Twain Museum Trust that restored the house and has been maintaining the building as a National Historic Landmark since 1963. The website, marktwainhouse.org, records:

> This commitment to experimentation is also revealed in the exotic and provocative interiors designed by Louis Comfort Tiffany and his partners in Associated Artists. Cultures and styles from around the globe are celebrated and reinterpreted in the dense network of pattern, texture, and colour throughout the first floor of the house. Northern Africa, the Far East and India are woven together in a bravura performance of a knowing and elegant eclecticism that helped set a new standard . . .

In 1896, Mark Twain, travelling extensively around the world, spent four months in India, and was soon to write eloquently about his fascination for and romance with the country in *Following the Equator: A Journey Around the World*. The book was published in 1916 and is replete with colourful descriptions of his complete enchantment with India. A passage from it reads:

> This is indeed India! The land of dreams and romance, of fabulous wealth and fabulous poverty, of splendour and rags, of palaces and hovels, of famine and pestilence, of genii and giants and Aladdin lamps, of tigers and elephants, the cobra and the jungle, the country of a hundred nations and a hundred tongues, of a thousand religions and two million gods, cradle of the human race, birthplace of human speech, mother of history . . . the one sole country under the sun that . . . all men desire to see and having seen once, by even a glimpse, would not give up that glimpse for the shows of all the rest of the globe combined.

Richard and Marie's first child, William Truesdale Bissell, was a year old when the family shifted to the Mark Twain house at 351 Farmington Avenue, Hartford, and his two siblings, Anne Carolyn and Richard Mervin (Junior) were born there. Though not corroborated in any way, it is an interesting thought that Richard Bissell's family might have followed the writings of Mark Twain not only because he became a reputed American author but because of their association with his house. The family lived there from 1903 to 1917, and William T. Bissell spent a large part of his childhood growing up in a space influenced by oriental design. Richard and Marie maintained a stylish lifestyle typical of affluent New England families of the time, with liveried chauffeurs and lots of servants. William, Anne Carolyn, Richard and their mother, Marie Truesdale, are shown posing very theatrically in the conservatory of the Mark Twain house in a photograph dated 1909 found in the archives of the Museum. Marie Truesdale was an extremely elegant, social and sophisticated woman, and lived long after her husband passed away in 1941. In fact she shared a very warm and close relationship with her grandchildren, as is evident from letters exchanged between her and her first grandchild, John Bissell, right until 1960.

Congratulating John on his twenty-first birthday while he was with the navy during the Korean War, she writes in a beautiful, flowing hand on 23 March 1952:

> I have found many joys in all the different stages of life—
> even the advanced one in which I now find myself. And
> one of the greatest is in my grandchildren. I am very proud
> of you and I love you very much. All my blessings.
>
> Granny

William T. Bissell (Bill) finished his studies at Yale, and married Elinor Latane in 1930 in Paris. Their son, John Bissell, was born in 1931, and daughter, Marie, a few years later. Elinor Latane also belonged to a fairly large family, with her mother having married twice. So she had three stepbrothers, and Bill had his two siblings, Anne Carolyn and Richard (Junior). By the time all of them married and had children, there was a third generation of more than a dozen cousins. The family maintained close ties with each other throughout their lives. Most of this extended Bissell clan have had a privileged childhood, studied in prep schools and Ivy League colleges in Connecticut, and are liberal democrats who still hold strong their New England values of community service and belief in the ideal of an egalitarian society. In a letter dated 1 April 1956 to his parents, John was to write of being surrounded by 'acute stimuli making you want to accomplish more, [to] start helping to make the world a better place to live.'

After graduating from Yale, Bill Bissell attended Trinity College in Cambridge and then the Sorbonne in Paris. In 1927 he started his career as a reporter with the *New York Herald Tribune*. In 1933 he helped raise money to start *Newsweek* magazine, and then worked there as an editor for several years. He became a member of the Foreign Economic Administration in Washington DC during the Price Administration and worked in the department of Indian Affairs (now called Native American Affairs) between 1943 and 1946. What followed was another series of interesting coincidences. Bill Bissell was a contemporary of Chester Bowles in Yale between 1921 and 1925, and the two were good friends. Bowles became administrator of the Office of the Price Administration during World War II, between 1943 and 1946, and asked Bill to work with him. Bill Bissell was sent to India for several months in 1944 in connection with the Lend Lease Agreement, a legislation enacted by the Congress in 1941 that empowered the US to sell, transfer, lend or lease war supplies to American allies during World War II. India, as part of the British Empire, was contributing forces and supplies to the war effort, and Bill came to administer the deal. According to his daughter Marie Prentice, he was very impressed with India:

> My father went to India and he had a fantastic time and great adventures. And he came back and told us all about them including meeting the Maharaja and Maharani of

Jaipur, which he thought was pretty terrific. He took photographs, and colour photography for amateur camera people was just coming in, and I remember the vividness of colour in India. I think that's what struck us all, the fabrics that everyone wore and of the colourful life there.

Other than experiencing India in a romantic way, Bill seems to have met up with Mr Birla whose jute mills, supplying jute bags for war supplies, were benefitting hugely from World War II. The idea of hand-woven material was to return to him ten years later. Bill Bissell's India connection did not end with his trip. When he was working with the Foreign Office in Washington, between 1940 and 1945, the deputy head of the Price Administration was John Kenneth Galbraith. Bissell and Galbraith obviously connected at that time. So Bill had two powerful friends in the US administration, both of whom became very close to India over the next twenty years. Chester Bowles was appointed US Ambassador to India first between 1951 and 1953, and then again between 1963 and 1969. John Galbraith was ambassador to India between 1961 and 1963.

Bill Bissell had already put in place several ties with India by the time his son John graduated from Yale in 1949.

John served in the US navy between 1951 and 1954, during the Korean War. The mission involved operations in the seas around Japan, and trips to bases in Guam and Japan were John's first exposure to the East. In October 1953 there is a letter written by Bill to John, who must have been on a short vacation to the navy base in San Francisco, informing him that he and Elinor were considering starting a business importing consumer goods from India. He requested John to examine the quality of imported Indian goods selling in the stores in San Francisco. John found nothing of worth other than the usual traditional handicrafts in ivory, brass and wood, and that was his first exposure to Indian products.

Bill had retired early to fulfil his desire to be a writer.

Thereafter he remained interested and curious about many things and wrote several letters to John about starting a business. Marie talks about her father:

> He really wanted to be a writer. He retired early so he could write plays. They never got produced but he worked very hard at them. He was a good writer and some of his greatest writings are his letters.

Bill's visit to India had sparked his interest in the colourful fabrics that he had seen there, and he decided to try his hand at import. In a letter to John he mentions having met Mrs B.K. Nehru in Washington (her husband was the Indian ambassador to the US), and she told him that the Indian government was keen on promoting the export of handicrafts to the US. She even showed him samples of Indian embroidery brought from the Cottage Industries Emporium in Delhi. At that time embroidered crafts attracted a 90 per cent import duty, so they could not be competitively priced for retail in the US. Father and son exchanged numerous letters over this idea in late 1953 while John was still with the navy. Bill saw too many difficulties and finally abandoned the plan. But John was to pick it up again, a year later.

It is really interesting to note that the Cottage Industries Emporium in Delhi had already entered John Bissell's life in 1953 (through Mrs B.K. Nehru), five years before he bounded up the stairs of the barracks in which it was housed that Saturday in August 1958! As the story unfolds, it is evident that every step from this stage was leading him towards some sort of association with India.

On 3 March 1954 John sent a letter to his father indicating concern for his own future. It is relevant to note that Chester Bowles had just returned from his first assignment as ambassador to India. His daughter Cynthia, a few years older than John, moved to India with her parents in 1951, and studied at the university at Shantiniketan in West Bengal. She was to write her book, *At Home In India*, in 1956, detailing her experience as an American student in India. The Bissell family had followed the Bowles' story in India with great interest. Marie said that stories about India 'inspired our imagination'. In his letter John wrote:

> Please give my best to the Bowles and ask Chet [as Chester Bowles was addressed by those close to him] if he could use the services of a capable leg man with charming discriminatory tastes and an insight into all the problems and solutions of any country in the world. I like to travel, meet people ... and will be available around 15th July having completed my assignment.

John left the navy in mid-1954 and became a salesman involved with the import trade in the West Coast. Along with a friend he bought handcrafted items from importers to sell to select stores at an average commission of 12 per cent. The two young salesmen travelled around the country trying to market handcrafted products from Hong Kong, Japan, Siam and India. For six months John moved from one city to another, from the West Coast to the East, in the US. In a letter dated 15 June 1954, John wrote of the following items:

> There was a 'complete line of rattanware: baskets, chairs, tables, handbags, and magazine racks'. There were bamboo objects, including Nagochi lamps from Japan, black and silver hand-engraved jewellery, brass and 'hand-blocked print goods, bedspreads, cashmere scarfs, turquoise jewellery, silk scarfs, ivory pieces and wood inlay.'

John learned about the trade talking to store owners who were concerned about the US trade-tariff policy. The importers were not organized enough to lobby the government to abolish or even lower tariffs. Another major impediment was the inconsistent supply of products from the manufacturers in Japan and India. The next year John joined the management training programme at Macy's, a large department store in New York, and worked there for a year and a half. He impressed the head of the Marketing department, Mr Leo Martinucci, and developed a close relationship with him that was to last a lifetime. But soon he was writing to his grandmother, telling her of his 'intention to think seriously about leaving Macy's by next fall', in a letter dated 25 March 1956. What is really interesting about this time is the fact that John was already so focused on the retail business, and his letters portray the evolution of his ideas about developing product lines, understanding customers and holding long-term buyer equity. In the same letter he continued:

> The volume of traffic and the complexity of operation in a large store is such that . . . merchandising executives like myself really don't learn very much about what they are selling to the public . . . There is very little standard policy in many of the departments; instead of developing and holding a large steady group of customers the trend seems to be for the quick one-time sale.

And further, 'Running along in all of this thinking is of course the idea of Foreign Trade; I am still as keen as ever on it, and getting more and more impatient to get started.' Mentioning India he wrote, 'I am afraid it will be sometime before I am able to get over to that part of the world. But I feel that I have enough experience now to be a pretty good salesman for some good importing house.'

And then more clarity from John Bissell in a letter to his parents on 1 April 1956 formulating his guiding principles for running a retail store. The context is a business begun by his mother a while ago. She had opened the Canton Green Store in Canton, Connecticut, close to where they lived, and was retailing mainly children's clothing. John's letter states:

> We constantly antagonize customers by being out of something, because we spread ourselves so thin and change

merchandise so fast in this fantastic effort for more business ... [leading] to a quite sharp and noticeable quality drop in the last few years ... The longer I stay with a big store the more confidence I develop in the strength of a small store, particularly in complicated lines such as apparel or anything where the personal and individual touch is important.

We know that John left Macy's and joined Far Eastern Fabrics in September 1956 and worked with them till July 1958. In his own words, Far Eastern Fabrics was a New York importer of handloom and hand-printed cottons and silks from India, Thailand and Japan. They sold to the ready-to-wear, home furnishings and accessory industries in the US. He says that it was an opportunity to see where and how the unusual, fairly high-priced, limited-quantity and highly styled fabrics were outsourced and used. Dealing with Thai silk at Far Eastern Fabrics, John would have been influenced by Jim Thompson who was living in Bangkok and had already established a reputation for organizing indigenous silk weavers into a successful business venture. The store on Madison Avenue in New York would definitely have been importing silk from the Thai Silk Co. Ltd.

Jim Thompson had arrived in Bangkok in 1945 a few days after the end of World War II, as a member of the Allied forces. Japan's sudden surrender had ended the war but Thompson stayed on in Thailand, captivated by a world he had never encountered before. An architect by profession, he initially joined a venture to renovate the Oriental Hotel, but soon moved to collecting old pieces of Thai silk. Within a few years he had located traditional Thai silk weavers, studied the techniques and produced enough samples to dazzle New York's sophisticated world of taste makers. In 1950 he set up shop in Bangkok and founded the Thai Silk Company to export silk to the US.

There is an amusing story that John related to Bim about one of his projects at Far Eastern Fabrics, which focused his attention on the problems facing US importers. The company was contracted to import fabric for costumes for a Hollywood film. *Anna and the King of Siam* had a huge cast of characters including the king, his hundred wives and their three hundred children. All the costumes were to be made with fabric imported from India and John made two important discoveries while in charge of this project. While appreciating the colour range and quality of handcrafted fabric from India, he realized that it was impossible to get consistency in colour or design when ordering large quantities. For instance, in trying to get matching saris for the wives, John found that he could barely import enough fabric for two saris in the same shade of blue. Even at that time he felt convinced that with suitable financing, guidance and training, Indian weavers would be able to have consistency of quality and sell anywhere in the world.

In the meantime, having gained independence, the government in India was struggling with huge problems of a fractured rural economy and the job of resettling millions of citizens displaced by the partitioning of the country. Right through the Free India movement, Gandhi had been stressing on the urgent need to rejuvenate village industry. British policies had turned agrarian India into a supplier of raw materials to feed their own industry and artisans had lost their livelihood. Gandhi wrote in *Young India* in 1920:

> I feel convinced that the revival of hand spinning and hand weaving will make the largest contribution to the economic and moral regeneration of India. The millions must have a simple industry to supplement agriculture. Spinning was the cottage industry years ago, and if the millions are to be saved from starvation, they must be enabled to introduce spinning in their homes, and every village must repossess its own weaver.

Following this ideology, during the First Five Year Plan (1951–56), the government allocated substantial funds for the development of village and small industries, and set up a network of All India Boards to deal with problems of the handloom, khadi and handicraft sectors. There were serious obstacles in enhancing the productivity of village units. Craftsmen and artisans did not have enough finance to procure raw material, the distribution structure was clearly inadequate, and the market was not interested in supporting outdated product styles. The Second Five Year Plan focused on setting up large-scale industries to supply the essential building-blocks of infrastructure while simultaneously working on a formula to revive the handloom and handicraft industry. The All India Handicrafts Board had already been set up in 1952 under the guidance of Kamaladevi Chattopadhyay to find solutions for this industry. Another government organization, the Cottage Industries Emporium, had been started in 1950 to provide a platform for traditional Indian handicraft and handloom textiles. But by now it was very clear that expert guidance was essential to tailor products to modern aesthetics and usage, especially for export.

The Cottage Emporium was housed in one of the old British Army barracks in Connaught Place, New Delhi. The Handicrafts Board's office was located on the second floor of the same building and Lakshmi Jain was the member secretary of the Board in 1958. He was in touch with the Ford Foundation which had established an office in Delhi in 1952 at the request of the Indian prime minister, Jawaharlal Nehru. The Foundation was committed to the Government of India to aid agriculture and rural development and to provide support to institutions working in community welfare. Douglas Ensminger was the Ford representative in India in 1958, when the All India Handloom and Handicraft Board asked for help. Ensminger invited Martinucci, who had since become one of the vice-presidents of Macy's, to consult with the Emporium on issues related to the marketing of handloom and hand-crafted items. The Board had already identified three international experts to help redesign and develop products from the crafts sector for export. The Foundation agreed to fund these designers to come and work in India. Then it was decided that another person was required to help coordinate the activities of the experts with the Board and the craftsmen. There were no resources available with the government in the shape of manpower or finance, so Martinucci was asked to recommend someone to take charge of this job.

Bim gives us this part of the story as narrated to her by John.

Martinucci arranged for his son to take on the assignment and move to India for a year. Well, as was destined, or so we believe in India, Marintucci's son went to Florida for a holiday before leaving for India. There he fell in love, and very soon the couple married. After that, he declined the assignment because he wanted to stay on in the US. Being compelled to search for someone else to send to India, Martinucci remembered the bright young man who had worked with Macy's two years earlier and who had spoken to him of his interest in India. So he contacted John Bissell who was still in Far Eastern Fabrics, and asked him if he would go to India as advisor to the Cottage Industries on a Ford Foundation grant. Since the matter had been pending for weeks John was requested to leave for Delhi in two days if he was interested in the assignment. And so he did.

It is important to understand the environment in Delhi at the moment in history when John Bissell arrived. Ten years had passed since Independence and the mood was still positive. Economic priorities had been identified and institutions were put into place to deal with them. Failures were treated as teething problems. Political leaders had the mandate and were excited about nation-building. Administrators were still talking about learning from early mistakes. In Delhi the elite felt themselves to be an integral part of the socio-political process, and were optimistic about their role in the empowerment of the nation. John Bissell's limited interest in the standardization of Indian fabric for import to the US was actually a small part of the great story of the revival of the Indian handloom and handicraft industry. That they coincided is one of those accidents of history that propel people to centrestage. John was surrounded by such leaders as Kamaladevi Chattopadhyay, Pupul Jayakar and Lakshmi Jain to name a few. Kamaladevi had launched the programme for handicrafts and handloom development in 1952, and Pupul Jayakar and Lakshmi Jain were active members of the All India Handicrafts Board. It was the process set in motion by these icons that eventually brought John Bissell to India. And, of course, he had spent years unwittingly getting ready for his part.

At that time there was a group of committed women working in Cottage Industries who were also part of the social elite in Delhi. Among them were Prem Bery, Teji Vir Singh and Bim. Bimla Nanda joined Cottage in March 1958 as an advisor in the export promotion department to work directly under Lakshmi Jain. Bim was an integral part of the Punjabi community that had made Delhi its home after Partition. It was a small world in those days for the educated middle class in India. Everyone knew each other, by kinship or by association. By default, John became the centre of a very interesting symbiosis comprising the American diplomatic and international aid community, the government administration and their beneficiaries (the craftsmen and artisans), and the network of Punjabi clans that formed the social fabric of the city of Delhi.

John Bissell arrived in New Delhi on 15 August 1958. It was a national holiday, and the driver who had been designated to pick him up at the airport, was on leave. Since there was nobody to receive him, John looked up a guide book and a map and hired a taxi to take him to the Maidens Hotel in north Delhi. The next day he reported for duty up the rickety staircase into Bim's office on the second floor of the Cottage Emporium. A few months later John introduced Bim to his parents in a letter, stating simply: 'Bim is a young woman who works in the All India Handicrafts Board'.

The Handicrafts Board and Cottage Industries were two separate departments of the Government of India, with very different mandates. The Board was to function as a design centre to improve existing crafts by upgrading the skills and technique of craftsmen. It already had a few Indian designers like Riten Mazumdar (a well-known hand-block printer and sculptor) and Shona Ray (one of Delhi's top interior designers in the '60s) working with the team. The decision to hire international designers, or experts, was taken with a view to develop products for export. This was where the Foundation had stepped in with an offer to provide grants for the experts and the consultant staffer who had been recommended by Martinucci. John's role was to facilitate and administer this programme with the 'experts', on behalf of the Board. This included field trips around India, identifying artisans, weavers and craftsmen whose products were interesting enough to be redesigned for export. There were three experts who had been invited to participate in the process. 'Madame Gres' from Paris, called 'the designer of designers' by Lakshmi Jain (who admired her versatility), Roger Model, also from France, who was a specialist in handbag fittings, and Peter Kaufmann, merchandise manager and director of the Globe Department Stores in Zurich. Another staffer from the Board would accompany John and the experts on these trips, to deal with other arrangements, and act as translator.

The Cottage Emporium functioned as the social marketing centre. Teams were sent out to procure samples of crafts from different villages. These products were tested in the Cottage showrooms through special exhibitions and promotions, and those that elicited a good response from the market were ordered. These orders were paid for in advance, at least in part, so as not to burden the craftsmen with capital expenses, since most of them were living in poverty. Redesigned crafts from the design team were also put through the same process before they were approved. The idea was to build up market knowledge, take it to the craftspeople, and help carry the financial burden of the upgradation of their skill base. However, all further retail beyond the Emporium in Delhi had to be taken on directly by the artisans. In this way the Cottage Emporium served a social mission—linking the urban centre to the village industry. Its environs became a place for people to meet and interact. Bankura, comprising a café, bookshop and flower shop, was opened on the premises, and Delhi's professional and social elite turned up with heart to support the concept. Tickets for cultural events were sold at the bookshop, journalists gathered there for coffee, and lunch at Bankura became a fashionable outing. The Cottage showroom became the first option to shop for handicrafts as presents for functions and gifts for the ever-growing population of international consultants and collaborators in India's economic development programme.

There was also a separate Refugee Handicrafts Committee that utilized the skills of thousands of displaced women living in camps who had to be rehabilitated in post-Partition India, after losing their homes, families and livelihood in the cause of Independence. This project was handled by Mrs B.K. Nehru and Kitty Shiva Rao (vice-president of the Handicrafts Board) amongst others. Incidentally, it was after seeing some of these samples of embroidery made by the displaced women in Washington, way back in 1953, that Bill Bissell became interested in starting an import business with India!

Since they were responsible for his trip, the Ford Foundation offered John a home in Sundar Nagar or Golf Links, upmarket residential areas in central Delhi. But John had come to India to understand the local culture and the community. He found himself a home in south Delhi, refused the use of air conditioners in his house, and settled for an Indian car, the ubiquitous Ambassador. John sent a rough floor-plan of the house to his parents in October 1959. The single-storey house, D-247 Defence Colony, was large enough to be shared with another family, Luc

Mrs Richard M. Bissell (John Bissell's grandmother) with her children in the conservatory of the Mark Twain House. Anne Carolyn & William (John's father) are standing, and the youngest, Richard, is in his mother's arms. Connecticut, 1909.

From left to right: John with his parents, Elinor and William (Bill) Bissell, his sister, Marie, and her husband, Tim Prentice. Connecticut, 1960.

Bill and Elinor Bissell arrive in India. Delhi, 1960.
From left to right: John, Bim Nanda, Elinor and Bill Bissell.

Rajasthan, 1964.

Townsend Swayze photographed artisans and their homes when he and his wife Felicity accompanied John and Bim on trips to villages around Delhi in 1964.

From left to right: Madhukar Khera, John, Anand Sagar (Madhukar's father), Tulsi Dass (Madhukar's grandfather) and Vinay Khera (Madhukar's brother).

John Bissell at the Bharat Carpet Manufacturers (BCM) factory. Panipat, 1972.

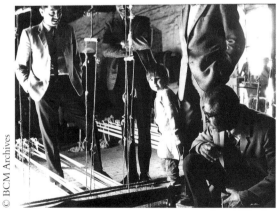

William Bissell in the BCM factory with the Khera family. Panipat, 1972.

Fabindia, inc.

440, MATHURA ROAD, JANGPURA, NEW DELHI-14
TELEPHONE : 74914   CABLE : WEAVERS, NEW DELHI

April 24,1967

Bharat Carpet Manufacturers
Panipat   Attn:Mr.Madhuker Khera

Dear Mr. Khera:

1 We sent an order to you on Saturday - please let us
know when you will be able to deliver it.

2 In the new sample 3' x 5' you brought us last week, in
some places the yarn is a little thin and the warp shows.
Please make very sure that the yarn stays thick and the
weaving very tight. We must maintain the quality all the time

3 I agree with you that colours do not look very good in
Ajanta quality. Do not proceed with the colour blanket at
present. Instead:

Please make us 1 Ajanta durry 3' x 5' in olive, to
match attached sample. DYE WARP SAME COLOUR. DO NOT
PRESELECT YARN - DYE AT RANDOM.

Please do this at once so that if the sample looks
good we can prepare additional samples for my trip
to the U.S.

Sincerely,

John L. Bissell

Encl:

An example of the letters exchanged between John Bissell and Madhukar Khera, as they
finalized designs and colours for durries.

Durrie weavers in the BCM factory. Panipat, 1972.

Bobbins of handspun cotton yarn at Handloom Cottage, Mr R.A. Agarwal's weaving unit. Muradnagar, 1974.

Spinning yarn at an artisan's home. Panipat, 1965.

John Bissell with Achan Khan. Delhi, 1964.

Achan Khan started working for John in 1960 as his cook, but soon
became Fabindia's first office assistant. Achan died in 1988 while still
in service. His daughter, Chaman Siddiqi, worked in Fabindia for many
years on the shop floor.

Durand, his wife Michele, and their three children. Luc was one of the many friends John would make in those early years, who were participants in the building of a new nation, and who, later, would lend their talents towards fulfilling John's dream.

Luc, now eighty years old, is a leading figure in modern Canadian architecture. In 2009, a museum in Montreal held the first major retrospective of the 'wonderfully diverse work of the young Quebec architect in 1950s India, a unique period in the history of modern architecture.' The 23 March 2009 issue of the *Monitor*, Quebec, says: 'Durand turned his hand to many different fields, helping to plan neighbourhoods in New Delhi and Calcutta and designing furniture and structures as well as rugs for Fabindia stores.'

Having settled into his home in Delhi, John moved into a whirlwind of travel around India, meeting craftsmen and weavers, designers and administrators, developing contacts and discovering the country. At this time (February–March 1959), John's letters to his parents are as full of descriptions of the landscape, architecture and people as of the excitement of seeing so many varieties of colour and form in crafts and fabric. Sending vignettes of his new life in Delhi he writes on 6 April 1959:

> I generally try to get through three newspapers every morning. It is not much of a problem because they are all short—only 10 or 12 pages. The Statesman which is sort of British and business oriented—published in Calcutta, the Times of India which is the old mainstay and the Hindustan Times which actually I like the best—that is published here in Delhi. Remember that 85% of the news is about India and it is mostly economic news. There is an incredible lot going on here—new roads—new dams—new factories ... grain stores & fair-price shops. Lot of news every day on the border violations ... The Prime Minister is always on the front page. I counted at least 4 speeches which were reported on one day. There is nothing like it at all at

home. The amount of coverage which he gets and which Mrs Indira Gandhi gets now that she is President of the Congress Party . . .

There is also a transcribed letter from an audio tape recorded by John (received by his parents in April 1959), rendering a full account of the prolonged trip around India with the international 'experts'. On a drive from Delhi to Moradabad he came across the Ganges:

> The high point of the trip was crossing the Ganges. We crossed at a place which is about 12 miles wide, though the river is only 100 yards wide at this time of year. But the land is so flat that the river spreads out for miles at the time of the monsoon and this leaves a sandy, shallow river-bottom on which nothing grows and on which no road has been built. This time of the year it is crossed by a pontoon bridge. It is absolutely a spectacular sight, because at one point all that you can see is just sand, nothing else and the huts of the caretakers of the road and the sun warm but not hot, and the sky fading from an incredibly intense blue gradually into the sand colour. It was a very Salvador Dali kind of landscape.

Then at the Rambagh Palace in Jaipur:

> It is a lovely place . . . it is big, and it is spectacular and it is wonderfully fun to stay in. I don't have to clean it. I can just stay in it. The gardens are superb because at this time of the year everything is blooming all over the place. In the evening as the Moghul poetry says there was a real perfume in the air. You could smell it all over the place, sitting out there in the evening.'

He adds, '(Incidentally Bill stayed in this palace as the guest of the Maharajah in 1945).'

About Bombay he says: 'Bombay is getting old hat for me—my third trip—and a good deal of fun as far as I was concerned . . . I know my way around now to the places to go for handicrafts.'

On one of these trips to Bombay, John met Patwant Singh who was running a design magazine at the time. Patwant says that John Bissell came to India as a person who was 'wide-eyed in Wonderland'. To him India was a unique experience. He was here to learn, to absorb and to register an ancient civilization. He had come 10,000 miles to experience the country and the people who were producing such wonderful crafts. Singh says that John was very clear, right then in 1959, that India was the place for him.

John also wrote about Trivandrum in this series of letters:

[It is] a completely tropical part of the world. And wonderfully attractive, rich and fertile, covered with palm trees. In small valleys between the hills and all the open places they grow rice . . . There is almost a continuous line of villages along the main road. You look back through the palm trees and there is a hut every few yards. Again spotless—every little dirt courtyard swept clean—no sign of refuse. Even the meanest hut of clay bricks and thatch roof—whitewashed. And the people friendly . . . Poverty does not strike you so much here. No one needs much to wear . . . there is a gayness, a quality . . . you expect them to burst into song, a lilt to their walk, their language . . . We went off the main roads and it is really lovely—terribly pretty—lovely places to work—girls working in a shed with open sides—spinning yarns for handweaving . . . this is a completely Gandhian concept. To be self sufficient—gives people work.

John says Madras was his favourite city:

It is a tropical city and very green and fertile and [there is] a magnificent beach . . . We did a good piece of business in Madras. There is an excellent store there—easily the best store in all India and is the gathering place for all work in south India. And there I found some carpets made of hemp. They are sturdy and washable. They need help with colours and designs. I think this could be a very successful item.

So he followed these carpets to their source which was a small village near Tirunelveli, 400 miles south of Madras. There John made one of his most important discoveries:

I went there to see ... the production of 'Sun Hemp Druggets'—a natural fibre carpet to be used in houses for the summer. It is damn exciting—the fibre has a rough interesting texture, it dyes into the most super colours ... It is called a drugget because it is woven not handknotted ... The loom is upright [and] made of bamboo, the warp is cotton, and this fibre already dyed is woven in the weft not by a shuttle but by hand—this I think could be changed to a shuttle which would make it faster. I saw it first in Madras but in very bad colour combinations[,] so gave them some specific suggestions which they accurately followed, with I might say in a modest fashion, spectacular results.

Unwittingly, John was setting the pattern for his continuing participation in the production of handwoven fabric in India. This sympathetic comprehension of material and technique formed the building blocks of the business he would soon start, which would span the two countries that he called his homes. In a letter dated 9 May 1959 he wrote about the weavers at the production unit run by the Madras state government:

I spent one afternoon, and part of the next morning, watching them work, talking over new ideas, going into the fields to see the fibre actually growing—it is a tall slender reed 6 ft high at maturity—[it] is grown in the dry season

[now] between the two yearly crops of rice—the fibre comes from the stalk[,] the leaves are left in the fields for fertilizer or can be fed to livestock ... I feel this kind of work is much the most productive that I or for that matter any 'handicraft consultant' can do out here, and it certainly is what I like to do best.

The journeys went on: Cochin, Cape Comorin, Hyderabad, Bangalore, Mysore, Calcutta, Banaras, Kashmir. The trips were repeated with each of Martinucci's team of consultants, and often with Mr D.N. Saraf, director of the Handicrafts Board. The experts' recommendations for products with export potential were noted by the government, but that did not seem good enough for the growth of the trade. Handicraft sales had stagnated over the year. On 4 August 1959 John wrote: 'I really think ... that the attack has to be on the Handicrafts themselves—let's make something exciting then follow up on the production and quality problems so we can market it commercially.'

Bissell learnt a lot about India and the handloom industry in that first year. He learnt that new ideas needed to be financially supported beyond the design stage, and samples had to turn into consistent and firm orders to be economically viable. The weavers were too poor to take such risks on their own and the Indian government was already stretched dealing with multiple problems to take on more of a stake in this sector. The market had to be developed aggressively for retail within India and for export. John's ideas did not conform with those of the Board as is clear from a letter to his parents on 6 September 1959:

The showrooms in Bombay, Madras and Calcutta are supposed to be for the export trade. In my estimation they are premature, because there just isn't enough new and exciting [stuff] to sell. It is too bad to spend the time and the money on this rather than on the really immediate problem of developing new things ... In spite of export figures that show trade has not increased in three years, in Handicrafts there is an avoidance of almost even mentioning the problem of stagnation.

When the first year got over, John was very worried that his contract would not get renewed and that he would be asked to leave. He wanted to stay on as a 'freelance' consultant to the Board and made a series of suggestions to Lakshmi Jain, including the setting up of a Handicraft Information Centre, developing more design cells to help follow up the recommendations of the experts, and starting a Craft Creativity Centre. John sent a summary of his plans to Martinucci in August 1959:

> I am enclosing a copy of my memorandum to Mr Jain on Mr Kaufmann's suggestions for an Indian Handicrafts Information Centre. This is a rather major undertaking and will take some time to become a 'going' concern, but I hope I can help with the details on setting it up ... The Handicrafts Creativity Centre—a forum for good design—is a more modest undertaking ... A good space over the Central Cottage Industries Emporium in the centre of New Delhi has been allotted ... [It] is the synthesis of a year's study on how best to follow up your ideas of indigenous stimulation to create new marketable products.

His suggestions went through the whole process—Lakshmi Jain sent them to the Ford Foundation, where John had made a friend named Jean Joyce. The letter then passed on to Douglas Ensminger who asked Martinucci in New York for advice. Once again Martinucci supported John and the contract got extended. John was all set for another year in India. He wrote to his friend Martinucci on 20 August 1959: 'The beginning of the second year finds my enthusiasm undimmed and now tempered with a little experience. I hope you will come to India this winter and help us achieve a solid creative breakthrough in handicrafts.'

During the second year of his assignment, John was actively seeking out and developing new products and adapting existing ones. He would then follow up production and quality problems and order material for himself, to turn it into apparel for his mother's shop in Connecticut. He had found a good tailor who was inexpensive and asked his mother to send him clothes' patterns 'so I can try this tailor with some RTW [Ready to Wear]. I would suggest some ladies' shorts, skinny pants, tailored sports' skirts and both men's and women's sports shirts ... there is a good range [of] striped fabrics that are ... colour fast and inexpensive ...' He sent out 'Madras Sisal Fibre table mats in sensational colours', aprons, tablecloths, bedspreads, ready-to-wear skirts, shirts, shorts and beachwear. The response was good at the Canton Green Store and John felt very encouraged. But there were shipment problems. He was sending all these packages to the US through the services of the Cottage Industries who had a 'shipper' to handle export. But shipments had to wait for months to get government clearance. The apathy disturbed him. He was 'disillusioned by the moral fibre or character of so many in government office'. He wrote to his parents on 10 July 1959: 'You know the only solution is working for myself—and one of these days I am going to start.'

John was exploring every possibility to start business in India. He had discussed some ideas with Mr Kaul, a 'private handloom fabric producer who I have seen a lot of and like very much. He seemed enthusiastic to have me come to work for him ...' Also John's trips around India were producing results and he wrote excitedly to his parents on 20 September 1959, asking for patterns to design shirts or shorts for the Canton Green Store:

> I have just received some pretty exciting hand-blocked, indigo dye prints from Andhra Pradesh—not seen on the American market, and colour-fast; I was going to send the fabric, but decided to have it made up into clothes that would be easier to sell. There are 10 different patterns—9

yards of each one, but colourings mostly blue combinations with two or three reds.

Walter Freidenberg, a journalist friend who first met John in early 1959, sent a detailed account to Bim of the year he spent as John's 'roomie' in the Golf Links' flat:

> I admired and respected John's work as a Ford Foundation sponsored advisor to the Indian handloom industry. He would go off to various ramshackle handloom workshops in the Delhi area and come back and tell us about his efforts, usually gratefully welcomed, to teach ways of improving the fabrics, dyes and design in order to increase production and thus affect livelihoods ... As the sponsorship drew closer to an end, John would tell me how much he wanted to stay in India, start a company and continue his work in improving and expanding the Indian handloom industry.

There was another bit of excitement brewing in John Bissell's life. Bim Nanda's friendship had become very significant for him. He travelled with her family, even learning to ride at Bim's family home in Hissar over ten days in December 1958. 'I enjoy it even more than Wyoming,' he wrote to his parents enthusiastically. He said he visited Bim's uncle and aunt in Bangalore and 'enjoyed it tremendously'. But it was on an extended summer holiday with Bim and her family in Kashmir in June 1959, with long walks in the mountains, picnics in the forest and fishing in the streams, that John fell in love with Bim. Back in Delhi, he wrote: 'As you probably guessed from the letter I wrote ... from Kashmir, I had an absolutely first-class time there. And of course the real reason was Bim ...'

After this trip John referred to Bim in almost every letter to his parents. On 15 July he wrote, 'Bim is back and it sure is nice.' After that he described the nursery school Bim ran in Delhi, and said that he had been helping her get ready for the opening of the post-monsoon term.

> I have been spending quite a lot of time helping Bim get her school ready for the opening . . . This is kind of fun because it involves building things, going into the wholesale markets, and of course, seeing a lot of the Director [Bim], which just might be the best part.

On 21 August Bim's youngest sister Meena came over to John's house and tied 'rakhi' on him, traditionally making him her brother and thus a part of their family. John comments: 'It was a gentle and thoughtful little ceremony and I must say I was quite touched.' On 20 September 1959 he writes again to his parents:

> The summer is coming to an end; today we went on the first picnic of the season—just at sunset an assortment of young Delhites including Luc, Michele, the three children. Bim, her sister Meena and cousin Rava . . . all went down to a fine grassy green tomb called Haus Khaz. There we explored ruins in the fading light, had a high tea consisting of cold coffee, coca cola, beer, scotch, sandwiches, and pastries, and quietly went away under a sharp bright sky to the sound of a solitary flute player adding the proper note of serenity.

By 7 October 1959 John and Bim were spending time together every day, 'and she is pretty remarkable company', he writes. 'I still don't really know her very well, and feel the same impatience that I do with her country. It is an impatience to know, to understand, essentially to establish a rapport at as many levels as possible . . . I would like very much to fit here easily and with no more than the normal irritations of living anywhere . . .'

Bim says that John had such a natural, open personality that it was easy for people to like him:

After the first year John thought he could make a difference. He felt that he could resolve most of the problems the weavers were facing. When he talked to them about what needed to be done to export the stuff, they understood what he was talking about.

Patwant Singh too remembers John's easy manner, his smile and his informality. 'He was very adaptable, visiting villages and working with craftsmen for days, getting along fine without even knowing the language.'

It was very clear that John had no intention of returning to live in the US. He had established a substantive interest in the business with his letters full of excitement about sourcing fabrics and styles for stitching and exporting to the US to sell at the Canton Green Store. He seemed to be thoroughly disenchanted with the Handicrafts Board's 'slow and ineffective . . . delivery', and knew he could do it better on his own. Till the end of 1959 there are descriptions of more trips with Bim, and a full social life in Delhi, making new friends, entertaining visits of old friends and participating in festivals like Diwali and Christmas. John's parents, Bill and Elinor Bissell, finally visited India in January 1960, and spent two months travelling around the country with John. There is a letter from John requesting them to bring gifts for his friends in Delhi, and identifying exactly what he wanted for each person—for the servants, the driver, his office secretary, for the girls, for Bim, her parents and hosts of other relatives. Then he adds delightfully, 'With this list you won't have space for clothes, just bring what you can and that is it. Anything that looks American, with good machine finish and useful, is appreciated—no handicrafts!' And more seriously, he says in the next letter that his 'future looms large as we get nearer the end of my Ford contract' and that he 'wants lots of sage advice from his parents' before they leave India.

Soon after his parents leave, John is fully immersed in business plans and discusses his future with his ex-boss in Far Eastern Fabrics. In a letter to his parents on the 28 April 1960 he reports:

> Kunzman wrote me a letter asking me about my future plans; I have just replied outlining my ideas for starting a production unit for handloom fabrics and asking him if he thought it was a good idea. I also inquired what his future plans were for Far Eastern and if he thought I could have a place in them.

Then he reconnects with a friend, Jim Fraser, from his school, and shares his plans of trying his hand at his own import business. 'I got a nice reply in which he said it sounded like I needed some capital, and he would be interested in helping me get started. He mentioned the idea of a partnership or profit-sharing arrangement.' By 28 April John is totally committed to leaving Ford Foundation and beginning on his own. He writes:

> I have started saying my official goodbyes and without regrets because I am looking forward to being on my own. It has been twenty months of wandering around without much sense of direction or purpose except for the brief periods when one of the experts was here. It was a good chance to look around and learn some things, now let's see if I can put this to productive use. I would love to come home right now . . . to re-acquaint myself with the USA and the fast-moving merchandise world. [But] I have to come home with something to sell; some things that are new, designed for the USA market, and procurable at reasonable prices with a standard of quality, reliability of delivery and continue[d] supply. I haven't found them yet. To come and talk to people about what I can do for them in India without something to show, that they will want to buy . . . doesn't seem to have much chance of success . . .

And further in the same letter, John's leitmotif, the concept that lay at the foundation of the company he was soon to begin:

> It is tough and hard and sometimes dreary 'going it alone', but from time to time something is made that is good and new, a craftsman gets a little encouragement, and some business. This makes me realize how much I want to establish a place where they can come for direction, encouragement . . .

He received complete support from his parents for his ideas. Bill Bissell wrote on 24 May 1960:

> We both got a big kick from your last letter—written as an unemployed entrepreneur with good projects in mind . . . and hope that before you are able to get established, you'll be able to get a few commissions on things sold to Kunzman and others . . .

The rest of the summer in India was spent shifting house from Defence Colony to 43 Golf Links where he rented the first floor from Lakshmi Jain, who lived on the ground floor. His friend, Walt Freidenberg, also shifted in with him and they hired Achan Khan as cook and general assistant, another relationship that was to span generations.

Recently Walt wrote a very lively account of the three months he shared with John at the time:

> I had just returned to India after a month-long absence and was in need of a place to live. John was renting half-a-house in Golf Links. He agreed to take me in as his roomie. The apartment was decorated with colourful Indian handicrafts: furniture and certain fabrics, bowls, toys, hangings, and a huge multi-mirrored Rajasthani umbrella suspended from the ceiling over the sitting area . . . John and I shared household expenses, the services of Achan as amiable and efficient multi-tasked bearer, and a lot of

evening and weekend free time. We sneaked into the swimming pool at the new, posh Ashoka Hotel. We played a little tennis. When the hot season arrived, we would sleep on our charpoys on the flat roof of the house. When the sun peered hot over the horizon and began to raise a sweat on my forehead, we'd get up and dash to some tennis court and play until the sun became too hot to bear. We volunteered to drive Jean Joyce's car up to Kashmir, with young Lois Bennet as passenger. Here we were stopped at a checkpoint at night and faced the possibility of having to spend the night on the road. Right there, John suggested that Lois put a bunched-up shawl under her dress and we tell the guards that she was pregnant and we had to rush to the hospital in Srinagar. They let us through.

Jean Joyce worked with the Ford Foundation in Delhi and had become a good friend of John's. Lois had come to India to spend some time with Jean, who was her aunt. She says that her parents were close friends of John's parents back in the US, and he was very kind to her. He would visit and have dinner with Jean and Lois, and take them on several trips. She remembers many wonderful, adventurous journeys that she went on with John and Walt. Recalling a trip to Kashmir with John and his friends, Lois says, 'I remember John taking long, long walks on that trip because I think he was trying to figure out how to get Bim to marry him.'

Going back to Walt's story:

John had introduced me to a friend of his, Bimla Nanda (Bim). She was beautiful, intelligent, witty ... sociable, thoroughly modern in Indian and American terms, and accomplished. [She] was simply a knockout, a very attractive woman, savvy and fun to be with, as John's date. As double-daters we went out to dinner and to parties. We went to music concerts in a shamiana at All India Radio.

I recall hitting tennis balls with Bim on the springy grass at the Gymkhana and thinking, 'Wow, she is good—and powerful!

Walt returned to the US in June 1960. He continues:

I don't know when it happened between them, but after I had to return to the States . . . it dawned on me: Bim and John's friendship had deepened and become love . . . I had been a front-row witness to a Great Indo-American Love Story with a Most Happy Ending.

John was comfortable with the house in Golf Links, for it was very centrally located. On 28 April 1960 he wrote to his parents that he was 'only 3 miles to Connaught Circle offices etc. Easy to come home for lunch and particularly when I have no office it will be good because easy to go out for small errands.' His focus was now only on how conveniently he would be able to work from home.

He was getting organized to start his own business. He had found a screen printer in Delhi who was preparing samples to send to Kunzman at Far Eastern. He wrote to his parents on 13 May 1960:

I spent yesterday morning going through old block designs at a nearby printer's. He has some damn exciting designs— especially the ones used for the borders of sarees. I have had my first set of screen print samples done by him. They turned out very well I think, and will send them on to Kunzman. It is a single colour simple all-over delicate flower design that I found on one of his printed sarees. I have used different cross-weave handlooms and in most cases printed either the warp or weft colour to give a tone on tone effect . . . there are a total of 10 different combinations.

There was a garment manufacturer who seemed keen to work with John—a 'big quite well-organized shop on a production line basis.' He enjoyed going to such places and talking to the workers in 'broken Hindi and English. They are pretty amused by the whole performance and consider it a direct challenge to make what I want. This kind of experience reinforces my belief that a lot can be accomplished if one supplies patient direction.'

There were some people producing rugs from whom he would collect colour samples. Mr Kaul had offered him the facilities of his power-loom factory and would offer John a commission on anything he could develop there. 'I am going to work up some good colours using jute and cotton in combination', he wrote, which might work well as webbing on beach chairs for the US.

Then he found a shipper, 'a young chap who had a small company of his own', who would handle all details and get a commission on sales. This company was called India Loomcraft and had an office in Shankar Market, near Connaught Place.

But most importantly, Jim Fraser committed $5000 to John Bissell, in a letter dated 25 June 1960, to help make new samples to carry to the USA. Jim planned to visit John in Delhi in August to discuss the business. Writing to his parents, John said, 'I will pull out all the most charming young ladies at the Emporium in their newest Salwar Chameez and he [Jim] won't have a chance! ... I am going to work hard on getting my business affairs very well organized ... by the time Jim arrives.'

By July 1960 John had given his first order for 250 yards of a new drapery fabric which had no buyers yet, but he contracted exclusivity with that quantity. Nobody else would get to that product before him. The fabric cost him Rs 3 per yard and this Rs 750 was John's first documented risk capital for his new venture. In a letter to his parents dated 19 July 1960, we find the first mention of an upholstery fabric that John had obviously been buying from Cottage Industries over the last year for his client, the Canton Green Store: 240 yards of Delhi Homespun Cotton (or DHC), one of Fabindia's bestsellers, and a product that has sold there continuously through fifty years of its history!

On 3 August 1960 John successfully exported a number of items through India Loomcraft, including bedspreads, handbags, scarves, skirts, aprons and twelve dozen placemats, to the Canton Green Store and wrote to his parents that they were his best export customer! He hired Sarabjeet Singh as his secretary to work in Golf Links, and left for the US to meet his family. His intention was to raise capital by offering shares to the extended Bissell clan he grew up with, including his parents; and along with his own share capital ($20,000 left to him by his grandmother), to incorporate to the Fabindia business a company in Connecticut, that would operate as a buying house for his export business in India.

A month later Fabindia would be born. It was just two years since John Bissell first bounded up the wooden staircase to Bim's office on the second floor of the Cottage Industries Emporium in Delhi.

FABINDIA INC.
1960-76

T he cable read:

ARRIVING NEW YORK 1430 FRIDAY AUGUST 12
AIRINDIA 109 GREAT JOY LOVE JOHN

It was 1960 and John Bissell was on his way home to Canton, Connecticut, after two years in Delhi. He was carrying a 'small selection' of hand-spun fabric samples and a well-crafted proposal for the incorporation of a new company in the US. He was also looking forward to attending his 'little sister' Marie's wedding to Tim Prentice. John and Marie had been very close as siblings, and she gives valuable insights into his personality:

> He had an extraordinarily generous nature that just came instinctively to him. That was a quality everybody loved . . . God knows where John's business sense came from, I don't even remember him selling lemonade . . . He loved India and that was the thread that got him there.

Leaving Delhi had its share of anxieties. John's Indian visa had expired on 12 August and he had to get it renewed before he left, but it was necessary that the Income Tax Department clear him before he could apply. The Indian government granted visas valid only for a year at a time, and the tension of applying afresh each year, not knowing whether he would get another extension, bothered him for years. It is relevant to remember that the world

37

seemed much 'larger' fifty years ago than it does now. The seamless communication we enjoy today through different forms of media did not exist then. A trunk call had to be booked through a central telephone operator to speak to someone in another country. The call was 'booked' and took hours, even days, to materialize. Messages were sent through cable (literally), and had to be written out and physically carried to a telegraph office, or relayed by phonogram. The post office was the custodian of communication systems, nationally and internationally. Travelling from Delhi to the US took days. Air India, the official Indian international airline, operated services between Bombay and London only on certain days of the week. Before jets (Boeing) were introduced, Super Constellations had to make numerous refuelling stops between Bombay and London, hopping down at Cairo, Geneva or Paris. Pan Am flew across the Atlantic from London to New York with two refuelling stops, Shannon in Ireland and Gander in Newfoundland. Luckily for John, Air India had just introduced its inaugural Bombay–London–New York non-stop flight with the new Boeing 707 in May 1960. But this flight out of Bombay operated only once a week. On 3 August John wrote to his parents: 'By the way if you are looking up the flight it leaves from Bombay not Delhi. Direct all the way!' Understanding these constraints is necessary to be able to appreciate the boldness of John Bissell's dreams in 1960, and therefore the compelling motivation of his belief that Indian handicrafts could bridge the distance of 11,000 km between the US and India.

Once in the US, John contacted his cousin's husband Milton DeVane, a corporate lawyer working in New Haven, to help him form a corporation in the state of Connecticut. It was to be named Fabindia Inc. Inviting his father to join the company, John constituted his first board of directors. They were John L. Bissell, William T. Bissell and Milton DeVane. The first business that the company undertook was to raise money for what John wanted to do. A bank would not have been interested in funding such an enterprise, so John called upon the Bissell clan for support.

The interesting thing about this family was (and still is, fifty years later) that their homes were situated in towns located only a few hours away from each other. With the nucleus in Hartford, the extended family still lives within the small state of Connecticut.

At the time, John's parents were occupying a large, rambling house in Canton, a small village near the capital Hartford. A few miles away stood the Canton Green Store owned by Elinor, John's mother. The house at 44 Old Canton Road had an attached barn, one side of which had been opened up to make a porch for family gatherings on pleasant evenings. It was on one such evening in September 1960 that John presented the concept of Fabindia to his family. Milton reports that there were equal numbers of family and friends in the porch that evening. The friends from Hartford were mostly of Bill's generation who were attracted by the idea of John's project. Some members of the family still remember that discussion very clearly, including Margie, Milton's wife. She says that John made a wonderful presentation of what it would mean for the US and India to have this company in India, making beautiful traditional hand fabrics for export. 'Wait till you see what I'm going to do!', said John to them and spread out the samples he had brought with him. His excitement was palpable to everyone including his cousin Hector Prudhomme and his wife Erica, who were also present, and who have related a similar account of that evening, almost fifty years later!

John had prepared a paper to explain the concept of the company, and the clarity of his thoughts is so laudable that it is necessary to give a full report of the Fabindia Prospectus, as he called it:

The creation of Fabindia is to give corporate form to a business which I have been engaged in for the past 6 months, namely the development of Handloom and Hand-printed Fabrics made in India for sale in the United States and other Export markets.

The principal markets for these fabrics should be the Ready-To-Wear, Home Furnishings, Accessory and Retail Industries. In addition, related products will be explored for sale to the same markets. Ideas for the immediate future include Sun Hemp Druggets (a type of casual floor covering), Bedspreads and Table Linen, and perhaps Clothing.

The United States market is searching for the 'new and unusual'. There is a definite increase in the demand for 'distinctive, attractive, off-beat' fabrics which are only available in relatively small quantities so they retain their 'new' look.

The Handloom Industry in India is second only to Agriculture in the number of people that are employed in it. The tradition of weaving and printing is a deep-rooted one that has produced many attractive and unusual designs. There is at present, a large unused capacity and coupled with this a firm Governmental policy of encouraging Exports. Handloom and Hand-printed Fabrics can be made at competitive rates in India, and Fabindia will concentrate on those fabrics which cannot be easily duplicated on a machine.

In other words we have the situation of a real demand and place for Indian Fabrics in the US and the potentially productive facilities of the Indian market.

He said that he had been working on the project since May 1960 and could report some 'encouragement' from the international market:

Far Eastern Fabrics is now buying the entire production of one type of fabric. A store in New York City has agreed to experiment with selling one-of-kind fabrics at retail . . . We have sold fabrics to Charlotte Horstmann, a fine Hong Kong store, and in New Delhi to the United States Information Agency, and Technical Corporation Mission.

The immediate task before us is the creation, by adapting the indigenous skills and designs, of an interesting group of fabrics, and the arrangements for their production. This can only be done by personal exploration in many parts of India—by working up detailed suggestions to make fabrics suitable for our market, and by regular supervision, to make sure instructions are understood and followed, and production commitments fulfilled. (One reason more Indian products are not sold here now is that suppliers have not had a chance to understand Western tastes, standards, and trade practices). Fabindia will concentrate on 'new' textures, colours and prints—new in the sense that they have not been offered commercially before.

John predicted that his sales during the first year of operation (1 November 1960–31 October 1961) would be a modest $20,000, with a profit margin of $4000. But between the third and fifth year Fabindia would be rolling out sales worth $100,000 and that would be the break-even point of the business. 'This is a small fraction of the Indian Fabrics sold in the US market—a market which is anxious to buy more, but cannot because of the difficulties of getting attractive merchandise,' he said. Then he approached the problem of funds. 'To build a business large enough to achieve stability, and acquire a good reputation—and to earn substantial profits—will require outside capital.' But shareholders could not expect dividends on their investment till the fifth year of business:

It is going to take this long to build up a volume operation, but once in this position I believe there are many opportunities for profitable growth, and Fabindia would be in a strong position in what has always been a competitive business. India has the basic problems of Raw Material Supply, Design for a Foreign Market, and Standardisation and Volume of Production in the export of its handicrafts and Handloom Fabrics.

And lastly he added:

Fabindia has been organized specifically with these problems in mind. For the immediate future my base of operations will be India where we can cope with these difficulties as they arise. In two or three years when we are on the way to solving the problems of production in India then it may be advantageous to shift the head office to the US. This is an American Company incorporated in Connecticut.

The presentation continued with John stating the capital requirement and the number of shares being offered to the potential 'stockholders' collected on the porch. He had already invested $4000 in Fabindia, from a small inheritance left to him by his grandmother, and another $30,000 worth of shares was on offer. The family seemed to think this was a great idea and were very impressed with the mixture of idealism and practical experience John demonstrated in his presentation. The general consensus was that John was on to a good thing, and should be supported.

Reminiscing about that day, Marie says:

I remember the meeting we had at my parents' house—an old farm house in Connecticut—and John showing fabric samples enthusiastically. He had a proper meeting to tell us about the company. This is to potential stock holders, basically family members and friends—a small gathering. The amount involved was so tiny I can hardly believe today that you can start a company with that! I think we bought $500 worth of shares, but I'm guessing. I know it wasn't a huge amount but it seemed a lot then because we were young and didn't have very much.

Hector Prudhomme, John's cousin, thought that he and his wife Erica could not have bought more than $200 worth of Fabindia shares at the time. 'We were a young married couple and had no money.' Between October 1960 and October 1961 different members of the family, including John's parents, invested over $3000 in Fabindia Inc. A few friends present that evening chipped in with another $1000. James Fraser, John's old school friend, also made good his promise to finance John and invested $5000 in Fabindia Inc. the following year.

It was decided that a portion of this share capital would remain in the US for expenses incurred on the import side of the business, and the rest would be transferred to India to pay for Fabindia's expenses on the ground. Milton DeVane was appointed to handle the legalities involved with Fabindia Inc. in the US, and Bill Bissell would administer the bank account and all correspondence between the Delhi and US businesses. John had drawn up an expense budget for the Indian office, and estimated his minimum salary for the first three years to be $5000 for the first year, $5500 for the second year, and $6200 for the third year. Of course, he didn't manage to withdraw even that much during the first three years.

John had appointed a representative in New York to stock sample cuts (5-20 yards) of fabrics which seemed to have the best market reaction. The firm would try to sell these fabrics and procure orders for Fabindia. The Indian office would ship the merchandise to the firm or to the customer but invoice only through the firm. In addition, Bill and Elinor, John's parents, would stock some samples and merchandise in the Canton Green Store to offer to their own clients.

By the middle of October 1960 John Bissell was back in India, explaining to Bim that Fabindia was for fabrics and India, not 'fab' India, the slang derivative of 'fabulous' made famous by

George Harrison in his song *When we was fab* around the same time!

Bim Nanda had left Cottage Industries that same month and joined the American Embassy as social secretary to Ambassador John Kenneth Galbraith. She would work there for the next twelve years, facilitating social and cultural networks between Indians and the US administration in India. She would also continue to manage the Playhouse School, a nursery school initiative started by her in 1955. From the next year, John Bissell was to play the role of Santa Claus at every Christmas party in Playhouse, substituting a camel for the sledge drawn by the reindeers in the conventional story. This institution would endear him to generations of children who were initiated into Santa on a camel, 'because Santa Claus wanted to give every animal in the world a chance to take him around'. So said John Bissell (as Santa) to a six-year-old Indian girl studying at Playhouse who was precocious enough to ask the question in 1961.

It is important at this point to describe the logistics of the Fabindia operation in Delhi at its inception. John had it all worked out in his head, but like all ideas the weight of reality needed enormous organizational skills along with the requisite funding to achieve a viable balance.

As has been mentioned before, John was living in the first-floor flat above Lakshmi Jain in Golf Links, in central Delhi. So, 43 Golf Links became the first official address of Fabindia Inc. John lived and worked there, with Achan Khan as his cook, valet and office assistant. One secretary hired in the summer of 1960 had left and John was looking for another person to assist him with office work. Bim and Playhouse School came to his rescue, and for the next couple of years a series of young teachers from Playhouse assisted John in his office after school hours. This was to be a part-time solution till John found permanent staff.

There were a number of small production units John had experimented with over the last one year while preparing fabric samples for the international market. Between them different combinations of material and design had been woven into new products. These were the suppliers Fabindia started with in 1960.

There was a handloom-weaving factory about fifty miles from Delhi. It was Amrit Lal Batra's company, National Textiles, based in Panipat, and producing fabric since 1956. Lakshmi Jain had introduced John to Batra in 1959, and the association continued for decades. Like many influential people of the time, Amrit Lal Batra was a Congressman and closely allied with the Cottage Industries, supplying napkins and cushion covers to the store.

John knew a group of cooperative weavers in Delhi making cottons and cotton and jute mixtures. (They were actually several very small units who had banded together for marketing purposes). And then there was one screen-printing shop and a hand-block printer in Delhi (for cotton and silk printing) who had been working with John since 1959. (All the children who studied at Playhouse School were taken to this unit at least once a year to experiment with printing their own fabric with a block of their choice.) There was also a small machine-powered webbing and braid-making factory in Delhi, a group of cooperative weavers around Hyderabad, and one big handloom factory in south India that agreed to give exclusive export rights to John for certain fabrics.

In the meantime John had established connections with a list of buyers who he was supplying merchandise to, in very small quantities. They were Far Eastern Fabrics, New York; Charlotte Horstmann, Hong Kong; Joe Hyde's Shop, New York; Jack Lennor Larsen, also in New York; Philip George Inc., the agent appointed by Fabindia in the US; and, of course, his mother's Canton Green Store where he continually experimented with clothing, furnishing fabrics and table linen. In addition he had a couple of institutional clients in Delhi, both Indo-US government initiatives, as mentioned at the family presentation.

On his return from the US John visited the Commercial

Attaché at the American Embassy and registered Fabindia on the approved list of merchant establishments in Delhi for potential American customers. He had also been in touch with Jim Thompson in Thailand who had sent him a list of potential buyers for Indian handloom fabric. In a letter to his father on 18 October 1960, John wrote that he was waiting for the Charter of Corporation from Milton DeVane in the US to be able to register as a branch of Fabindia Inc. Then he would be in a position to export directly rather than through India Loomcraft, the agent he had earlier appointed to clear and ship his products out of India. That would remove one expense from the books and perhaps speed up the process of freighting and shipping.

A few weeks later Fabindia had a cable address, Weavers New Delhi, and could communicate and receive orders much faster. John wrote to his father on 27 October 1960:

> Auspicious day yesterday: our cable address was used for the first time—Charlotte Horstmann cabled an order—just a few yards, but a nice feeling of urgency.
>
> I am working damn hard; no orders except the one from Hong Kong for Rs.1000, small but encouraging ... A few samples have been made that are quite exciting ... it is a real new look, expensive however—Rs. 8.10 a yard 48" wide ... I am very impatient and want all the bright new ideas to be done the next day.

The product list was still small and exploratory. The main fabric being exported at this time was 'a hand-spun, woven fabric, flat coloured' called Delhi Homespun Cotton (DHC) developed by the Cottage Industries. Other samples in preparation were jute and cotton mixtures, druggets and some fibre placemats. John had tried bedspreads, table mats, skirts, aprons, shirts and dresses as well.

The challenge of the business was that samples had to be continuously produced in the search for exciting new designs and fabrics. John was in constant touch with his weavers, working with them on different products. To get a design onto the loom meant committing financially to several yards of fabric that would have to be paid for, regardless of a buyer. The weavers were not in a position to invest in experimentation themselves. John had already understood this problem while working for Cottage Industries. So throughout those early years he invested in samples, running through capital without enough market support. The process was relentless. To push the market he needed new products. To get new products he needed funds. To get funds he needed buyers.

There was an even more complicated problem. To get an order from a client on the basis of a sample and then not deliver yardage on time due to lack of funds, bad planning or shipping delays was fatal in a speculative market situation. So John would buy up sufficient stocks of fabrics that he felt were promising and then face a cash crunch in the office because he had no orders for them. This tension persisted through 1960-65 and was reflected in the correspondence exchanged between John and his father, Bill, in Canton.

On 19 November 1960 the first two orders were shipped from Fabindia, one for Rs 1500 and the other for Rs 500. Excitedly he wrote to his father: 'It is a modest beginning but represents Fabindia's first earned income and Foreign Exchange Balance!' Then: 'Its damn good fun to be running your own show— thinking up ideas & getting something accomplished.' He had a long meeting with 'the big shots' in the Handloom Export Organization of the Ministry of Commerce and Industry, and found them very supportive. They would help in several ways when administrative regulations governing the export industry became tedious and restrictive in India.

Equally impatient when the pace slowed down, John wrote to Bill on 3 December 1960:

No orders for about 10 days and that is always discouraging—
as you know we can't expect lots of business to start off
with ... I miss sometimes not being in the market in the
sense of being able to run over to 7th Avenue and get a
quick reaction to a new fabric.

Since his return there had been no response from his agent in
the US, and no order from the Canton Green Store against the
samples left there in October. John asked, 'Is it the location,
clientele, etc. of the store or the merchandise which is the
problem if they are not selling well?' He urged his father to send
more samples of different handloom products lying with the
Canton store to his agent in New York in the hope that
something would happen.

Against this backdrop of slow business the relationship between
Bim and John was blossoming. On 3 December 1960, he wrote:

Everything is rosy here—one perfectly beautiful day after
another—we have gone on a few walks ... I delight a little
more each day in the time spent with Bim; there seems to
be a steady stream of visitors, family members etc. coming
to town and we are feeling selfish about time together—but
I don't think this is the first time people have felt this way.

John was getting closer to Bim's social circle. There were dinners
at friends' homes, trips to the country with Bim and her family,
and a growing familiarity with the Indian concept of nationhood
that would stay with John all his life. He developed a sensitivity
within the precious space he occupied in Delhi of being able to
perceive different realities and to maintain an honest and
transparent position that seemed fair to everyone who met him
over the next thirty-five years.

On 11 December 1960 he wrote to his parents:

As I am accepted more and more by the Nandas' friends
... this very deep, strong and critical feeling of us is more

apparent. As you know this is a very Western oriented group in many respects . . . they lead rather independent, social, comfortable lives . . . There [are] a lot of irritations for them living and working around foreigners. The diplomatic corp. has succeeded in wrecking the rent structure in many places [in Delhi] . . . and they consistently make money because of their export–import privileges . . . the comparison between East and West is a daily one . . . as is hearing India discussed—her problems, her customs and her development schemes . . . I think the only thing to do is accept the situation . . . helps to be less critical . . .

He had already made good friends 'and I much prefer time with them to the round of sloppy dinner parties occasioned by the diplomatic environment' (20 December 1960).

John Bissell's generosity and warmth continued to draw different types of people into an ever-expanding circle of friends spread across personalities, professions, income levels, cities and nations. There were designers and architects, bureaucrats and politicians, economists and lawyers, diplomats and journalists, business leaders and statesmen, artisans and dancers, weavers and craftspeople, social-workers and students. A few years later, with Bim's formidable charm at his side, John's boundless energy would find a home. Between them the Bissell couple would establish a vast network of friends around the world who would soon form the core equity of the Fabindia brand.

In the meantime Fabindia continued to struggle through 1961-62. Orders were regular, but small—'from Horstmann in Hong Kong, an interesting Australian buyer, and a new client from London'. A merchandising woman from a department store in Miami visited John, and took samples and prices. Far Eastern Fabrics was still the most substantial client. John also sent samples to Jim Thompson's clients in Thailand, and there was a trickle of customers in Delhi, friends who had started visiting Fabindia to buy fabric for their homes. 'We are also doing

business almost daily here—small orders—but good for the morale—
they add up and use up all the odds and end of material.' There
were however problems with transporting, freighting and shipping.
Goods had to be sent to Bombay and be loaded onto ships. But
all merchandise needed to be custom cleared before loading. It
was a time-consuming process. Air freight was more efficient but
expensive. Faster delivery also meant quicker payments but funds
were too tight for them to explore this option.

John enjoyed travelling around India to meet new suppliers. A
trip to Hyderabad, Coimbatore and Calicut yielded interesting
material made of natural fibre. 'Some new fabrics are coming
along which I think we will sell . . . I am learning pretty fast, I
hope, & building confidence in being able to . . . adapt ideas.'

In Delhi the government was beginning to recognize John's
worth. He was appointed Chief Consultant to the Men's
department at Cottage Industries. Fabindia fabrics were displayed
in the Handloom Board exhibit at the Indian Industries Fair in
Delhi. The company won an order to furnish the newly built
India International Centre. John remarked that it was 'only $800
or $1000—but it is a feather in our cap as the building will be
quite a showpiece & the architect, Joseph Stein (an American) is
very particular.' Riten Mazumdar, a good friend of John's, invited
him to display his fabrics in a new retail outlet he had opened in
Delhi. John wrote about his efforts at 'keeping the looms full',
but the shop did not attract enough business and had to be shut
down. Also by this time inventory worth $7000 had piled up in
the Golf Links office. 'I feel in deep water & am proceeding very
slowly.'

With the earlier arrangement having failed, a new agent was
appointed in the US who was contracted to buy merchandise on
consignment. But the contract did not stipulate the minimum
orders required to keep production moving. Hampered by
conditions of exclusivity John could not strike out on his own.
He also felt that the agent was not generating enough business.

The agent, on the other hand, was restricted by lack of ready stock in the US. Cash flow was a constant problem. In those early years John's father provided a lot of support, coordinating with the agent and encouraging John to be patient. On 7 August 1961 he reassured John that the agent (and her partner) 'want to sell Fabindia's products . . . they've done and are doing as good a job as you could hope for—in investigating possibilities, contacting big, small & medium prospects; analysing problems . . .' On 30 August he tried to persuade his son to come to the US and explore the market himself. For 'the only person who can effectively sell stock in a one-man outfit is the one-man himself . . . in short, for your own interests you'll have to come home at some point.'

Capital was running out and John urgently looked for new investors in the US. The family in Connecticut came to his rescue again. His sister and her husband bought shares in Fabindia, as did other cousins. And then Bill and Elinor decided to bail out their son. His father wrote to John on 25 September 1961:

> Your new capital requirements will at least partly . . . be satisfied by us . . . by the time you get this letter an agreement will have been made for me to buy $4500 worth of Fabindia shares . . . we wish at this point to help stake you in your promising and adventurous enterprise.

By November it was clear that John had not managed to turn over even $20,000 in sales the first year. He posted a net loss of $6000 on the balance sheet. On 14 February 1962 he wrote: 'I took all this on when I decided to start Fabindia—sometimes it takes all the strength I have.' And his father replied:

> I'm aware that you didn't meet your goals the first year . . . but I'll bet nobody (including myself) really thought you would. People seldom do—even in a familiar domestic business, let alone a foreign field . . . the thing is you did

> get started—did discover new products & sources—and now
> have (some) orders coming your way . . .

The association with the US agent, Design Imports, was fraught
with problems and after three years of wrangling about breach of
contract, broken commitments and unsatisfactory sales, the
agreement was wound up. Thereafter Fabindia Delhi exported
merchandise directly to Fabindia Inc. in Connecticut to buy,
hold as stock, and sell directly to US customers. Bill Bissell
managed all the administration of the business in Canton with
Milton DeVane as the company Secretary for many years.

By the middle of 1962 there were signs of more activity at
Fabindia. The business attracted two competent girls to handle
the small office. Amrita Malik arrived in the summer, worked for
a few months, and then left to take care of a sick mother. She
returned later in 1963 and stayed on for eighteen years. For a few
months Meena Rai worked at the Playhouse School till 12.30 and
then came in to Golf Links to work till 6 p.m. After Amrita left
Meena joined Fabindia full-time and stayed on to form the
backbone of Fabindia for almost forty years. Meena's story, which
we will narrate as we go along, provides an interesting account of
the history of a successful company, but more importantly it is a
valuable documentation of the efficient office procedures set up
by John Bissell during the evolution of Fabindia.

Most of the staff who joined Fabindia during the early years
were entirely guided by John. Both Meena and Amrita give us
insights into John's personality and the ideology that informed
his work. John taught them office and administrative skills,
supplier and client interface and most of all, to value and
recognize good-quality Indian handcrafted products. Amrita says:

> I did most of my learning from him about Indian fabric—
> what it meant, and why it was more beautiful than machine-
> made pieces from England. He showed me that the warp
> formed the length of the fabric and the weft went across

the fabric. If the warp was green and the weft was yellow, they combined to form a textured fabric. The texture only came if the warp and weft were different. John loved textured fabric. He taught me a lesson about Indian fabric every day and would take me to the looms to meet the weavers and understand the difficult conditions in which they worked. He showed me why the colour of a handloom fabric changed. If a man weaving some cloth took a break and his wife worked the loom for the next eight yards, it would show—because if the hand changes the fabric changes. Just looking at a length of handloom fabric could tell you that the hand had changed because the texture was different. One day he decided to tell me about shading bars. He went down on his knees with a white hanky and rubbed the hanky across a bright red Delhi Homespun fabric lying on the ground. In two minutes the white hanky was red and he said that was the colour bar and that's the beauty of the fabric. Only those who understood this could appreciate the beauty of it rather than see it as a defective piece.

Meena speaks about John's sensitivity to Indian colours and how excited he would get talking about the annual camel fair in Pushkar, seeing all the different colours worn by the people of Rajasthan:

Since my father was an Animal Husbandry officer we had to go to Pushkar every year for 12–13 years. It used to be dusty and hot and all you saw were animals and men. I never focused on how colourful Rajasthan is. I just had not looked at it that way. It is after I came to Fabindia that I started thinking colour and began looking at it.

The first-floor flat in Golf Links was organized very simply. At the centre was the drawing room in which there was one desk in a corner, a dining table with stools around it, and an alcove at the back covered by a *chik* (bamboo blind). This alcove held samples of fabric and other things John had collected for reference. Then there was John's bedroom, and a back verandah with another room that became the stock room. Behind the verandah was the kitchen leading to Achan Khan's living quarters. Meena remembers the time when only John, Achan Khan and herself comprised the staff at Fabindia. Typically John would give instructions and leave for lunch and expect the work to be done by the time he returned. Achan Khan would direct Meena to the relevant files lying around the room to collect the information needed to complete the job. Meena went to typing class after office hours to train herself for the office, and then had to re-learn some details according to John's requirements. Here is an amusing example related by her:

> There was a way things were done. I don't remember John giving specific instructions but he established some procedures and we followed because it seemed the methodical thing to do. One such was letter writing. I had learned that a letter starts from the left-hand corner and ends on the right. That's the way I had done it all through school and college. Also letters were started with 'Dear So and So' and ended with 'Thanking you, Yours sincerely'. John said lets cut all that out. The letter must start on the left and end on the left. Doesn't it look much neater, all left-aligned? He also said don't waste words. Leave out the 'Thanking You' and 'Hope to see you soon' bits. The letter should be concise, informative and to the point.

John stimulated people to do their best for him. Like a good teacher he motivated his staff 'without looking over my shoulder to see whether I was doing things right or whether I was doing things wrong'. Leaving them to work things out 'became such an inner challenge that you wanted to do it right'. Fifty years later, these same ladies remember details with amazing clarity. There was Mrs Austin, who had started coming in to help in the afternoons. Also working at Playhouse in the mornings, she was deputed to make samples at Golf Links, cutting and chopping fabrics to make six-inch pieces. Often the weavers were asked to weave different colours of yarn onto one single colour on the warp. This fabric, very much like a patchwork quilt, would then be cut up to get individual colour patterns. So, over and above the name given to the generic fabric, each colour pattern would be given a number starting with one. Mrs Austin's task was to ensure that each sample had the number sticker on one particular side of the fabric and not the other. She sat and worked behind the chik in the alcove in the central room. She had to stick the samples onto paper and file them in a fabric reference file. When more colours were added to the same fabric they were all put onto that same sheet of paper. She also made sample sets which were sent out to different customers. This procedure was followed meticulously for years. Even today, when a client needs to select from among a variety of fabrics, swatches are cut out of the fabric and stapled with the name, number and price before being handed over for reference.

This leads us to the story of the naming of the fabrics. There is, of course, much to be written about the nature of the products themselves—the fabrics, durries, carpets and clothing—and their genesis, the suppliers and designers, but that will be dealt with later. When Amrita and Meena joined there was only one type of fabric being sold at Fabindia and that was Delhi Homespun Cotton. Available in six different colours and procured from the Cottage Industries, it was produced in Delhi and so carried the name of the city. The next fabric added to the inventory came from Panipat and was called Panipat Handspun or PP Handspun. In the beginning there was an attempt to name the material according to its place of origin, but there were so many weavers based around Delhi, that the procedure became inconvenient to follow and another one had to be adopted. 'When a fabric came in everybody sat around, looked at it and admired it and John would say, Now what should we call it? Somebody would say, Simla, or Manali, or Goa.' Some fabrics were named after towns associated with people. So there was a Hissar fabric because Bim had lived there for several years. Or there was a Jaipur fabric because the weavers were based there. There was a Dhanaulti because someone had just returned from a holiday there. And so it went on . . . with Barmer, Bhagalpur, Bombay, Barabanki . . . 'You name it and we had all the places you could think of on the India map.' Fabrics kept coming in and names ran out. Gradually the names had little to do with where the fabrics were coming from. Bedspreads came to be named after people. The Shaila bedspread was for Meena's daughter; the Padma bedspread for Bim's sister who was printing bedcovers. And then the durries were given girls' names—two of the most popular ones were called Haseena and Sangeeta. Though naming fabrics was a lot of fun it was taken very seriously by everyone in the office, and after it was done Mrs Austin would cut the swatch and name the sample meticulously before filing it. The good thing was that everyone knew what was being referred to including the regular customers who started asking for repeat fabrics by name. So a DHC-54 was the red Delhi Homespun fabric, while the green was DHC-55 and so on. The names have carried on to this day, as have some of the fabrics, and those who participated in the naming still retain a strong affinity to the product. This was one of the processes that ensured ownership of the brand amongst the staff.

Once Meena started handling the office, John was a little freer to travel around the country meeting new suppliers and searching for that special product that would make the difference. He also visited Thailand and was very impressed with Jim Thompson's professionally run business. 'I have a little way to go to catch up,' he wrote to his father on 9 December 1962. This was a good year for building capital. Fabindia sold another $6000 worth of shares to friends including a wealthy businessman from New York and a friend of the Bissell family, Harold Hochschild, who was impressed by John's commitment to the cause of hand-woven fabric.

New buyers were showing up in Delhi, a few from overseas but more from within India. The contact with the American Embassy too was yielding results. Since Fabindia was on the list of recommended retail, officers posted to Delhi would come to the Golf Links flat and choose fabrics to furnish their homes. According to Meena, the American Embassy had given the families of these officers a choice of three colours of pile carpets—rust, blue and green. The house had to be furnished around these colours. Ladies would come in with the carpet colour and Meena would sit with them and help them choose fabrics to match the carpets. Meena says: 'To help people decide we started making little charts with the three colours and matching colour samples for the curtains, and the upholstery. Maybe I learned a little about design this way.' The tailor who worked for the American Embassy introduced John to a group of weavers around Delhi. However these weavers had only worked with small quantities of fabric and had to be trained to weave up to 50 m of cloth. John, in the meantime, was experimenting constantly, 'looking to create that outstanding fabric that would sustain itself'. Soon Meena found herself sitting with the weavers reworking colours and designs. She learned about yarn counts, and that 'using 2-singles or 4-singles would make the fabric thinner or thicker'. Stripes and checks were tried with different colours. Colour wave samples filled Mrs Austin's alcove, and those that looked promising were woven into new fabric. To accommodate the new walk-in clients Fabindia started carrying stock. Fifty yard bales would have to be kept of the popular fabric because two sets of clients could use up to twenty-five yards each for their curtains. As stocks built up, bales filled every room in the flat. At one point even the garage was used to accommodate material. A couple of years later the stock-room floor developed a crack with the weight of the material lying on it!

In the late afternoons a deluge of friends and acquaintances would storm John's office and discussions would carry on into the night. Visitors sat on bales of fabric in the drawing room sipping tea. Patwant Singh says, 'the walls were stacked with bales of handwoven material. It was everywhere—under the bed, over the bed and on the floor!' According to Meena, John seemed to know everybody. He was equally at ease with buyers from Macy's and Neiman Marcus as he was with young professionals who had returned to India after their studies abroad and wanted to change the world! There was optimism and excitement about industry, manufacturing and economic development. There were discussions on politics and war, foreign affairs and khadi. Indians were waking up to Indian products, wanting to throw the colonial legacy of chintz curtains out of the window. This group was part of the larger circle of people formulating the ideas that brought in the cultural boldness of the '70s.

Meena remembers Chester Bowles dropping in with his wife. He had been appointed ambassador to India after Galbraith. Not only was he an old Bissell family friend, he was also close to Bim since she worked with him. There were social commitments in the evenings, picnics to old family country-houses with friends, and trips around India. John and Bim were now unofficially a couple and wedding plans were in the air.

In early 1963 John's sister Marie and her husband Tim visited India on a cultural tour. John drove them to production units in Rajasthan and introduced them to his weavers. Marie has since returned to India several times, but has never forgotten how impressed she was on that first trip by the aesthetics of traditional Indian architecture in the villages. Through the years John utilized every opportunity to share his excitement and involvement with India with his family. He would tell them, 'There is heart in India!'

On 23 September 1963 John Bissell married Bim Nanda, at 17 Rattendon Road (now Amrita Shergil Marg), the US Ambassador

Bowles' official residence in Delhi. The Bowles represented John's parents at the wedding and his good friend Patwant Singh was the best man. Families on both sides were delighted, and John was inducted formally into the Nanda household, figuratively and physically. He shifted out of Golf Links and moved in with Bim to the first floor of their house in Defence Colony. Bim's parents occupied the ground floor of D-387, and the young Bissells settled in above them. Like a good Indian couple, John and Bim lived within the expansive circle of the Nanda clan for many years, carrying the family with them when they shifted to their home in Friends Colony ten years later.

John and Bim returned from their honeymoon in the Kullu valley to find that August and September 1963 sales at Fabindia had been very good. In August, export sales recorded $1550 and the home market was $3200. In September, the figures were $1300 and $3100 respectively. A total of $9150 in two months! That was better than ever before.

However in the US there were serious problems with the agent, Design Imports, and a disagreement was in progress. John needed a minimum monthly order of $3000 from them, since Fabindia production was running between $4000 and $5000 a month. That was the minimum viable output to scale up the company. But the agent did not buy more than an average of $700 worth of merchandise a month in 1963. John wrote to them: 'Fabindia will face bankruptcy by the end of this year if we do not expand sales to the US immediately. This is a solemn fact to be understood and acted upon.'

In early 1964 Bill impressed upon John the need to come to the US to cancel the contract with the agent, meet buyers personally and increase his client base. '[Y]ou'll be able to do more about the US market when you are here ... seeing the trade here ... may give you some ideas that wouldn't occur to you at 43 Golf Links.'

So Bim and John Bissell made the first of their many trips to

Connecticut as a married couple. On his return John commented that he had 'learned a lot' from visiting the markets in New York and London. '[T]he new customer in London is absolutely terrific ... and [they] are obviously doing a roaring business—they feel the homespun cotton will be very successful.'

After this John's letters to his father are supplemented by the continuing correspondence between Bim and her in-laws, showing the mutual warmth and respect that would characterize the relationship between the Bissell families, now extended across two continents, for years to come.

On 19 December 1964 Bim wrote:

> John and I are trying to plot ways and means by which we may be able to entice you to come and visit us in Delhi ... we want you very much to come ... nothing could give us as much joy and happiness as to have you come and visit us ...

And then on 7 May 1966:

> We are overwhelmed by your letters—please don't thank us—it's we who want to say what a treat, delight, privilege and utter joy it was to spend a little time with you ...

In September 1964 there were celebrations in Fabindia, for sales had crossed $9000 in a single month. Bim wrote to John's parents in Connecticut: 'Fabindia business is booming. The best month yet—Rs. 44,000 in sales—50% better than the best month so far. John has given everyone a bonus—including us—for we go to Mussourie for the weekend!'

Thereafter Fabindia continued to grow and the final accounts at the end of 1964 reported a small profit. From this year John's financials would show a steady curve of increasing sales. By the end of 1964 Fabindia recorded sales of Rs 205,082 within India, and Rs 184,318 from export, which converted to a total of $81,966, at the current rate of Rs 4.76 a dollar. However it was still short of John's anticipated break-even figure of $100,000.

In addition to John the office now had a staff of three, with Chitra Chopra having joined Meena and Amrita. There seems to have been clearly designated work responsibilities though it was not obviously stated. John looked after the export work while Amrita handled all his correspondence. Meena was in charge of the office, including accounts and walk-in customers. Chitra assisted Meena. On 27 July, after returning from the US, John had written: 'Meena did an absolutely superb job in every way.'

This confidence in Meena's competence allowed the young Bissells to maintain a lifestyle which followed the same pattern over the next thirty years. Typically winter was the time when family, friends and clients landed in India. Months in advance, detailed itineraries were planned to coincide with the arrival of guests. In a letter persuading her in-laws to visit in the winter of 1964, Bim wrote: 'We are expecting no guests after the new year begins, and so we are going to dust out our best sheets and have the room ready just in case . . .' John was passionately interested in visiting every Indian state and studying its culture and craft first-hand. He wanted to understand people in their natural habitat, and made every effort to talk to them personally. It is true that all reports point to his struggle to master spoken Hindi, but it is also true that everyone mentions that he was a great communicator regardless of language. Soon after starting Fabindia John had appointed a Hindi teacher named Benjamin Singh who taught him for many years without great results but became a good friend. Monsoon recalls that her father had long conversations with Benjamin but they were not about Hindi. They were about politics. 'What life is like and how much are you earning and how do you make ends meet and how much do you spend?'

Those were good days for travelling around the country. Friends recall long drives to different parts of India with the Bissells in their second-hand Ambassador car. There was one ten-day trip in particular, when the Swayzes and the Bissells drove all the way to Jaisalmer in Rajasthan, that is remembered with great affection and amusement. Bim says they cruised through the desert trying to figure out what lay just beyond this hillock, or that plateau, stopping to find out as much as they could about the lives of the villagers. 'John always wanted to know what they did, what they made and how, and what they thought of the world.' On these trips Bim often served as the translator and the interpreter, but the Americans sometimes tried to make it on their own.

Tounsend Swayze, or T, and his wife, Felicity, were among the Bissells' closest friends. Felicity worked with Mrs Bowles as her secretary while Bim worked with Chester Bowles during 1964-67. Here is an account of a journey in T's words:

John and I had both laboured to learn Hindi and Benjamin Singh was our Hindi teacher. John was somewhat further advanced than I was but we both kind of struggled with a very basic Hindi. John was not shy and he made great efforts to communicate. He was very effective because he had such an engaging presence about him and people could not help but respond warmly to this man as we explored the bazaars in small villages. John was extraordinarily inquisitive, he just wanted to learn about everything and I was equally interested in rural India. I remember on one occasion our questions may have seemed silly because we were trying to find out all about that particular person we were speaking to. He was a farmer and we wanted to find out about his farming, what he grew, how much he grew, and how and where he marketed his goods. I remember one point in this conversation, we saw a man walking in the distance and John and I asked, in our broken Hindi, who that person was. The man we were talking to said simply, 'Oh, he's just another man, like you and me.' It put us in our place and I cannot forget that . . . John was so wonderful in relating to these people, in encouraging them, talking to them, [e]specially with his weavers. It was a relationship of trust and great care.

On another trip, T mentions that John and he came across a local fair where a handmade wooden Ferris wheel was spinning with many children on it. It was only fifteen feet high and John and T were fascinated by it. John had been buying all kinds of interesting things in Rajasthan like camel saddles and rough, handmade goat-wool rugs, and they considered buying the Ferris wheel too, but couldn't figure out where to keep it in Delhi. Of course they didn't buy it but John talked about it many times later, regretting that he had not brought it back with him. Even thirty years afterwards, paralysed and unable to talk, John would remind T about the Ferris wheel that they had left behind in the desert.

So winters were spent taking guests around India, and in the summer the Bissells would plan their US holiday, spending up to six–eight weeks with the family in Connecticut. On these journeys John and Bim often stopped over with friends in Europe and England, where John would also meet new clients or regular buyers to check out the market and discuss work. John often travelled alone to hold Fabindia board meetings and attend to legal and administrative work in Connecticut with the directors of his company.

Early in 1965 a decision was taken to find a larger space for Fabindia. There was not enough room on the first floor of 43 Golf Links. Business had grown and the landlord was upset about the bales of cotton fabric that threatened to break through the floors. Also it was thought advisable to search for office premises in an area more accessible to customers.

That summer John visited Connecticut to attend the first meeting of the board of directors, and the annual general meeting of the shareholders of Fabindia Inc. On 9 July John Bissell was appointed president of Fabindia Inc., and Meena Rai named Manager, India office. Patwant Singh was elected as a director in the US company, along with Bill Bissell, Milton DeVane and James Fraser. The corporation voted to sell some shares to Bob and Blakie Worth, an American couple who were friends of the Bissells. John reported that there was enough capital in the company to build up stock, by storing popular fabric in Canton. With the possibility of faster delivery he was confident of better sales in the US. He announced that Fabindia was beginning to turn around and had earned a small profit in India due to local customers and a few good international buyers.

For the next ten years we have lively letters from John's father who, along with his wife, was supervising the US Fabindia office, mainly out of the Canton Green Store. His play-writing skills come into play at every opportunity and provide amusing and dramatic details of otherwise routine office affairs. On 5 November 1965, Bill wrote to John and Bim:

> At the Canton Green store—at the same instant—arrived two great trucks, dwarfing the store and all its outbuildings, and also the church, with their cargo ... It looked like a crisis, much as though the troops of Hannibal and of Napoleon had encountered each other at the Alps' summit. But finally the two transportation commanders acknowledged each other's presence—saluted, shook hands— and ended by helping each other to unload.

Here he is referring to the simultaneous arrival of two Fabindia shipments! Both were best sellers in the Fabindia product line. One was the Canton Carry-All, a canvas bag that John's mother Elinor had developed, which sold very well at her store. And the other was 'bolts of beautiful fabric', that is, 600–700 yards of Delhi Homespun, destined for their now regular buyer Design Research in San Francisco. Here is another delightful description of 'Pa and Ma' working at the Store (in the same letter), having just finished erecting a new five-shelf rack to accommodate rising imports:

You ought to see the natives working here on Fabindia, in their picturesque costumes consisting of dirty old pants & sneakers. They're reasonably conscientious, and it's the very cheapest labour you'll get, even in India! The old barn's full: we'll have to sell, to make room . . .

Back in India the political climate was changing. There was trouble brewing on the border with Pakistan. Since the 1962 debacle with China, India had been attempting to build up its demoralized army to deal with contentious neighbours. Political analysts reported that India's best-loved prime minister, Jawaharlal Nehru, had died a 'tired and broken man in 1964 . . . unable to come to terms with the fact that China had hoodwinked India . . . and to realize that no amount of rapid industrialization had helped create a well-equipped armed force.' Lal Bahadur Shastri was now the prime minister of India. Notwithstanding his gentle demeanour Shastri had taken some key economic decisions and initiated the Green Revolution which would eventually lead to India becoming a food-surplus nation. Mrs Bowles (still the US ambassador's wife), along with Bim as translator, visited Mrs Shastri and found her to 'be a lovely person'.

John's letters to his father at this time were full of anxiety for India on issues ranging from communal trouble to American military aid to Pakistan. He wrote: 'It makes me sick at heart to know that we have such imbecile leaders in Washington to keep permitting Military Aid to be sent to Pakistan.' Amazing prescience led him to worry about the plebiscite in Kashmir. If Kashmir separated from India it could lead to the rise of communal forces that would coerce India to abandon its secular state. Declaration of war in August 1965 sent the weavers, mostly Muslim, back to their homes fearing violence. Almost every Punjabi family known to the Bissells in Delhi had at least one member in the armed forces who was actively involved in the war. Bim's uncle, General Sibal, was in command of a section of the 'front', and John managed to visit him after the ceasefire. He wrote: 'I had never been to an actual battle area before—it was pretty grim—everyone is dug in and on the alert.' And then again, strong views on India: 'I have had a lot of critical things to say about my second home, but it is a Secular state; it is a functioning democracy, & it certainly is not belligerent . . . And should be supported by the US at the UN and everywhere . . .'

On the Fabindia front, war had seriously affected business. Production decreased because weavers had run away to their villages and shipments suffered due to delay in international flights. But two significant events took place in 1965 that carried the company to a new phase in its corporate history. In October Fabindia moved into a new building with two floors and a Fabindia sign above the entrance. 440 Mathura Road had the showroom on the ground floor and the office on the floor above. It worked really well for Meena because she was getting married and her fiancé (the architect, Morad Chowdhury) also lived on Mathura Road, just across the street from the new office building. Meena Chowdhury's staff had by now been supplemented by men who would handle the stock, look after the showroom and pack the shipments. There was Mangal Singh, Paan Singh and Achan Khan's son, Abdul. John liked the idea of recruiting people who were related to existing members of the staff. He felt that this strengthened the loyalty factor and built permanent relationships. So we find several generations of kinship coexisting on the Fabindia shop-floor—parents and children, uncles, brothers and cousins.

The Fabindia–Conran association also started in 1965. There was a lady whom John had got to know while working with the Cottage Industries. She had since gone abroad to study design and returned to India in 1965. Her name was Sonia Pandhi (née Thadani). Sonia introduced John to a friend, David Hicks, a very successful designer, who was married to Lord Mountbatten's daughter, Pamela. This couple in turn introduced John to Terence Conran who was looking for an Indian contact to buy products for his UK company, Conran Fabrics. Soon Terence founded his next business, Habitat, to retail home furnishings, and opened stores around the world within ten years. The Habitat connection catapulted Fabindia into financial security for the next twenty-five years and fulfilled John Bissell's dream of finding the perfect buyer.

In Terence, John found a partner to fuel his creativity. Terence loved the fabric Delhi Homespun Cotton, and decided to introduce six colours of DHC into his line. He devised the Conran fabric card which looked like a book mark with cut-out windows. The six colours of DHC were stuck onto the card and showed through the windows. This card was then sent out to Conran's buyers to promote the fabric.

Bim tells the story of the original Punjab cotton durrie that had caught John's eye. Traditionally, families in the Punjab had slept on string cots (*manji*) covered with rough cotton durries. A tough but thinner cotton mat, called a *khes*, covered the durrie. Both the durrie and the khes were typically multicoloured so that dirt did not show easily! Above the khes would be spread the cotton bed sheet. Bim's mother must have carried a number of such items in her dowry when she got married. In the cities string cots had given way to the bed-with-mattress combination, so the durries were used as casual throws on verandah furniture. John decided to develop this durrie as a Fabindia product and set off to Ambala to meet Mr Shyam Sundar who was producing them. He was also looking for bedspreads—reworking the khes concept in a way. Shyam Sundar's cheerful durries suited the Indian taste for colour but were too strong for the Western market, so John decided to rework the designs. That was the year Terence came to India and John took him along with him to Ambala to see this product. Meena Chowdhury accompanied them 'for the first time to Ambala', and these are her recollections of that trip:

> I remember that Terence got so excited with this product
> that he didn't just squat on the floor, he almost lay on the

floor and wanted a piece of paper and threads of yarn, and right there he worked out a colour width. He selected three yarns and said that those three colours would look beautiful together. The weavers who were sitting at the loom actually wove a portion right then and Terence was so happy he couldn't stop himself and worked out more and more colour waves on the spot. There was a black & white which was a very classical one, an orange & red, and blues & greens, all of which were a great combination of colours.

The product had to be named and Meena suggested 'Haseena'— thus a bestseller was born, which soon featured in the Habitat catalogue for the next year.

A year later in 1966, due to Shastri's untimely death, Nehru's daughter, Indira Gandhi, became prime minister. She had to deal with serious economic problems during her first two years in office. India was still very deficient in food grain and desperately dependent on the US under a public loan scheme called the Public Law 480 (PL 480) through which it imported fifteen million tons of wheat in 1965 and 1966. Many US government officials moved to Delhi during this period to monitor the programme. These officers, along with the Peace Corp volunteers (Kennedy's project to promote world peace and friendship attracted many Americans to work in the developing countries), constituted a large part of Fabindia's clientele in those years. But persistent food imports, along with the import of arms, industrial machinery and technology, created a serious balance of payments crisis. In June 1966, bowing to pressure from the International Monetary Fund (IMF), the government announced a huge devaluation of the rupee–dollar exchange rate—from Rs 4.76 to Rs 7.50. Overnight the value of Fabindia's exports almost doubled in Indian rupees.

In June 1966 a boy was born to Bim and John Bissell. He was named after John's father and also carried Bim's maiden name.

The following was Bill's response to the cable announcing the arrival of William Nanda Bissell on 10 June:

> Your cable got us up at 7.30 this morning here and we nearly exploded with happiness ... how deeply touched and proud I am to have him named partly for me ... how delighted the whole tribe will be ... and ... Devaluation of the Rupee should help exports in general and WNB's father's business in particular ...

The devaluation of the rupee coincided with William's birth, and typically for the Bissells, both events were discussed with avid interest in the same note. The characteristic quality of both John's and Bill's letters was that the scale of information covered the personal and the official in equal measure, one often leading to the other as though connected in some way.

John was optimistic that year and wrote to his father on 26 June:

> [The m]onsoon arrived right on schedule ... Now we hope for steady rains about every 10 days ... it really is so crucial. You have read of import liberalization—the big step that had to be taken after Devaluation ... now it is up to Industry to get going ... Mrs Gandhi has been strong, honest and courageous in her speeches and actions—and inspires a lot of confidence.

He reduced the prices of items post the devaluation of the rupee and got a favourable response from some buyers. A London client 'seem[s] to think the new rate is great' and increased his order subsequently. However, notwithstanding the devaluation Fabindia sales did not make it to John's magic figure of $100,000 even that year, and it needed another product, another special, sustainable item to make the difference.

Well, the year that William Bissell was born, another life-long relationship was forged around just such a product, woven in wool and based in Panipat.

John's old employer and also an occasional client, Macy's, was looking for 'embossed woollen hand-knotted rugs' from India. They contacted John who asked his old friend and supplier of PP Handspun, Amrit Lal Batra, to put him in touch with a supplier of woollen rugs. There was such a company in Panipat called Bharat Carpet Manufacturers (BCM). So John wrote a letter to BCM on 17 May 1966, addressed to Anand Sagar Khera, inquiring about samples in 'both embossed self-coloured designs as well as European patterns' for several sizes of rugs. He clearly stated that though he was representing Macy's, BCM must do the export directly to earn the incentive themselves, for 'we take no commission, but merely try to find the best suppliers for Macy's.'

There was a postscript to the letter requesting Mr Khera to make a sample that John was interested in. He had sent a length of yarn with the letter, and wrote: 'please make me a sample of a carpet using this yarn in a golden colour similar to the swatch attached, in a medium quality with a very long pile, i.e. about 1½ in.' Similar requests though describing different yarns, colours and designs would make up the reams of correspondence that would be exchanged between John Bissell and three generations of Kheras over the next few years. Letters sent by post and by hand, phone conversations noted on the backs of invoices, purchase orders in thousands, and finally faxes and computer print-outs fading into illegibility–these comprise the archive of a forty-year-old relationship between the two companies. When John wrote that first letter Anand Sagar Khera was fifty years old, his father Tulsidas eighty and Madhukar, his son, just entering the business at twenty. Together with John, BCM would create a product that would identify Fabindia in India, and more so in the Habitat stores around the world.

Starting from that first letter in May 1966, right up to May 1967, John and Madhukar continued experimenting across Delhi and Panipat making samples of different colours, strengths and sizes in thick, hand-spun natural wool. The communication focused on the creation of these druggets is fascinating:

14 September 1966: John Bissell asked for samples as soon as possible of 'thick hand-spun natural wool, 6 knots per sq. inch, ¾ inch pile' and also one of a 1-inch pile, 'woven very tightly so the quality is fine.'

28 October 1966: John wanted samples of the hand-spun wool qualities called Ajanta and Ellora in brown/natural mix, and also placed the first order for both in different colours of natural mixed wool. 'Please dye all the woollen yarn in 1 bath so as to deliberately get variations in shade.' Drugget names had been mentioned for the first time.

29 March 1967: 'I have been looking at the 9' x 12' Ajanta durrie—it is really a very nice piece, and, I think, should be a very saleable item.' He wanted the sample size of 6' x 9' urgently, and clearly stated: 'Please purchase at once at least 200 kilos of brown/natural mix yarn—we will guarantee to use it up'.

3 April 1967: Madhukar replied: 'There will not be much difficulty regarding the availability of natural colour brown yarn in any period of the year.'

6 April 1967: 'Please get us 6'x 9' durries with all possible speed.' And 'I am asking you again to please stock some yarn, so we can speed it up.' Again he requested: 'I want it woven just as tightly as possible, so it will be firm.'

13 April 1967: 'We are very anxious to get the sample drugget . . .'

15 April 1967: Madhukar replied: 'I can really imagine and appreciate your anxiousness . . . The position is that the yarn in our hand was not enough for 6' x 9' drugget . . . Now with enough yarn at our disposal the sample druggets will be ready in the next couple of days . . . I am also working on getting this hand-spun yarn made at Panipat . . . Tomorrow I shall try to dye white yarn, using different techniques to get the uneven effect. If this method works, it shall be very easy to dye bulk quantities.'

22 April 1967: There was an order for one Ajanta-quality

durrie: 'Please make the weaving very tight and yarn thick.'

24 April 1967: Feedback on the sample: 'In some places the yarn is a little thin and the warp shows. Please make sure the yarn remains thick and the weaving very tight. We must maintain the quality all the time.'

26 April 1967: Another order for an Ajanta durrie as per sample.

25 May 1967: Finally the result—a big order to BCM for 504 pieces of Ajanta-quality woollen druggets in different sizes. This was accompanied by a letter specifying the number of looms to be used and the days required per loom for each size of drugget so as to be clear about the delivery dates.

For Fabindia this was the largest order to date. The triumvirate of John Bissell, Madhukar Khera and Terence Conran would supply thousands of natural, hand-spun mix-wool rugs to homes across the world for twenty-five years. And in 1967 Fabindia finally crossed $136,000 in total sales!

In 1967 general elections were held in which the Congress lost six states to regional parties. Indira Gandhi returned as prime minister and John looked forward to a more liberal trade policy. But that was not to be. India didn't have enough internationally competitive industries to reap the benefits of a significantly devalued currency, and the precarious balance of payment situation made Mrs Gandhi suspicious of any form of economic liberalization. She was determined to set India on an inward-oriented, license-driven, government-directed growth path, under an anti-rich socialist mantle. Working steadily towards gaining absolute control of the Congress she introduced various measures to alienate the older members of the party. She nationalized fourteen major Indian banks and insisted on her presidential candidate for India. In 1970 she formed a new Congress (R) after being expelled from the Congress and was joined by a large number of the cadre who had crossed the floor of the Lower House to support her. Within a year she called for early elections using one of India's greatest political slogans '*garibi hatao*' (eliminate poverty). Campaigning tirelessly she became the face of a new India, and won by a large majority. Indira immediately drove home her electoral advantage. Her mandate was to reduce poverty by taxing the rich, subsidizing the poor, creating greater state ownership of the means of production and imposing regulations on the conduct of business. There were severe import controls through high tariffs, which were often in three-digits, and multiple quotas that restricted free trade. Strict restrictions on the use of hard foreign currency led to the practice of under-invoicing of exports and over-invoicing of imports, with the cash being kept in foreign bank accounts. Exporting required filling up many forms, securing different clearances and seeking permission every step of the way, thus unleashing a tide of corrupt officials who lined their pockets through every procedure. It was a frustrating time for anybody in business except the few who were influential enough to wield serious political clout.

John's letters at this time reflected his concern over port and truck strikes, the food crisis, political unrest and business recession, but Fabindia exports continued to grow. In a letter to his parents on 28 March 1968 he wrote: 'Everything is fine here; we have almost $20,000 in export orders pending which is terrific—helps a great deal in planning.' He was now looking at diversifying into silk, for 'it looks as if we will be able to buy Tussor yarns and use them on our looms in Delhi. This will make a great difference as there is considerable interest in heavy silk fabrics, but we haven't been able to make them previously because we didn't have the yarn.'

Along with durries and woollen rugs, Fabindia added bedspreads and table linen to its line of merchandise. There were now five girls in the office which was in 'the smoothest shape it has ever been . . . Meena has done a beautiful job and I am delighted.' At the end of 1968, Fabindia sales recorded over $195,000.

On 23 November 1969 John wrote that it was an 'exciting

week for business as we got an order for about $32,000 from
Habitat in London for cotton durries ... Things are looking
glorious.' And then in December the Bissell family was complete.
A daughter was born to Bim and John, and was named Monsoon
after India's favourite season. In a letter to his father John gave
an amusing description of the baby: 'She is a kind of cheruby
little creature—quite long—very round fat-cheeked face—some hair.
In short everything is just lovely.' A month later Bim described
Monsoon's first morning to her in-laws: 'John was there reading
your cables, and there were beautiful roses and sunshine ... and
it was altogether a wonderful feeling to be alive and living and
have so much to be grateful and happy for.'

The next year Fabindia rented an additional space near the
office to store, pack and ship the expanding line of floor coverings
'which are bulky', and also opened a retail outlet in one of the
rooms for the sale of durries and rugs. John was keen to produce
a larger variety of floor coverings and local sales would give him
the opportunity to experiment with this product. A small line of
clothing had also been introduced for export, with kurtas and
kaftans made from handloom fabric and hand-block prints.

The nature of the Fabindia operation, with its head office in
the US and its main business located out of India, created some
peculiar financial problems. Some percentage of the initial
investment in Fabindia had been transferred to Delhi to enable
John to start the business. Shareholders had been informed that
dividends would only be distributed once the company had
stabilized. But dollar profits could not be repatriated from India.
Also between 1969 and 1971 taxes were raised to absurd heights
with corporate tax moving up from 30 per cent to 65 per cent
and personal income tax to 96 per cent!

On 16 June 1969 John wrote: 'Our Indian accounts have just
been completed and show a before tax profit of about $5300,
after taxes $1600 ...' But, two years later on 27 November 1971,
the profit margin had changed: 'Everything is actually going

along very well in office ... we are going to show quite a large profit this year i.e. about $30,000—nice except we have to pay tax on all this before the end of the year i.e. about $20,000, which means we have to accumulate this much.'

The profit after tax (now 70 per cent of revenue) was retained as working capital for the India office. John wrote: 'I have planned all along that stockholders' dividends should come from the profits made at our Head Office'. But the Delhi office had a constant cash flow problem due to its emphasis on buying stock and holding a large inventory. On the other hand since Fab-Canton, with few overheads, 'operated like an independent distributor: buying from India with its own funds, selling, collecting and depositing the proceeds', there was more than enough dollar income to pay for Canton purchases and build inventory. On 18 May 1970 John explained his position to his shareholders: 'I have concentrated, in India, on developing sales, possibly at the expense of a smaller profit margin.' The idea was to increase sales through competitive pricing and maintain a higher level of production. That would directly ensure more employment to the weavers since everything was handmade.

There are a few beautifully handcrafted annual reports (printed on hand made paper with real fabric samples inserted in the pages) that have survived the years, and still preserve the personal statements and sales analyses worked out by John Bissell for his US shareholders between 1969 and 1972. John presented his export sales figures for each country with detailed explanations. Large international buyers from different cities had started figuring in the list: Trade Action from Australia, Habitat from the UK, stores in Copenhagen, Germany and Brussels, regular clients from Mauritius and Hong Kong, an excellent store, La Renascente, in Milan, and many more in the US, including Bloomingdales, Far Eastern Fabrics and, of course, Fabindia USA.

Between 1969 and 1974 the Fabindia sales curve rose steeply, reporting a 200 per cent increase in five years. This growth was achieved despite the continuing constraints of economic policies in India at the time. The first of these was that export quotas had been imposed which forced companies to push their shipments through 'a first come first serve basis'. Second, multiple permits, clearance certificates and regulatory licenses slowed down the delivery process and contributed to increasing business overheads. Third, the duty drawback and cash incentive system available to exporters encouraged unethical practices such as under-quoting and slashing rates to profit only by the incentives. The result was that craftsmen were forced to decrease their margins and so the industry suffered. John fought with the Handicrafts Board to cancel these incentives. He saw that the quota system was 'really rough on . . . thousands of weavers and printers, and tailors [who] will be out of work . . . it is damn cruel'. Amrita Verma recalls that the Textile Committee was required to check all merchandise before they were packed for shipping, ostensibly to avoid the malpractice of under-invoicing. But the system bred corruption rather than ethics. There was a 5 per cent bribe to clear dishonest shipments and a 2.5 per cent bribe to pass merchandise that was clear. She reports that Fabindia had a policy of not paying bribes to any department regardless of the delays caused by these principles. Eventually the inspectors learned to respect the fact that John Bissell's office was not amenable to negotiation. Bim remembers that John used to go to all the offices personally. He would sit outside every place where he needed a permission or a license. And he would get it finally, without having to compromise his conscience.

But there was worse to come. India's resounding victory over Pakistan in 1971 and the liberation of Bangladesh had further strengthened Indira Gandhi's political position in India and she pressed for more economic sanctions. In 1973 she passed a draconian legislation, the Foreign Exchange Regulation Act. FERA was valid for any enterprise which had a 40 per cent or more foreign equity and prohibited it from a) carrying on existing activities without periodic approvals from the Reserve Bank of India, and b) expanding capacity or output. Processes became even more cumbersome. Import quotas became sacrosanct and were administered through endless licenses. Every act of spending or earning foreign currency involved multiple clearances and documentation. And yet it was found that the incidence of poverty had only increased in the past decade.

At first John was excited about developing 'Indian solutions for Indian problems' (1972), and on a private visit to the prime minister with his good friends Charles and Monika Correa was impressed with the 'relaxed leader of 550 million people discussing flowers and Japanese gardens . . .' with them. But soon his optimism suffered with the 'real problems of unemployment, scarcity of raw material, terrific shortage of electricity, wholesale evasion of income tax, terrific lowering of educational standards and suffocating bureaucracy . . .' On 20 April 1973 he wrote to his father: 'Economic growth is pretty good for the elite & the middle class, but not much percolates down to the bottom . . . is there another democratic alternative?' Then again in September 1974:

> Often I feel I would like to do something else . . . be the Finance Minister or Commerce Secretary . . . most rewarding . . . would be the job of leading a quiet peaceful democratic but successful revolution to implement in great haste all the reforms that are imperative if we are serious about insuring 1500 calories a day for everyone.

The voluntary quota system for 'made-ups', i.e., durries, bedspreads and clothing, agreed upon between the US and India in 1970, finally affected delivery to Fabindia US. There were fixed expenses on 'made-ups', therefore margins were low. The rush to send shipments out within the allotted quota period resulted in increased costs on air freight. Sea freight was a lengthier process and often resulted in the shipment missing the time slot allotted.

US protectionist policy along with the general quota embargo in India created a serious problem for the struggling business in Canton. In 1973 the Canton Green Store was in financial distress and John considered renting the store as a warehouse for Fabindia stock and retail. Large export orders that had not been dispatched due to the quota restrictions were lying around as stock. Canton also had a stock pile-up of non-saleable items. This was inevitable since 'almost everything we do is new to the market'. With excessive money tied up in stock Fabindia faced a cash crunch and John was back to the essential problem. To control the pipeline was an endless adjustment between orders—production—dispatch. Tired of coping with unrealistic economic restrictions, John complained about the 'muddling bureaucracy' and the quick money that was being made by 'cornering quotas'.

But in mid-December 1973 Fabindia got a 'rather sensational order from Habitat!!!' The value of the order was $500,000 and 'this seems to be only half the order ... This is larger than our total exports in 1973. It is overwhelming and tremendous and quite a challenge—I am going to try and take it up—the largest part is for the woollen druggets ($200,000)—our weavers in Panipat are excited and willing to take on the challenge of doubling their production.' The rest of the order was divided between cotton durries, bedspreads and fabrics. John admitted candidly: 'We certainly won't be able to meet their delivery schedules—they must have realized that when they sent the order ... these are the challenges ... in India.'

The India office had expanded to six people. With the large order from Habitat in their hands the financial crunch was over and shipments were leaving Bombay 'fairly smoothly'. John was excited by what was happening in his office. But the euphoria was short-lived. Within a year Habitat cut down the order and the spectre of over-production hung over Fabindia once more. On 2 August 1974 John wrote: 'Just too bad to cut back when it has been really rolling—which was fun—& more seriously, weavers will be out of work.' In addition he saw trouble in India: 'The economy is in bad shape & I don't think the planners know what to do.' Recession had hit hard, inflation had increased by 35 per cent and 'weavers have kept bringing in fabrics etc. very fast because they all need to work so hard to keep up with inflation'. The monsoon too had been bad that year and there were crippling power cuts in Delhi. On 22 November 1974 he felt, 'Morality around here continues to sink slowly but very steadily.'

Gradually stirrings of discontent rose against Indira Gandhi's economic policies across the country. Students protested against government inefficiency and corruption. Jayapraksh Narayan, a national figure respected for his incorruptibility, challenged the government. He led a silent protest in Patna against hunger, inflation, injustice and corruption, and talked of the need for a 'total revolution'. He was subsequently joined by George Fernandes, a fiery trade union leader, who engineered an all-India railway strike. Protests increased throughout the state. Jayaprakash Narayan led a protest rally in Delhi which was attended by lakhs of people. This movement became Indira Gandhi's greatest challenge to power. And in 1975 a maverick politician Raj Narain won a legal decision against Indira Gandhi at the Allahabad High Court that declared her election to Parliament in 1971 null and void. She had to step down from power but decided to take the challenge head on. Spurred on by her ambitious son Sanjay Gandhi, she got a pliant President to sign an ordinance declaring a state of internal emergency in the state of India on 25 June 1975.

All key Opposition members were put behind bars, including Jayaprakash Narayan. There were severe restrictions on newspapers and magazines. Power supply to their offices was cut off. No editorial material was allowed into India. Anybody criticizing Mrs Gandhi's policies was arrested under the deadly Maintenance of Internal Security Act (MISA), including student leaders and writers. Many of John's friends were journalists and were 'thrown out of India at 24 hours notice'. 'Quality of life has changed, one goes out less', he wrote on 28 August 1975. Conversation was inhibited especially with reporters and the press. On 2 October 1975 John wrote to his father: 'We have little idea of what is going on in India as all the news is subject to the guidelines of the censor'. Jacques Leslie was arbitrarily asked to leave, 'a very nice thoughtful, serious, sensitive guy ... Los Angeles Times correspondent, writing low-key articles, critical but never based on speculative gossip, [who] stayed off personalities, we thought [was] very good writing under mighty difficult conditions of censorship.'

That year however was good for business at Fabindia. In Canton, Jacquie, who had been appointed by Fabindia to handle the US office, was reporting better sales. Buyers were responding to quicker delivery due to available stocks lying in the store. 1974 closed with $835,222 in total sales, more than 68 lakhs in Indian rupees. However due to increasing expenses—mainly production and shipping costs—the profit margin had been low. After the Emergency was imposed, incentives were reintroduced in 1975 and Fabindia cashed in on a percentage on exports of cotton fabrics, durries and bedcovers. Import licenses issued against export could be officially leased out for a fee and added to the profit margins. John took advantage of these policies and reduced rates again. There was more good news. Fabindia won the income tax case that had been filed in 1972 and was granted exemption from paying tax out of 'profits made as a result of export purchases by a non-resident company'.

By 1975 the Mathura Road office was getting cramped and John was keen to move to a larger office in a commercial area. Meena and John had also discussed opening a retail store for all the products handled by Fabindia. Meena thought that Indian customers were ready for the Fabindia product. The export showroom had seen a steady increase in walk-in clients over the past few years. Some people visited regularly to keep in touch with new developments, even though local sales had initially been introduced to clear leftovers and non-exportable designs. She said, '[Fabindia] had the supply base, and the staff so why not retail?'

The space where the durries were stored and sold was located in the Greater Kailash (GK) N-block market. In those days the market was a dump with some small general goods stores, a tea shop, a hairdresser and a furniture unit. John saw the potential this market had and decided to invest in it. The ground floor at N-14 was the first retail space rented by Fabindia and within a few months the first floor was taken on. Within ten years, Fabindia would move across the market picking up another four shops, and would start maintaining the central park within the market. By the '80s the market was called the Fabindia market. It was John's foresight or luck but as it happened, Delhi expanded towards the south, and between 1970 and 1980 many residential colonies were built around the area. Geographically, the N-block, GK-1 market occupied the centre of South Delhi by the mid 1980s.

In 1976 John Bissell decided that he needed to set up an Indian company to be able to deal with the enlarging scope of his business. Increasing regulations were making it difficult to operate a US-based import house through a branch office in Delhi. Foreign companies could not be set up without a majority stake by an Indian partner. The process was initiated in early 1976 and would take a year. Fabindia Inc. at Mathura Road would transit to Fabindia Overseas Pvt. Ltd at N-block, GK-1 market, New Delhi.

·3·

THE BUILDING OF AN INDIAN BRAND
1976-90

As far as Delhi is concerned Fabindia started in 1976. Any talk about Fabindia's fiftieth anniversary in 2010 gets people worried. Could they have aged so fast? Post-Independence Delhi babies born in the '50s remember buying their first chic khadi kurtas from Fabindia in the late '70s when they were in university. More specifically those who studied in the Lady Shri Ram (LSR) College in 1976-78 argue about the year Fabindia started. Everybody knows that Fabindia's first retail outlet was in the N-block, GK-1 market, a stone's throw from LSR, the fashionable women's college in South Delhi. So if these girls were teenagers in 1976, how could they have aged fifty years since? Was it not in the '80s that they furnished their first homes with Fabindia bedspreads and durries with their meagre incomes?

All this is true. Fabindia engaged its clientele so completely while developing its local retail business that it became a Delhi landmark within ten years. Whereas Fabindia Inc. had built itself up as a successful export company from 1960, it was only after the shop started in 1976 that the popular Indian brand was born. The Fabindia style has carried thousands of young men and women across the threshold of their first homes, typically in Delhi 'barsatis', to fancy apartments across the metropolises of urban India over the last forty years.

But we are running ahead with the story.

Fabindia Inc., still at its office on Mathura Road, had turned over a hefty $716,000 in export sales in 1975. In those days the figure translated to an appreciable Rs 58 lakh, and John Bissell felt comfortable leasing additional space in the GK-1 market. By the end of 1975 Fabindia had taken over the basement, ground, first and second floors of N-14 GK-1. Space was required to stock and pack large cotton and woollen durries and fabric for the expanding order book in the Export department. A decision was also taken to open a small shop in the front portion of N-14 to check out the response to Fabindia retail.

The Indian government had warned the company that it was illegal to operate out of the residential premises on Mathura Road, and advised them to shift to a commercial space. The Emergency was still on and it would have been indiscreet to ignore the notice. Fabindia signed the lease for the building in the N-block market and John turned to his friend, Riten Mazumdar, for help with the design of the new store and office.

The two men had been friends since their first meeting at the design centre of the Cottage Emporium in 1958. Since then Riten had trained with the iconic Finnish textile designer, Armi Ratia, in Marimekko, a company founded by her in Helsinki in 1951. Armi was one of the first entrepreneurs to see the potential of a designer-led textile house. In 1961 Riten opened his own studio, M Prints, in South Extension in Delhi, to design and print saris for Delhi's fashionable elite. At that time John Bissell had also kept some Fabindia stock in his store for local retail. However the shop was not a success and Riten closed the business. An extremely talented artist, he continued to work as a graphic and textile designer in Delhi, and became one of John's closest friends over the years. John wrote to his parents on 21 January 1976:

> Riten will help with planning the new premises for office and shop and much as I hate to move from this very satisfactory location, I feel cheerful now at the move . . . Meena as usual has been a great help and I think will be

able to organize the whole thing with a minimum dislocation of exports. I will be seeing the authorities this week to see if there is any urgency in our move—and after that we will work on some kind of timetable, but we have lots of space to move the fabrics to.

Talking about those days Bim says that John was worried about Sanjay Gandhi's drive to move businesses out of residential areas. A policeman had recently visited the Fabindia office on Mathura Road asking for a bribe to allow them time to move out. Upright and law abiding to a fault John felt threatened and depressed about the state of affairs in the country. His letters reflect his helplessness: 'it is very sad because so far there are no specific policies, no resurgence of the economy & no indication that the poor are getting to be better looked after.' A good friend of his, Larry Lifshultz, 'a good, sober, low-key, check-out-the-facts guy', working for the *Far Eastern Economic Review*, had been asked to leave India within twenty-four hours. John was so affected by this that he personally drove Larry to the airport even though he had been advised not to openly show his association with journalists who were out of political favour.

The political climate notwithstanding it was business as usual for Fabindia. As happened every year, March 1976 brought buyers to India and John took Terence Conran and his wife, Caroline, and their designer, Jeremy Smith, on a trip to different weaving centres around India. They visited Hyderabad, Madras, Cochin, Calicut, Kerala, Goa and Bombay. 'John worked without taking time out to breathe', says Bim. Bim took a couple of days off from her job at the World Bank and joined the group for two days in Goa along with young William. At the end of the trip Conran left Fabindia with an order worth $225,000. Detailing the order in Indian rupees, John said that there was Rs 6 lakh worth in orders for new items and 12 lakhs in reorders of old items. John wrote to his parents on his birthday, 23 March:

I had an absolutely terrific trip with the Conrans & Jeremy Smith. All the arrangements worked well, they were very turned on by what they saw, a real rapport was established with the suppliers who were most hospitable . . . he is also our prime customer . . . and an easy, convivial, humorous relationship developed.

The government was acting tough and Bim's letter to Canton in April 1976 expressed concern about the fact that the authorities had cut off water supply to the Mathura Road office and 'so the entire office will be moving very soon. In view of these circumstances, John has been extremely wise in getting two new premises. One on the same side as the shop and the other across the park [in the N-block, GK-1 market].' The same year a letter arrived from the Reserve Bank of India (RBI) stating that under the FERA, foreign companies were banned from operating in India. Fabindia Inc., a company registered in the US, could at best own 40 per cent shares in an Indian company. John Bissell along with Mohinder Puri, Fabindia's chartered accountant, tried to work out a solution and a letter was sent to the US stockholders on 29 July 1976. It stated:

> Basically we will form a new company in which Fabindia USA has a 40% share, the maximum allowed. The new company will be called Fabindia Private Limited . . . The authorized and paid up capital would be Rs 500,000. 40% i.e. Rs 200,000 would be held by your Company and the balance Rs 300,000 offered to a few people here who understand and are in sympathy with Fabindia's aims. In addition to making profit, our aims are constant development of new handwoven products and the maintenance of quality on which our reputation stands.

While hoping to become managing director of the new company John requested that he be allowed to continue as president of Fabindia USA. The Indian company would appoint four or five new directors and all employees would maintain the same positions and salaries as before. He continued in the same letter:

Our accounts would be audited as of the close of business September 30. These figures will then be used to establish the net worth which should be around Rs 850,000. The difference between this figure and Fabindia USA's investment in the new Company (Rs 200,000), i.e. Rs 650,000 would be due to Fabindia USA.

John Bissell stated very clearly that the money would be remitted as soon as the RBI permitted it, a procedure that could take a couple of years. He was also clear that it was in everybody's interest to continue this business in India since closing it down would 'jeopardize the security of our employees, the weavers who work for us and the source of supply for our own Head office (Canton).' Quoting the sales figures for 1975 and 1976 he says 'we are doing well, as you see.' The sales in 1975 were $716,000 (Rs 5,800,000) with a profit of $81,000 (Rs 648,000). The 1976 January–June sales were $525,000 (Rs 4,200,000) with pending export orders of another $600,000 (Rs 4,800,000).

Over the next few months the chartered accountant firm, Mohinder Puri & Co., argued with the government that the company should be allowed to retain its old name, Fabindia, for the new concern. There were restrictions on the use of certain kinds of names. Bureaucratic procedures and delays at the office of the registrar of companies ensured that the suspense continued for some time. After sixteen years of international trade the name had become synonymous with superior Indian handwoven soft furnishings and John Bissell did not want to lose a hard-earned identity. He wrote on 10 October 1976: 'We still don't have permission about the name; using names like Fabindia are not being allowed to anyone i.e. basically a proper name . . . Mohinder thinks with enough of a battle we will get permission . . .' By the end of the year their persistence paid off. Mohinder Puri managed to get this exceptional permission from the Government of India. John wrote to his father on 9 December 1976:

> Finally, it is now practically an anti-climax, we will change over on December 20th to become Fabindia Overseas Private Limited . . . we have now a firm promise to get the certificate of incorporation at the end of this week and inventory will start today.

Fabindia Overseas Private Limited was incorporated on 14 December 1976.

In compliance with the Reserve Bank order and with the approval of the shareholders of Fabindia USA, John called a meeting in Delhi on 16 December 1976 under the chairmanship of Gen. H.K. Sibal (Bim's uncle) to enable Fabindia Pvt. Ltd to take over the original company as a going concern. The aim was also to appoint a new board of directors, with John Bissell as the managing director, and to resolve to 'continue with the business of design and fabric development, merchandise administration and export of handloom, textile and woven floor covering fabrics and various kinds of handicrafts.' (From the minutes of the meeting.) With Meena Chowdhury as promoter, the Indian company named her, Gen. Sibal and Madhukar Khera as directors. John Bissell became the managing director; Mohinder Puri the auditor. This session would initiate the business of setting up the financial and administrative structure of Fabindia Overseas Pvt. Ltd. The first set of shares was allocated to the directors, the Bissell family and a few members of the staff and friends of Fabindia. 40 per cent of the stock of Fabindia Overseas was held by Fabindia Inc., USA. The directors resolved that all profits due to Fabindia Inc. would be remitted as soon as possible, including 60 per cent of the net worth of the operation in India taken over by Fabindia Overseas.

The remittance of profit had been held up due to a case regarding tax rebate on profit earned by Fabindia Inc. that had been going on in the courts for two years. Legally foreign companies trading out of India were exempt from paying tax on profit earned by them. However complications had arisen from the fact that a large component of Fabindia profit was the cash incentive received from the government for exports. The lawyers were close to winning the appeal, and if that happened Fabindia would receive a large tax refund of $65,000. As John had explained to his shareholders in the USA, the company was not actually paying corporate tax in the interim but was carrying it as a liability on the balance sheet. Since its incorporation in 1960 the company had not even paid dividends to its shareholders in America. If it won the case it would mean a very large windfall for the shareholders.

In the meantime the office shifted to N-14 GK-1 with Meena Chowdhury in charge of all administration and retail operations. The store was on the ground floor, with the office and Export department upstairs on the first floor. The move prompted a 'spring cleaning' and a huge sale was organized to clean up excess stock from the Mathura Road office.

Early Fabindia sales made history in Delhi and stories about them are related by faithful Fabindia customers till today. Having once participated in this Delhi tradition, nobody can forget the sight of the crowds pouring through the doors of the Fabindia store. Since most of the customers attending the sale knew each other either through family or association, hurried greetings were exchanged with eyes darting quickly to the rapidly increasing 'bundle of stuff' in the 'other's arms' just in case there was something there that 'this one' had missed. And oh the joy, and ah the grief, when one said to the other, 'I'm afraid this stock is over. I was just in time to pick up the last five pieces!' At the beginning Fabindia fabric was available only to those who knew that stock could be bought from the export warehouse in Golf Links and Mathura Road. These were all typically friends of the Bissell family, and their homes draped in the elegance of cleanly woven handloom from John Bissell's stable created an exclusivity restricted to those who had access. But gradually, through word-of-mouth publicity, there came to be a large group of people in Delhi who waited for the Fabindia sales to satisfy their desire for good handloom products. There was a belief among the customers that these sales were for real—prices were truly slashed by 25-50 per cent and not mark-ups brought down, as so often happened with other branded products.

The process remained unchanged over the years. Different products were placed on tables around the room. Each table was 'manned' by an intimidating lady from Fabindia along with her 'bouncer' from the packing department. The tables carried the label describing the item and the discount on it. For example, napkins—50 per cent off, bedspreads—25 per cent off, etc. On the first day of the sale the store would be packed with so many people that doors had to be closed to stop others from coming in. Mountains of colour descended rapidly through the day and evening left a debris of leftovers strewn in the sorry corners of the battle-ground. People would rush around picking up armfuls of material and then place the bundle down on the floor to free their hands to collect more. Some families sat a child down on the package to keep it from being picked up by another customer, sometimes an elderly person would 'guard' the collected 'booty'. It was considered inefficient to attend the sale alone since one person could only deal with one armful!

Fabindia changed its sales strategy many times in an attempt to refine this process. In 1976 John wrote that he was trying a new experiment with pricing. He divided the stock equally into six parts, one for each day of the sale. The first day saw a 25 per cent discount on everything and every day there was a further 5 per cent markdown till it was 50 per cent off on the sixth day. The idea was to encourage people to visit on different days. John wrote to his father in April 1976: 'Theory was that those who wanted the best selection would come on the first or second day, and the bargain hunters would be in on the last day.' But this strategy failed because Delhi's 'shrewd customers figured out that there was lots of stock right to the end', and it was cheaper on the last day! So they came on the morning of the last day waiting for the shop to open. The queue snaked around the park of the Fabindia market (as it is popularly called) in two loops! On 18 November 1977 John would write: 'We had a two-day sale—with such a crush we had to close the doors for awhile—at the end every shelf was bare.' He specified that the average selling price per item was a mere $3, so the $11,000 made at the end translated to many items sold!

Talking about the '80s Charu Sharma says that Fabindia sales were all out of export orders that had been made in excess or cancelled. Sometimes a whole colourway would get rejected. Since nothing was ever returned to the suppliers, the warehouse would fill up. The home market 'shelf' could only sell a few pieces at that time and often colours made for one country (Switzerland for example), like pink and purple, would not work in India. Sale prices would then hit rock bottom, sometimes even lower than the cost prices. 'And it was crazy. We had to get twenty people inside the shop, pull down the shutter, exit them out and then bring in the next twenty.'

Attempts were made to streamline the process by sending out invites in different colours to segregate people into separate times of the day. Madhukar explains: 'the blue invitation means you come in the morning, yellow invitation means the afternoon.' Lists were sent to permanent customers, 'But how do you tell others not to come?' Of course John Bissell made certain that his office staff had priority by designating a day for them to pick up their items before the sale started. Charu says that the girls working at Fabindia shared a joke among themselves: They were so excited with the products sold in the shop that they would buy something or the other almost every week, thus, 'What we earn in Fabindia we spend in Fabindia!'

1976 was a landmark year in many ways. The export order book was already full for the whole year in July. Returning from his annual trip to Canton John sent a cable to his parents on 21 July 1976:

FABINDIA HAS OVER 600 THOUSAND DOLLARS IN ORDERS THE WHOLE TEAM HERE HAS DONE A WONDERFUL JOB

By October Fabindia was shipping $100,000 worth of goods every month. And in December John wrote: 'We have crossed one crore rupees in exports this year ($1,100,000) . . . And [we have] a good many orders in hand.' Though John had consistently referred to money in dollars to his parents so far, he now started writing the rupee equivalent to get them used to Fabindia as an Indian company.

Increased production led to another lease for storage space, and the company took on 4000 sq. ft in Nehru Place close to a smaller basement which had been rented earlier. John wrote on 9 December 1976: 'it is a good space and will give us enough room to increase our sales even above as much as I think we will be able to.' This was the first time that he had voiced a desire to grow the company substantially in his letters to his parents. Three years later, on 9 December 1979, John would outline the problems inherent in the expansion of the handloom industry in India:

We certainly are reaching the stage of thinking about optimum size—it is getting hard to control quality, and our shipments got very far behind this year—partly because of the increase in business, but partly the management of it all—we need systems—transcribing precise instructions of a wholly automated German buyer to a weaver in a grass-covered shed who operates 10 looms on handspun yarn with no education, no finance, no phone, piece-rate workers who come and go . . . Our producers cannot be automated (which is what it is all about) and often the smaller units give us the fabrics in most demand . . . At the same time we need pretty big customers . . . and some of the ones in Europe tend to shop around . . . price a big point with them. Habitat continues to be loyal . . .

It was just this sensitive understanding that Fabindia had with the weavers that made it so useful to Habitat. Priscilla Conran, Terence Conran's sister, and a designer herself, would accompany the Habitat team every year to shop for the prestigious Conran store in London. She says that she would sit with the weavers and John, along with Jeremy Smith, (the Habitat designer), and shift a design here or there to get a sample made. Then Fabindia would make sure it was interpreted correctly and exactly as it was conceived by the people making it.

> This is absolutely vital for production in large companies and Fabindia did it so well. I think the management of Fabindia was extremely important. They did deliver on time, they did do very good quality control, and you know that's the most difficult thing to do out of India. John would never let something go if it wasn't right and I think he brought that value to Indian exports at the time.

While business was booming John was getting increasingly disillusioned with the sociopolitical climate in Delhi. Referring to the Emergency he wrote on 14 September 1976:

> It is getting more oppressive all the time . . . The quality of life continues to creep downhill . . . for omnipresent values connected with money and position are transmitted firmly into society . . . I don't think we should nor can I ignore what is going on around us. And mostly Big brother continues to act in a most autocratic manner.

During those years John felt vulnerable as a foreigner living in Delhi. The fear was not unwarranted as Bim discovered some years later. Her father had a friend in the home ministry, Sardar

Nawab Singh, who told him that there was a thick file with information on John in the ministry because the government suspected him of being a CIA agent. The reason being that John had once sent a telegram to Bim from Darjeeling, joking that there were spies hiding behind the tea bushes!

As had become routine the Bissell family took a winter vacation, this time to Sri Lanka (Ceylon in those days) to stay with friends. John's account (10 January 1977) of the new Tamil Nadu Express train that had been introduced between Delhi and Madras is quite entertaining:

> [It is] a new, fast train that arrives there in 30 hours . . . We travelled using a new service called Air Conditioned Sleeper or better known as AC Second Class. The 'bogie' is sealed and AC, making it free from dust & noise etc.– everyone has a bunk upper or lower in groups of 4 with a curtain in front of each compartment which is pretty small–a good way of travelling, it costs the same as ordinary first class . . . As you may have guessed–trains are my way of travel.

Soon after they returned from their trip Indira Gandhi lifted the Emergency, dissolved Parliament and announced fresh elections in the country. She was sure she would return to power with a huge majority. It wasn't to be. In March the Congress was voted out decisively and Mrs Gandhi was wiped out in her own constituency. There was 'dancing in the streets of Delhi' the night the results were declared and faith in India's democracy was restored in the eyes of the world. John wrote on 7 April 1977: 'the change in the Government has made us feel an awful lot better–it has made the most terrific psychological difference. . .'

That year John Bissell and Meena Chowdhury decided to experiment with printed bedspreads for the Fabindia store. Many years earlier Riten had printed some fabric with a paisley design which had proved to be very popular with friends. But funds had been scarce in those days and local retail was not considered. This time Riten was given a free hand and he designed a line of bedspreads with bold, colourful tantrik patterns—large red and orange circles on black and white squares, and black and red lines running diagonally across the fabric. The experiment also included printing different types of fabric which could be used for curtains, bedspreads or cushion covers as required. The designs were an instant success and the Fabindia team quickly assembled a line of products from their stock to complement the Riten Mazumdar look. So there was PP Handspun cotton fabric for curtains, natural woollen durries from Madhukar Khera in Panipat, the bright Haseena cotton durrie from Ambala, and Riten Mazumdar's bold geometric bedspreads and cushion covers. As Meena describes so eloquently, the idea hit the Delhi public in the eye and overnight a Fabindia look was born. To complete the style low chairs and *moorahs* and grass matting, which had been brought in from Mr Prasad's factory near Cochin, were added. Meena says:

> You put a grass mat on the floor with a bright Haseena durrie on top of it, a Riten Mazumdar bedspread on the bed, scatter some cushions with Riten's designs on them, and you were done. It was different. It was stylish and it was very affordable.

She recalls a young couple walking into her office at the back of the shop and thanking her for having made it possible for them to furnish their entire home within a budget of three thousand rupees! She adds that the favoured Riten bedspread, named Target (with an inner circle of orange and a thin outer circle of red orange) literally became the focal point of a room whether it was used on the bed or as a wall-hanging. Suddenly young professionals were keeping their bedroom doors open while entertaining guests in their drawing rooms. Fabindia products had become a status symbol. Meena Chowdhury points out: 'I think that was the turning point as far as Fabindia [retail] was concerned. Riten's collection of designs had made people sit up and notice Fabindia.'

Riten Mazumdar's continuing association with Fabindia from this point onwards is worth relating. Meena worked closely with him for ten years till he went to live in Shantineketan, West Bengal, in the late '80s. Riten was mostly designing bedspreads, cushion covers and table linen, and Fabindia offered him a consultancy. Being very particular about his art, he wanted to supervise the colours and make sure his geometric designs were being printed perfectly. So it was arranged that he would come to the office every Tuesday at 3.30 and meet the printers who would bring in the previous week's assignment. Meena and Riten would check every piece to make sure the colours were right. Conscientiously telling the printer where the colour had spilled over the line, he would turn to Meena and ask her what colours had been used in that particular print. This happened so regularly that Meena says she thought she was being tested, till one day she asked him why he was doing it. 'Don't you realize I am colour blind?' he replied.

Meena was amazed—he was so sensitive about colour tones that it was almost impossible to spot his disability. There were some colours he just could not see, for example green, but he could decipher a shade difference immediately and his mastery over the medium was so complete that he worked with tones like others did with colour. Riten would write down the colours for her within the design, 'blue will come here, red and orange here', before it was handed over to the printer.

The dominant colours were bright reds and oranges with black, as in the classic Target that transformed the Fabindia style. Each product carried Riten's signature as a stamp on the reverse side. Since designs were printed in several colours and on different types of merchandise continuously, a special financial arrangement was worked out for Riten by Meena. He was paid royalty on every

Early Fabindia Inc. annual reports were designed by Riten Mazumdar and printed on handmade paper. This cover was block printed by Abdul Gaffar. Each annual report credited the designer and the printer inside the back cover.

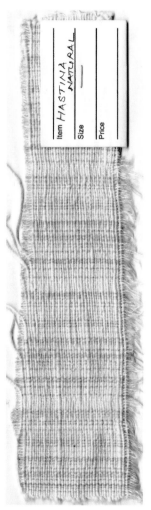

Delhi Homespun Cotton (DHC) was the first fabric to be sold by Fabindia and still remains a bestseller fifty years later.

Hastina was inspired by the Haseena cotton durrie and created in the mid '60s. It continues to sell in Fabindia even today.

Fabric sample swatches have been cut and stapled with the name, number and price exactly like this for the last fifty years at Fabindia.

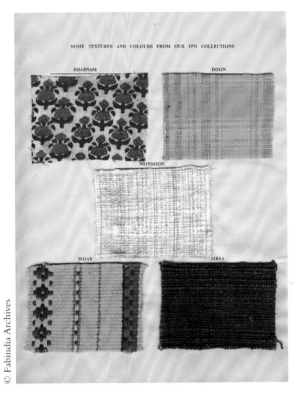

SOME TEXTURES AND COLOURS FROM OUR 1971 COLLECTIONS

SHABNAM

DOON

MONSOON

BIHAR

SIRSA

Real fabric
samples presented
in the 1971
Fabindia Inc.
annual report.

Renu Bery and her nephew
Jaiwant model a collection of
kaftans and kurta pyjamas for
Fabindia. Delhi, 1969.

Poster promoting an exhibition of Riten Mazumdar's collection for Fabindia at the Jehangir Art Gallery in Bombay, 1978. This was Fabindia's first contemporary design collection using traditional techniques. It was a complete sell out.

Riten Mazumdar painting his signature circles. Delhi, 1977.

Map locating
Fabindia's first
retail store at N-14,
GK-1. Delhi, 1976.
Till as recently as
1994, only sixteen
years ago, this was
the only retail
outlet. Today there
are 112 Fabindia
stores across forty-
one cities.

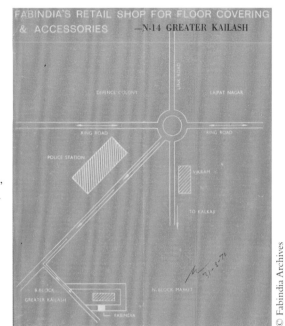

FABINDIA'S RETAIL SHOP FOR FLOOR COVERING
& ACCESSORIES   —N-14 GREATER KAILASH

Interior view of the first store. Fabindia Overseas Pvt. Ltd. Delhi, 1978.

John Bissell in the Fabindia store. Delhi, 1978.

At this point the store stocked only soft furnishings and a very small selection of men's kurtas and shirts.

piece of merchandise and every yard of fabric carrying his design, as they were ordered by Fabindia. There was a higher percentage of royalty paid on export orders since they were sold at a better price than at the store. So Riten's income was calculated weekly, and on volume orders. The popularity of his prints ensured that the income increased steadily over the years.

Even after Riten left Delhi for Shantineketan, his prints continued to sell and payments were sent to him regularly for years. Fabindia carried those designs in their store till 2000, when Meena terminated the contract and closed his account with one final flat payment.

At the end of 1977 John wrote to his parents: 'Local sales are good but I haven't checked yet to see if the PM has paid his bill!' Morarji Desai was the prime minister at the time and though a staunch Gandhian, was in favour of business and free enterprise. His daughter-in-law had been shopping at the store, and John regretted that he did not recognize her, but he had heard that 'the PM likes simple plain homespun weaves' as furnishing fabrics.

A year later khadi shirts were introduced made from the standard khadi available at the government-owned departments of the Khadi Gram Udyog. Tara Sahney, working in the Production department at Fabindia, remembers going with her team to the large Khadi warehouse in Karol Bagh in 1978. From then on every year the girls in the office would make a trip to purchase khadi during the first week of October because discounts were offered on the occasion of Mahatma Gandhi's birthday (2 October). Tara says:

> We would have it all taken out to look at it. It was so badly kept that it was dirty and stained with holes in the fabric, and it was not consistent. But it was a good price, and we would buy thousands of metres of the white khadi fabric. We found that the hand-spun look was so good!

Very soon khadi kurtas joined the shirts on the shelves, and the journey towards Fabindia's popular garment collection began.

John Bissell's Hindi teacher Benjamin Singh knew how to stitch. He was the one who made the initial khadi shirts and kurtas. John's standard outfit consisted of a khadi kurta worn over cotton trousers made from Fabindia fabric. In winter a khadi jacket was added to the ensemble. John liked khadi and stated that it was the most satisfactory fabric to be worn in the summer because it 'breathes'. On 18 November 1977 he informed his parents that garments had now been introduced in the shop: 'We also are selling the std. khadi kurta (i.e. the traditional one). I enjoy this image of selling the pure stuff enormously.'

The first size of kurtas to be stitched and sold at Fabindia were fitted to John's figure which was a size 40 (in inches). With this as a standard sizes were calculated two fits up for larger people and three fits down for slimmer bodies. According to Madhukar Khera he wore the smallest Fabindia kurta which at the time was a size 34. What was not discovered till much later was that John Bissell's extra-long arms had created an erroneous sleeve length running through all the sizes. Madhukar and his brother-in-law Mr Banga finally complained and sleeves lengths were shortened to the Indian standard. Charu says:

> Our kurta and shirt sizing was all done in-house. We never worked with an international size standard, and would size them by trying them ourselves. And it has remained like that. For thirty years we have sold kurtas and shirts with hardly any change to it.

Kurtas were unisex and ideologically trendy. Most university students wore kurtas over their jeans and Kolhapuri chappals, and carried cloth sling-bags called 'jholas'. That was the 'look', and the hand-spun style served the Delhi-born teenagers of post-Independence India very well. The young women of Lady Shri Ram College across the road from GK-1 found the Fabindia facilities a great improvement on the Khadi Bhavans from where they had earlier purchased their kurtas. There were no trial rooms in the government shops, so kurtas had to be tried by stuffing them on top of the clothes that the girls were already wearing. Power failure was common and the shops were badly designed, so there was no natural light, and kurtas had to be carried out into the daylight to check the colour. Popular sizes were always out of stock, and the shop assistants were disinterested and unhelpful. On the other hand Fabindia had trial rooms, the fans worked, the staff was female and friendly, kurta colours were interesting and the prices affordable. Those college girls became the youngest brand ambassadors of the Fabindia style.

Soon cotton pyjamas made from soft mill-spun cotton and stitched by the Cheshire Home were introduced to complement the kurtas. These homes had been founded by Lord Leonard Cheshire, a Royal Air Force pilot of World War II, to assist people with disabilities around the world. John Bissell was very committed to supporting the underprivileged and stitching Fabindia pyjamas was a good source of income for the residents of these homes in India. The white kurta–pyjama from Fabindia became a fashion statement and was worn to cocktail parties in the social circuit. In a letter to her in-laws in 1979 Bim wrote:

> The shop downstairs has become the thing to do in Delhi, and so he [John Bissell] enjoys seeing the great cross-section of people walk in, and I imagine that these days, he dreams and sometimes even plans to expand into a Habitat type store for the house & not just a soft goods place . . . last week there was a fantastic film festival in town . . . well the story around town was, that if you wanted to meet any of the stars, you just had to go to Fabindia & they would all be found shopping there!

On the political front the hastily created Janata Party had no clear leadership and was 'fumbling with unclear policies'. The only thing that unified them was to make Indira Gandhi and her son Sanjay pay for their crimes. Eight enquiry commissions were appointed with the Shah Commission being the most important and talked about. In fact it turned out to be a political and public relations disaster for the Janata Party, with both Indira and Sanjay using it to establish their victimization and martyrdom. There was chaos for two years with governance given a backseat. There was a shortfall in food production, serious inflation, a severe diesel shortage which affected irrigation, power and transport, and a strike in the public-sector oil companies that grounded flights. The party had come to power with a surge of goodwill. But it squandered everything with corruption and 'venal, corrupt, selfish, egotistical, prejudiced & self-seeking men/ women who make the policy and in some cases carry it out.' (John Bissell, 17 July 1980.)

Cash incentives offered by the government for export had encouraged many people to get into the trade. Producers turned exporters were competing in the same market as Fabindia and offering furnishing fabrics at lower prices. The surge in export-generated income had resulted in conspicuous large-scale consumption in north India, with new money being spent on lavish displays of wealth such as large houses and convoys of imported cars. John worried about a business down-turn that had affected Fabindia's biggest buyer, Habitat, and wrote about the need to think about the future of Fabindia, 'and just where we all go from here'.

Notwithstanding John's concerns, the Habitat team continued to visit India every year for their annual pilgrimage to Fabindia. Their aim was to meet suppliers, initiate design and colour trends, approve samples, plan the monthly production and shipping strategy for all Habitat and Conran stores and fill up Fabindia's export order book for the year. The trip was made in the spring, normally between the months of February and March. John Bissell planned the itinerary in great detail in advance of the visit. All suppliers for Habitat, whether they traded through Fabindia or directly, were informed and asked to prepare new samples for the buyers. Hotels and train tickets were booked, and hospitable friends staying in different parts of India were contacted to host the guests so that they could visit new parts of the country. The Fabindia team prepared their schedules and brought in new samples to make optimum use of the trip. John loved visiting his weavers and searched for new suppliers and new products continually. He always said that travel energized him more than vitamins ever did. The programme was treated 'as a kind of a challenge to get it all to work out so that everyone has a good time and does what they want to do in India', wrote John to his parents on 19 February 1982. There was so much packed into each trip that in 1981 John wrote five letters to complete the description of the Habitat visit.

This is the story of a typical journey over two weeks in February that could have happened any year between 1975 and 1990:

> Habitat would be represented by a combination of the following people: Terence Conran, his wife Caroline, his sister Priscilla Conran Carluccio, the designer for Habitat, UK, Jeremy Smith, and Yves Combier from France. Though the designers for France changed over the years, Jeremy Smith remained constant right through the twenty years of the association between Fabindia and Habitat. 'Jeremy comes every year and we have a good working relationship as well as being friends.' (John, 21 January 1984.)

The first few days would be spent in Delhi working with the Fabindia team discussing new trends in design and colour, and taking stock of the previous year's orders. Schedules and budgets would be looked at transparently and in detail, with suppliers being called in to give cost updates in front of the buyers. John Bissell had an open-book strategy with both suppliers and buyers. The price mark-ups were constant and transparent, and every participant in the delivery chain knew the process that decided the final selling price of that item. There were no hidden agendas for either the artisan in his grass hut or the sophisticated importer in his glass building.

Evenings were spent with the Bissell family and their friends, drawing everyone into a close circle of comfortable familiarity—Patwant Singh, Mani Mann, the Thapars, the Devas, the Correas in Bombay, and family friends in Gorakhpur who had run a large sugar factory for four generations. John wanted everyone to experience the different influences that had shaped his fascination for India. So there were many work trips to small towns and villages. Bim would get away from her work at the World Bank to join the group for a couple of days either at the beginning or at the end of the trip. She often lent her expertise to help procure specialized products from the larger markets in Delhi and Bombay for the elite Conran Store that Priscilla managed.

Usually there would be a trip to Shertally (Cherthala), near Alleppey, where John had a good friend, Mr Prasad, who was the second largest exporter of coir products in India, and also a supplier to Habitat and to Fabindia. The unwieldy grass matting that had become such a success in the Delhi store was made here. These were rubber-backed 'rolls of coir 4 m wide and 30 m long, weighing 300 kilos' that had to be cut and stitched before use. John had met Mr Y.R. Prasad of Travancore Mats and Matting almost twenty years earlier when he was working with the Cottage Industries. The team stayed with the Prasads in their large bungalow within the factory compound for a few days. John mentions 'long walks amongst the palm trees, swimming in the Arabian Sea, eating off banana leaves & generally enjoying themselves.' The Prasads were special friends and John had described their home and habitat in great detail to his parents over the years. Cannanore, on the coast in North Kerala, 'with cashew trees, rubber plantations amidst rolling hills with red earth' had a large hand-weaving centre. The fabric produced there was called Cannanore by Fabindia and it sold well at the store in Canton too. It was 'a place I like', wrote John to his parents.

Another old friend John visited with the group was Mr Laxman, 'an expert technician' from whom John had learnt a lot and who was based in Chenamali. This master weaver had worked for many years with the Commonwealth Trust Co., a large, well-organized handloom weaving factory in Calicut, Kerala. In 1960 John had visited there trying to develop fabric for export, 'the blue, the grey & ... the brown stripes of a jute and cotton mixture', now stored in Canton 'in the barn behind the store'. John had always loved this fifty-year-old factory and bungalow with 'a long high thatched roof and gleaming tile floors'.

After a break in Madras, one of John's favourite places, to meet friends, shop and generally enjoy a large city, the group would move to Hyderabad. 'The city of Hyderabad decays along with many of the inhabitants from the old families; while on the periphery large new families come up with no thought to the terrain, the landscaping, the pollution or any kind of rational planning', John would write, and then in bold letters, 'BUSINESS AND INDUSTRIAL DECISIONS MADE WITH PROFIT AS THE PRINCIPAL GOAL DON'T HAVE MUCH TO DO WITH SOCIAL RESPONSIBILITY.' Under the shadow of the Golconda Fort the buyers were treated to dinner at a 'charming small farm ... the home of another old friend in the "trade"'. Suraiya Hassan handled handloom business and export durries to Habitat from production centres around Hyderabad. She had been associated with Fabindia for many years. The business was started by Suraiya's father in 1925. He was a freedom fighter who was credited with the revival of bidri work (a specialized metal handicraft) in the state. Suraiya's uncle, Abdul Safrani, had worked with Subhash Chandra Bose as his right-hand man and her husband, Aurobindo Bose, was Subhash Bose's nephew. Suraiya remembers that 'Gandhiji came to our house in Hyderabad and we had a bonfire of British products when I was five.' (*The Hindu*, 2 September 2008.) John liked to work with Suraiya because she was one of those 'sensitive, open, sympathetic people who treat weavers decently & practise a certain ethic in their business'.

Ikat weaving, practised in Andhra Pradesh for centuries, really interested John who thought it was 'a wonderful design for the climate'. The pattern was produced by first tying and dying the yarn and then weaving the fabric with the design resulting from the dyeing. Suraiya Hassan had come up with some great new ideas in ikat and John wanted to 'help her get better organized'. This of course implied offering credit facilities to the weavers for 'dyestuff and yarn at reasonable prices ... and some marketing assistance'. He was certain ikat had a great future. According to Meena Chowdhury:

> Nobody had ikat kurtas at that time but ikat fabric was developing in Hyderabad in those days. Fabindia was a pioneer in that. We bought ikat in bulk from Hyderabad and it was kept in our store for a long time, one or two years. We kept thinking about what to do with it and then we used it for kurtas. Then the ikat took off and everybody focused on ikat kurtas and where it was coming from.

During their search for ikat weaving on a trip in 1977, John Bissell along with Jeremy Smith came across a couple of interesting villages. There was Puttapaka with 'white houses and mud walls built on a stone plinth with peaked roofs with tiles.' The houses had a large central room with looms on the sides, with an 'opening to the sky in the centre and a small stone pool below'. Then they travelled to Koyallagudem, where John 'saw some very nice designs and sat for a long time on the stone floor just kind of savouring the atmosphere of a quiet Andhra village ... considerably cleaner than its counterpart in north India.' He would write on 7 April 1977: 'I feel physically very good travelling, lots of energy & sort of bubbling cheerfulness.'

In the south among the other places they visited was Karur, in Tamil Nadu, which had become a very large weaving centre for furnishing fabrics over the past few years. The whole town was exporting to Scandinavia and the rest of India. Their products were sold at very low rates presenting serious competition for suppliers everywhere, including Fabindia. Karur was known only for its fabric but they were beginning to produce durries and John thought it was time to find out for himself how they managed those low prices.

So in 1982 John visited them with the Habitat team. They spent the day with a large family who shared their experience and business practice very openly. Essentially wage labour was cheaper in south India than in the north. Weavers were paid Rs 10–12 per day, almost 50 per cent less than the Fabindia rate for its weavers (Rs 16–20), 'which in itself is nothing to be proud of', wrote John to his parents. The exporters handled all other processes directly—buying and dyeing the yarn before handing it over to the weavers, and picking up the finished fabric after it was ready. They worked with large volumes, maintained a goods dye house and kept a close watch on packing and shipping costs. The samples presented to their buyers utilized a mix of cheap and expensive colours. The products were designed with costs in mind and may have 'compromised' on the design therefore, but, as John knew, buyers were tempted by low prices. In comparison the Fabindia style was to keep working on a fabric till 'it looks right', and then calculating the cost. And that's the way it would stay.

Another place they visited was Kanchunpalli (128 km from Hyderabad) with Madhukar Khera. John was concerned about a production centre there that was producing a new and complicated design of durrie for Habitat, but where the weavers were being paid very low wages, equivalent to unskilled labour in the area. He wrote about it: '[D]urries actually tend to be woven in depressed areas where wages are low and the capital investment is very little.' John and Madhukar took the initiative of announcing a 30 per cent wage increase for the weavers on the spot. The factory owner was assured of a higher buying price from Fabindia, and therefore from their buyer, Habitat. John hoped that this would encourage weavers to buy more looms and therefore increase production, for 'there is no reason why we couldn't keep a 100 looms busy.'

In the north the Habitat team would be taken to Agra, where there was Agra Handlooms, a Fabindia supplier of durries, and then to Jaipur to spend some days with Faith and John Singh who had a design and production company called Anokhi.

Anokhi exported fabric printed with traditional Indian motifs and techniques, re-designed and re-coloured for the international market. It was a direct and regular supplier to Habitat, and also sold printed fabric to Fabindia when they started selling garments in the shop in Greater Kailash-1. Faith and John were good friends of the Bissells and the two families shared significant characteristics—mixed marriages and a deep commitment to Indian handicrafts and the rural artisan. On 26 March 1981 John would write:

> [T]hey make a considerable variety of hand-block printed home furnishings—bedcovers, pillows, table linen, etc ... and now ... some appliqué work done in villages near Barmer in Western Rajasthan and this seems very 'contemporary'—the layout and the stitching is their own— the colours selected and dyed by Anokhi. As usual it was a very interesting day with a long lunch in their garden talking over our roles in 'development', encouragement of the 'traditional', the limitations of an organization like Habitat etc.

There were also the Oakleys in Mirzapur, producing and exporting exquisite hand-knotted, hand-tufted and flat-woven carpets since 1920. Madhukar Khera remembers a trip with Terence Conran,

Caroline, Jeremy Smith, John and Bim to Varanasi to look at carpets. After spending the day at Varanasi, Terence had to go to the village of Badhoi, to visit the Taj Mahal Pile Carpet Co. before catching the train back to Delhi. The schedule was running very late that day and the group reached the village at night. There had been a power failure and the factory was in total darkness. Terence Conran saw the carpet collection in the light of kerosene lanterns and petromax (gas pressure) lamps. Then the group rushed to catch their train from a small station, also in total darkness, and managed to scramble onto the first compartment they bumped into hoping it was the right train. John narrates the same story in a letter written to his parents on 12 March 1981:

> We finally convince[d] them . . . to get a 'petromax'—the same gas pressure lamp we used to use at 'camp'. Dhurries and carpets are displayed, Jeremy and Yves make notes while I watch the faces of the 50 odd men and children, no women, who are watching us. One of those memorable moments—on the sub-continent.

Talking about John in 2009, Priscilla Conran says:

> I know there's the magic of India but I also know when you're developing something you cannot let it go, you have to keep at it all the time and in difficult circumstances. That was the most important thing about John. He was really able to teach Habitat how they should work in India. He had a deep sense of responsibility which he passed on to Habitat in those days.

And again:

> The most impressive thing from my point of view about John was that I think he was the ambassador for Habitat in India. I think he was incredibly generous about

introducing other suppliers and putting people in touch with each other. He wasn't possessive like so many other people are, and I think that earned him the most incredible respect right through India. He did an enormous amount of networking and introducing craftspeople to buyers right across India.

For John, 'It was all great fun, very interesting, stimulating & went off smoothly—all arrangements worked, planes were on time, lots of hospitality, hosts, etc. . . . most important, there was a wealth of possible new products.'

All those interested in buying durries were taken to Bharat Carpet Manufacturers (BCM), Madhukar Khera's factory, about 100 km north of Delhi. This is an account of a typical visit to Panipat narrated by John in a letter in January 1984:

> Madhukar as usual had arranged things perfectly . . . morning coffee at a small farm en route, a village visit with photos, lunch at the canal rest house and a tour of the Panipat factory which is always clean and busy & gives an appearance of everyone being pretty happy & knowing what they are up to.

About 200 km from Delhi, in a town called Naugaon, John had started working with a large number of weaving units who were producing fabric for Fabindia's regular buyers. This was a predominantly Muslim area and the weavers were all interrelated in different ways but ran independent production centres, each specializing in one particular product. At the beginning John found the environment in Naugaon very depressing, because 'even though the men we work with who have small weaving sheds are competent, good technically & god knows work hard', they had too many dependents to care for and absolutely no education. However eight to nine families from Naugaon remained steady suppliers for Fabindia improving their lifestyles as their incomes grew. Abdul Sattar from S.K. Handlooms says that their houses have been built 'brick by brick' through Fabindia. He quotes John: 'Build better now you are doing well.'

Another production unit in Muradnagar, UP, owned by Mr Agarwal, became one of the largest suppliers for Fabindia for the next twenty years. In Ambala, it was Mr Shyam Sundar who had been producing an extremely popular cotton durrie for Fabindia since the mid-'60s and in 1985 was still handling orders for the same product. It was the Haseena durrie that Terence Conran had helped develop years earlier.

There were many more buyers visiting Fabindia now. There was a new client from Hong Kong, Ann Prescott's Design Selections; another 'super company in Australia, Ascraft'; Toulemonde from France; Peter Simons who owned eleven 'Monsoon' shops in London; Gilbert Powrie from New Zealand (bought out by Philip Martin but continuing to import from Fabindia); some new Norwegian designers, and even (in 1982) the Indian government through the Handicrafts and Handloom Exports Corporation (HHEC) who were organizing a Festival of India in Britain and wanted stock for '18,000 sq. feet of space at Selfridges for two months.' In the meantime the Habitat group was accounting for more and more of Fabindia's export sales through its combined shops in the US, the UK and France.

Fabindia Inc. in Canton, USA, continued to do good business, even though Jacquie, their efficient and long-term manager, had to leave suddenly due to a severe illness. Jacquie Unsworth had worked in Canton from early 1973 to September 1979. John's parents returned to handle the Canton Green Store after she left and John advised them to increase their staff. Elinor and Bill Bissell were not so young any more and Fabindia Inc. was now regularly supplying products to architects and decorators, and to wholesale dealers.

With export sales crossing over $200,000 each month in 1980, Fabindia ended the year with a turnover of Rs 2 crore. John wrote about his ideal business model for the future:

After considerable thought I have come to the conclusion that Fabindia in India is a pretty good size—we shouldn't push for growth—as this means taking on orders & customers without much discretion. It also means not enough time to work on projects that may never mean much volume, but are fun & stimulation. Besides I think this is our 'role'—find, develop & then when a new fabric or durrie gets to be popular & demanded in great volume, let others pick it up (there are hordes of exporters now) & go on to something new.

Meanwhile John's letters got increasingly critical about the Indian political state with 'several leaders forming new coalitions with themselves as PM!' He lamented the 'deterioration in morality, values & goals in society'.

Writing about the Janata Party at the time, Ramchandra Guha in *India After Gandhi* says that the reign was at best remembered as 'a chronicle of confused and complex party squabbles, intra-party rivalries, shifting alliances, defections, incompetence and corruption . . . merely a bunch of jokers.'

Indira Gandhi returned to power in the 1980 Lok Sabha elections. Having proved her point she was determined to rule like a queen. Her plan was simple: she was her party and she knew how to govern, with her son as confidante, advisor and heir. But on 23 June 1980 Sanjay was killed while flying a private single-engine plane. His mother was devastated. In a letter written on 26 July 1980 John says:

Mrs G's bounce back has been fantastic—she maintains a v. controlled public image & appears in total control. However no decisions or sense of direction, or who or what will fill the vacuum created by Sanjay . . . Since he was running almost everything, you can imagine the sense of suspense that pervades the bureaucracy.

In July 1980 Fabindia Overseas Pvt. Ltd found itself in a position to remit the total purchase price of Fabindia Inc. Almost $460,000 was paid in to the account of the US company in two instalments. Now that left just the tax liability of $380,000 which was still being fought out in the court by Mohinder Puri. John also talked of doing 'something useful & constructive for the handloom industry'.

It is necessary to view these figures in a contemporary perspective to understand the value of the business achieved by John Bissell in those early years. Just a simple conversion at the exchange rate today would give us Rs 2 crore leaving aside the valuation after taking into account inflation over the last twenty years. In 1980 that was a lot of money! After the annual stockholders' meeting on 11 August 1980, John wrote: 'It really is a terrific piece of news—gives me a wonderful sense of security to be in such a good financial position. I think now we should really start to do something with this surplus.' The balance sheet was showing 'a good profit'—almost $250,000 before taxes and $90,000 afterwards. He continued:

> I shouldn't take all the credit for this prosperous state of affairs—we had some good luck . . . with our cash incentives for export & just generally with a mighty nice group of customers. I don't think there is much chance of having such large profits in the future . . .

John specified that he was not interested in 'wild growth as even if we have the orders I haven't figured out how to control it all'.

On the political front, disconsolate and alone, Indira Gandhi persuaded her elder son Rajiv to forgo his career as a pilot with the Indian Airlines and join her in politics. Rajiv was elected as MP from his brother's constituency in March 1981. But these were some of the worst years for India as the largest functioning democracy in the world. Nothing much was happening to the economy. There were little or no reforms, and the license-permit raj continued in full swing. Export drawbacks remained an administrative nightmare. Customs duties were astronomical as were corporate and personal tax rates. 'We have had the most enormous pre-tax profit of about $275,000 (Rs 22,00,000), but after corp. tax (which is more than 70%) . . . and dividends, balance only $22,000 (Rs 1,60,000) can be retained in the company', John reported at the 1981 annual stockholders meeting, and than added jokingly that this could put 'a great premium about cheating the IT [income tax] department' and that the 'bright side of high taxation is that it is a lot less painful not to make much profit!'

On 15 August 1981 John wrote a poignant letter to his parents:

> Today is the 23rd anniversary of my arrival in India—on a DC-3 [Dakota—WW II workhorse] from Karachi. No one from the Ford foundation met me as I was to have come the day before, but missed the connection from Karachi . . . In the next few days I met easily the most beautiful collection of young ladies at the Cottage Industries all engaged in handicraft development . . . A month later I went on my first trip, stayed in the wrong hotel in Madras . . . A month or two later I voiced ideas for projects, probably implied a little criticism of some of the Handicraft Board members without understanding all the complicated relationships, political overtones (including [the] ambition . . . to become Prime Minister!). After this I learned to swim with the current.

A little later he added: 'I am so incredibly fortunate to have such parents—your warmth + humour + generosity + unselfishness . . . gives me a feeling of stability . . .'

By now Habitat's successful business model was reflected in 65 per cent of Fabindia's yearly export revenues. John visited Terence Conran in Barton Court, in the UK. He would write: 'it is as serenely a "perfect design" as any place I have seen. Like the products selling in Conran's stores the house was "understated & wonderfully original".' Conran complemented John on his 'efforts in India'. Talking about their relationship Priscilla said: 'I think they clicked–chemically–very well. Terence certainly respected JB and I'm sure JB did the same. They were born the same year, 1931!'

By the end of 1981 the Fabindia shop had turned over Rs 37 lakh in sales, a healthy 15 per cent of the total turnover. With Rs 2 crore showing in the export account, 'Fabindia ended the year with a very cheerful feeling in the office' said John, continuing to describe the Bissell's annual Christmas brunch to his parents. 'The Christmas breakfast party went off well–about 100 including children.' Listing the menu he added: '[T]here were conventional ham and eggs, South Indian dosas & stuffed 'parantas' (North Indian).' On 31 December Bim reports: 'this [Fabindia] shop is the place in town to go to & is really the most talked of place– everyone knows it & everyone goes there.'

In 1982 John was finally able to redeem his promise to his family and friends. The Indian government had withdrawn its appeal to the Delhi High Court in the tax case. Fabindia no longer had a tax liability in its books. In a letter addressed to his US stockholders on 15 June 1982 John wrote:

> We now have a considerable surplus of cash over and above what is required to run the business. So the Company can offer to redeem its shares from its patient shareholders who have been investors for twenty years without sharing in the profits.

Fabindia Inc. offered to pay $1353 for each original share bought in 1960 for $100. That was a 12.5 per cent return on the investment made by those who had made it possible for John to realize his dream of developing Indian handloom fabric. It was twenty-two years later and Fabindia had become an international brand for furnishing fabrics and floor coverings around the

world. He ended the letter saying, 'It has been a great
encouragement to have had your support for so many years.
Many thanks. John'.

Later that year John's son William Nanda Bissell moved to the
US first to school and then to college in Connecticut, enabling
him to interact more closely with his grandparents and the rest
of the Bissell clan his father had grown up with. For John his
parents had been his best friends and he told them in a letter
written on 20 June 1982:

> Having the 'rock' of Old Canton Road has made it
> possible for me to tackle a few things in life with some self-
> confidence—You are without doubt the most perfect of
> parents—always setting the example to live by—while
> encouraging us to find out things for ourselves. With a
> great deal of love.

Through all the years that John had lived away from home he
had continued to share the smallest detail of his life with his
parents through letters typed and posted at least thrice a month.
After marrying John, Bim's letters to his parents also became a
monthly feature with graphic descriptions of their life in India.
As the children William and Monsoon grew up they were also
encouraged to correspond with their granny and grandpa, first
through cards and drawings, and then through handwritten
letters. School report cards, friends, illnesses, problems and joys
were all minutely detailed and dispatched. In fact the number of
days a letter took to reach its destination was often a matter of
much discussion. The postmark on the letter therefore carried a
lot of significance along with the date of posting, both at home
and in office. Charu Sharma recalls, 'When we opened a letter
[in office] the first thing we did was to look at the postmark and
write it on the envelope, along with the date of receipt of that
letter.' Letters were taken seriously by the Bissells in Delhi and
Canton.

In 1982 John lamented the deterioration of ethical and moral values in society. While the Fabindia shop turned over a record sale of Rs 400,000 in the month of August 1982, John wrote that 'the pace at which the leaders of India are substituting expediency & rapacious personal gain for the old codes of honesty, forthrightness & objective decision-making in the "public interest" is accelerating.'

Through 1983 business remained good. The buyer from New Zealand, Philip Martin, gave a continuing order for one container-load of fabric and durries per month, which would add Rs 200,000 times twelve (months) or Rs 24 lakh to the year's export billings. But frequent and prolonged power cuts affected sales in the Fabindia shop and John remarked that he was thankful he did 'not run a factory that depends on motors'.

1983 closed with record figures at Fabindia with a pre-tax profit of Rs 4,000,000. But due to high taxes profits were much lower—only Rs 1,200,000. So Fabindia took a decision for the new year. They would lower profit margins to deal with huge competition from other exporters. John reported that they had developed 'some very nice new samples', had a full order book and that their spirits were high.

Between 1981 and 1984 there was a complete breakdown in government institutions. The country was beset by some of the worst separatist movements that it had seen since Independence— much of these arising out of neglect as well as out of strategies that reduced chief ministers to rubber stamps and involved playing divide and rule with senior political persona. First there was an agitation in 'Assam for the Assamese', soon joined by Shibu Soren for a separate tribal state of Jharkhand. Regionalism grew in Andhra Pradesh with N.T. Rama Rao finally winning the assembly elections in 1982 with his Telugu Desam Party (TDP). The textile strike started by Dutta Samant, a powerful trade union leader in Bombay in 1982, involved 200,000 workers and carried on for two years.

The most significant uprising against the government led by Indira Gandhi at this time was in Punjab. Mrs Gandhi dismissed the elected Akali Dal Party, and swept in with the Congress, an action that pushed the already simmering Khalsa supremacists to support Jarnail Singh Bhindrawale's call for Sikhs to purify themselves and remove the Hindu yoke from Punjab. After a series of murders of prominent people who spoke out against Sikh extremism, there was the killing of ordinary Hindu passengers in a bus travelling in Punjab. In the winter of 1983 Punjab witnessed several atrocities against Hindus in the name of Bhindrawale. In retaliation in early 1984 Hindus burnt down several gurdwaras in Panipat and closed town for ten days. People stayed at home in anticipation of trouble. Most weavers, being Muslim, ran away to their villages in fear. Even though they were not Sikhs 'all kinds of elements get involved when there is communal trouble'. In Delhi shops closed to protest the government's lack of action against Sikh extremists but Fabindia remained open. John wrote in February 1984: 'This kind of situation makes me remember the hatred that religion encourages . . . Always best to stay neutral.'

The last letter written by John to his parents is dated 29 March 1984. Suddenly the communication was over. Bill and Elinor both passed away within four days of each other. W.T. Bissell died on 12 April 1984 and Elinor L. Bissell died on 16 April 1984. Bill had been ailing for quite a few years and Elinor had been diagnosed with cancer in 1983. They were both just over 80 years old. Between 1948 and 1984 John and his parents must have exchanged more than 3000 letters between them.

In India by mid-April 1984 the situation had got out of control. Bhindrawale and his supporters started fortifying themselves within the Golden Temple in Amritsar under Shabeg Singh, a former major general of the Indian army and a hero of the Bangladesh war. In response, Indira Gandhi unleashed Operation Blue Star on the night of 5 June 1984. The army smashed into the precincts of the shrine with tanks, and the militants were flushed out and Bhindrawale killed. This successful operation extracted its price. On 31 October 1984 Indira Gandhi was shot point-blank by her two bodyguards, Beant Singh and Satwant Singh.

Rajiv Gandhi was hastily sworn in as the new prime minister on the eve of the anti-Sikh riots which started in Delhi in retaliation against the murder of Mrs Gandhi. In December 1984 at the next general elections, the Congress swept the polls more comprehensively than ever before in the history of Indian democracy. Rajiv Gandhi now had the greatest mandate, more than anyone before him to quell the political fires and reform a limping economy. He opened a window of promise to a beleaguered country. Here was a clever, sophisticated, well-thinking young man, unshackled by political baggage. There was some easing up of the economic shackles by the finance minister V.P. Singh. He restructured the personal income tax schedule and reduced the maximum marginal income tax rate from almost 62 per cent to 50 per cent. Corporate income tax was brought down by 5 per cent and customs and excise duties were reduced for a series of products related to export-oriented industries. Directly impacting Fabindia was the decision to raise the duty drawback rate for the garment industry from 7.5 per cent to 10 per cent. Such reforms were lauded by the industry as the harbinger of economic freedom and the key to inducing greater entrepreneurship. Times were better for Indian business.

Fabindia did well too. In 1984–90 total sales increased by 100 per cent. December 1984 closed with almost Rs 2.5 crore in export and Rs 84 lakh in domestic sales. By the end of the 1991 financial year in March export sales fetched over Rs 5 crore and the home market more than doubled to Rs 2 crore.

At this point it is worth looking at the business processes that were responsible for this growth. It is even more important to trace the trajectory of the products that became the best-sellers in the Fabindia stable and carried the weight of success at the time and for years to come.

The N-block, GK-1 market consisted of two rows of double-storey buildings facing each other across a park. The park had been landscaped and maintained by Fabindia since 1977. In 1984 the company was occupying all three floors of the building at N-14, and the ground floor at N-13. Within the next six years Fabindia would spread to buildings across the park, first to N-5, then N-7, and finally to N-9. By the late '80s N-block, GK-1 market was being referred to as the Fabindia market. Each additional lease was in response to the growing Fabindia retail, and also to provide storage space for the enormous quantity of stock feeding the export business.

Meena Chowdhury was General Manager, Fabindia Overseas, and looked after the entire retail operation from her office at the back of the N-14 shop. A staircase led up from this shop connecting the ground floor to the main office on the first floor. The office was divided into three departments—Production, Export and Finance, each occupying a distinct space and handled by a fairly permanent core of women over the period of time being described. There was Tara Sahney, Enid Paul and Meena Sharma in Production. Amrita Verma was export manager for many years accompanied by Punita Singh, and after they left, the team comprised Charu Sharma, Madhu Mathur and Neela Sontakay. Sunita Berry worked in Finance for over ten years after which the department was led by Sudarshan Madhok, with Krishna Jaitley (who left and then returned after a few years), Monika Tandon and Anita Duggal. Though there were others who joined for brief stints, these nine ladies ran the show on the first floor. John Bissell sat in a room leading out from Production, and from all reports mostly kept the connecting door open. There was a sample room across the courtyard which could be approached both through the Production department and John's room. The retail stores had a small nucleus of permanent staff and a somewhat shifting population of educated young women to manage the clients. As with Bim's Playhouse School many years earlier, educated girls found it convenient to work in the upmarket Fabindia shop before moving on to more professional jobs. Meena Chowdhury also supervised a rapidly increasing workforce of men to handle the stock and packing.

Fabindia was almost entirely handled by this core of fifteen women and John Bissell in the '80s, along with a very supportive board of directors. It is important to note that the whole team had been trained on the job. There were no management degree holders in the office. It was a neat, tight operation and we shall describe below how it worked. To simplify the description we will divide the business into several categories.

The first category was the suppliers, who actually created the products. These could be the weavers themselves or entrepreneurs with production units who had invested in looms and hired weavers. As we have seen earlier in the story, John Bissell was working with suppliers from all over India. Fabindia maintained a daily interaction with artisans in Delhi, Panipat, Ambala, Chandigarh, Muradnagar and Naugaon. These were mostly weavers, but also included fabric printers and tailors.

We also have the ever increasing category of products which were in a cycle of continuous creation. An idea generated by one supplier often morphed through several combinations of material, design and colour, delivering successful products at every stage of the process. This course of evolution often involved inputs from several categories of people. It could be John suggesting a different colour; Meena Chowdhury a change in yarn; the buyer, Habitat, a shift in design; or even the weaver who inadvertently burnt the yarn. All these products for export could be simplified into a) durries, b) fabrics and c) made-ups such as bedspreads, table linen and napkins, and kitchen linen. In addition, there were garments made for the home market, often utilizing the same fabrics that constituted the made-ups. Meena Chowdhury commented: 'We wanted to show that the fabric that we are developing could be used for furnishing and with a bit of restructuring, a thinner version of the same fabric could be used for clothing.'

Production was distributed per category to each of the three girls in the department. So Tara Sahney looked after durries, Meena Sharma, bedspreads and table linen, and Enid Paul, fabrics. Meena Chowdhury was in charge of garment production, selection and retail. There was some overlapping especially since visits to and from suppliers were often shared, and the development of products was a participatory process involving the whole office.

Important actors in this activity were Fabindia's top ten buyers who had become an intrinsic part of the process, not just because they provided the wings for the products to fly, but because they participated in Fabindia's commitment to John Bissell's dream. They travelled to India and were taken to suppliers to understand the world of the artisan, and the constraints of the handloom sector. They worked with the team to 'tweak' designs to suit their market and accommodated the frustrating processes of the license raj. There were many who stayed loyal through the thirty-odd years that Indian handloom fabric remained a fashion in the international market.

These buyers were divided between the girls in the Export department who handled their orders and supervised their visits. Charu Sharma was in charge of Habitat UK and Neela Sontakay looked after Habitat France. Madhu Mathur's portfolio of buyers was spread all over the world. She dealt with Fabindia Inc., US; The Conran Shop and Habitat Group, US; Cornell Trading, Montreal and Toronto; Tomo Corporation, Japan; Dulton, Japan; Jean Paul Denton, Switzerland; Zibayish, South Africa; Becara, Spain; Ascraft, Australia; Martin Wright from Bazaar and Gibert Powrie in New Zealand.

On the face of it the work flow was simple and easy to follow. Let us trace a hypothetical path of the progress of a product from first acceptance to sale and closure of the deal after payment.

We start with a 12 inch sample swatch that a weaver had brought in to Fabindia, which was approved by the team and had interested John Bissell enough for it to be named. If it was a fabric sample, the girls would walk up to a map of undivided India hanging in the buyer's room, look for a place with an interesting name that was not already a Fabindia product, and christen the sample. Then a smaller swatch was cut from the fabric to be stapled with a card carrying the identification details. This 'identified' swatch was stored in the Fabindia sample room for future reference. The other swatches were sent on to suitable buyers by post, with accompanying details and cost estimates that might help in determining usage.

A few weeks later one of the buyers would respond with an order and there would be jubilation in the office. The lucky weaver would be summoned by phone or post (most likely) and he would come to the office to be given the order. The team collected around the weaver to discuss and finalize the price, the colours, the quantities and the date and the man was off to buy his yarn to fulfil the order.

The designated Export department person kept in touch with the buyer to keep him updated on schedules. In a little over the stipulated time, the weaver returned with his armload of fabric and an invoice in his hand. The fabric was opened up and examined for inconsistencies, colour quality, size and weight by someone from Production, and 'passed'. The invoice was signed for clearance and handed over to Finance, who promptly wrote a cheque for the weaver. Happy to be paid the weaver left, probably carrying another order for the same, or other fabric.

The fabric was packed into boxes for shipping and the Export department applied to the Textile Clearance Committee to inspect the goods before they were sent off. The inspector arrived the next day, argued about the lack of bribe, checked a few random boxes and handed over the clearance certificate. The

Export department prepared the relevant shipping documents and the boxes were packed off to the shipping agent in Bombay. The agent rushed around to get the shipment cleared by different customs departments, loaded the cargo on to a ship, collected more documents for proof of dispatch and the ship left in about ten days. The agent then sent back the precious documents to Fabindia to the Export department. Again all these documents were cleared by the Textile Committee and returned this time to Finance. Finance prepared the final papers including an RBI permit for this particular export order.

The whole set of documents was then taken to the bank, in this case the American Express, to process the payment. The bank held on to one complete set and the other was sent to the RBI for the record. The two banks corroborated the date and terms of payment which could either be immediate on receipt of the documents or after the buyer had collected his goods. Depending upon the agreed terms, payment was made. The cycle was complete.

Lengthy as it appears, this is just a sketch of the process simplified for quick comprehension. The real story lay in the details, some of which were frustrating and pertained to bureaucratic red tape, and some concerned the joys of the process of creation. Creation not only of a beautiful hand-finished products but also of office procedures which evolved to ensure fair and full satisfaction to the suppliers, the buyers and to the committed team at Fabindia.

Tara Sahney has an entertaining story about the process of building office regulations. When she joined in 1973 there was no official list of office holidays. Aside from the mandatory days that the government had fixed for all commercial establishments to remain shut, Fabindia often took last-minute decisions in this regard. Years later, when the turn-over had increased and there were regular supplies arriving almost weekly from outside Delhi, a holiday was declared on 1 January just two days before, on

30 December. Tara knew she had a supplier coming on 1 January and there was no way to tell him not to come. He had no phone and there was no speed post in those days. Not being informed of the change of date the supplier arrived on the appointed day and unloaded his truck. The shop guard stored the products in the only space to which he had a key—the shop floor. So when Fabindia opened their doors to the new year on 2 January, there was an untidy pile up of bedcovers all over the floor. After that incident the office maintained a holiday list, decided in collaboration with the staff every year and posted on the office notice board.

When Sudarshan Madhok joined in 1976 she was a shattered person. Her husband had recently passed away and she needed to rebuild her life. 'I put my heart and soul into this job,' she says, 'and till this day I am thankful to Fabindia for making me what I am and keeping me sane.' Sudarshan 'handled everything as far as finance was concerned'. She remembers home market sales being a meagre Rs 10,000 a day and export revenue just one crore in 1976. When she retired in 1996 Fabindia's total sales had crossed Rs 15 crore. Today, in 2010, Sudarshan is still a consultant to Fabindia, handling their landlords at the original GK-1 establishments.

Sudarshan Madhok described the incredible requirements of bureaucratic procedures without pausing to take a breath. She had lived it for twenty years. There was paperwork at every point of interaction with the government, and each transaction carried a price, either in cash or in perseverance. Since bribes in any form were non-negotiable at Fabindia the girls learned to be patient. Madhu Mathur reports on the Textile Committee procedure. An application had to be sent to the Committee along with the invoice to the buyer and a packing list with details of the goods being shipped. For export to the US the construction of the fabric needed to be detailed—the number of threads in the warp and the weft per square inch according to which the weight of the material was calculated. This was counted through a magnifying glass. The inspectors arrived within a day of receiving the application. Since there were no bribes being paid the 'babus' (government clerks) would refuse to inspect the boxes and say, 'What will you do if we reject this shipment?' John's orders were clear and the reply would be 'Reject it if you want but we do not pay.'" Ultimately they would return after a few days to inspect the goods. They would never find a discrepancy between the invoice and the quantity or sizes of the items in the boxes.

Other exporters often under-invoiced or sent smaller sizes than contracted. John's policy was to ask the weavers to make the pieces a little bigger if necessary and Fabindia would pay for that extra material. The order was always 5 per cent more than what was invoiced. Not being able to find fault with the consignment the inspectors often complained that their time was wasted because there was no money to be made at Fabindia. It sometimes took persuading but the clearance certificate would finally be handed over.

The next step was the compilation of papers to be sent along with the consignment to the shipping agent in Bombay. This was done by Finance and included a certificate of origin (GSP as it was called) which was a form with details of the client, of Fabindia, and of the number of boxes (or bales) being delivered, in addition to the invoice, and the Textile Committee certificate. L. Gordhandas & Co. was Fabindia's shipping agent in Bombay. The two brothers Dinesh and Mr Ramiah had built up a good relationship with the Fabindia team. One brother handled the office while the other 'ran around the docks getting everything cleared'.

Customs duties had to be paid at different 'nakkas' or check posts, and important documents collected and stamped for clearance before the shipment sailed. Customs were authorized to inspect the shipment and would randomly open boxes hoping to find fault and collect a bribe. Once the cargo was on the deck the agent had to ensure he had the following documents: a shipping bill which was proof that the goods were on the ship and a bill of lading from the shipper which gave details of the shipment on board, both with certifying stamps from the customs' authorities. The buyer's invoice had also to be stamped by the customs to prove that the goods had sailed. Gordhandas & Co. sent one set of these papers to Fabindia and kept one set in Bombay.

The papers held by the agent were presented to the government in Bombay against which a percentage of the customs duties were refunded as a 'duty drawback' incentive to the exporter. The responsibility for this tedious procedure lay with the agent, and due to the efficiency of Gordhandas & Co. (and without paying a 'kick-back' to anyone) the cheques would successfully materialize at Fabindia after some weeks.

The set of documents returned by the agent to Finance were posted back to the Textile Committee for yet another stamp of approval. But the job was not over yet.

'Are you sure you want to know all this?' Sudarshan asks in disbelief. But it is important to understand the scope of activities that had to be carried out in the course of Fabindia's journey to the success story it is today. These were a handful of people without computers dealing with a tangle of government regulations that took more than a 'pound of flesh' for every window they opened. History must document the first stumbling steps taken to appreciate the long road travelled.

The Finance department had another long haul to complete the process leading to payment. Like a memory game that adds objects at every stage to make it tougher, Sudarshan lists the final documentation required for the bank. There were the buyer's invoice, the Textile Committee certificate, the shipping bill and the bill of lading complete with customs' clearances. In addition there were the GR forms and the bill of exchange. GR or General Record Index was a set of numbered forms that were issued to exporters in a booklet authorized by the RBI. This ensured that each shipment carried a unique number. The bill of exchange was a form to be filled with details of the importer and the bank that would release payment to Fabindia on his behalf. These six precious documents would be carried to American Express, Fabindia's banker, to be processed and passed on to the client's bank. The GR was copied in triplicate, one remaining with Fabindia, and two going to American Express, where the third was passed on to the RBI.

This complicated procedure was necessitated by the paranoia surrounding foreign exchange transactions in India at the time. The payment was finally made against terms agreed to in the contract between the buyer and Fabindia. There were two options. The first was to Fabindia's advantage and was called 'documents against payment' which allowed for the release of payment from the customer's bank to American Express as soon as the bank cleared the final documents. Due to the close understanding between Terence Conran and John Bissell, the arrangement with Habitat was on these terms. The second option gave the buyer a credit period of thirty to ninety days in which to pay, and this often created a cash crunch in Fabindia.

American Express offered bridging loans to Fabindia under two schemes. There was an overdraft facility which had a crushing rate of interest of 16 per cent, and there were loans offered against 'bills purchased'. If Fabindia had a large enough invoice of pending payment, this invoice could be pledged against a loan from the bank at a more comfortable 6 per cent interest rate. So Sudarshan often found herself waiting for the Export department to send off a good order so that the large invoice amount could be pledged against another loan taken earlier, to pay off the overdraft facility, thus saving Fabindia a few interest points.

The last act in this tedious financial play was collecting 'cash assistance' from the government—a great incentive for exporters. The government literally gave back (in cash) a certain percentage of the Free on Board (FOB) value of the shipment. The exporter could get anything between 2–10 per cent cash back of the value of the products sold after submitting an application with the relevant documentation. The government had stipulated different percentages for different categories of fabrics and 'made-ups'. Incentives were offered to enable exporters to keep their prices competitive in the foreign market, and 'cash assistance' added up to 20 per cent of revenue to Fabindia's balance sheet in the good years between 1984 and 1994 (when Dr Manmohan Singh, as the finance minister, withdrew them).

Sudarshan says that she would go personally to the Central Licensing Authority (CLA) once a month to collect a cheque against the 'cash assistance' due to Fabindia. The same six documents would have to be compiled along with the application and a bank certificate stating the FOB value of the shipment. Sudarshan may have been one of a very small minority of women who visited the CLA monthly. She says, 'The CLA officers knew that there was no "hanky panky" in the Fabindia books of account and we were not going to pay anything as bribe. We would fight it out.'

There were also 'H' forms that had to be filled and submitted to avail of the total exemption on tax for exporting handloom and hand-spun fabric. A similar incentive was offered for selling handloom in the shop—reduction of sales tax on certain goods and even total exemption from tax for khadi. The story gets even more incredulous when the facts reveal that Fabindia availed of every incentive offered by the government for years without paying a rupee in bribe.

Sudarshan Madhok remembers questioning a deputy governor of the RBI while attending a meeting of the Federation of Indian Export Organizations, 'Do you want to help exporters or make regulations to make them helpless?' Sudarshan spoke from a position of strength. Fabindia had led the movement for the revival of Indian handloom in the international market. Referring to John Bissell as a 'pioneer of the revival', Joyce Burnard of

Ascraft, Melbourne, Australia, writes in her book, *Chintz and Cotton: India's Textile Gift to the World*:

> [H]e stayed on in India to set up his own firm Fabindia and played a big role in guiding village weavers to produce cloth in colours and designs that would appeal to Western taste. He was at the forefront of handloom exports.

Fabindia has helped develop hundreds of products since its inception but those fourteen years between 1976 and 1990 produced 'best-sellers' that the world could not get enough of. As Meena Chowdhury explains it is very difficult to get a clear sense of the most popular items in the Fabindia inventory. Sales figures are not entirely reliable because some products are more expensive than others and stand out in large numbers on the balance sheet but not in the inventory. Also demand varies in different markets. One specific fabric did very well in the UK but was too heavy for the Indian market. A particular bedspread became the rage in Australia but another size of the same had to be discontinued. A new woollen durrie hit the world like a storm when it was first developed but the demand did not last beyond a few years. And of course there are the perennials that are considered great value for money and have sold steadily for thirty years in the Fabindia stores.

All considered, there are interesting stories that relate to the creation, development and marketing of some of these Fabindia 'best-sellers'. Fifteen different sources have contributed to this narration, and each person has identified and named items worthy of historical description. Here is an account of some of those special products introduced between 1965 and 1990.

Abdul Sattar from S.K. Handlooms in Naugaon says that John Bissell used to give ideas to the weavers for designs and colours and request them to make samples within the 48 inch width of the cloth. Woven with four different colours in the weft this one piece would constitute sixteen samples to be carried to Delhi to be shown to the Fabindia team. Suppliers were free to create new patterns since they were compensated even for their experiments. Fabindia always paid double the cost of the sample to the weavers because John knew that wastage was very high when samples were made.

Tara Sahney remembers the Rajput bedspread was a 'big, big seller'. It was conceived by one of the weavers who brought in a sample (like a patchwork quilt) which was 'loved' by Fabindia. He had made this with a single colour of warp, and different coloured wefts and 'it was beautiful'. This was in the early '80s and everyone was there including John, Meena Chowdhury and Charu Sharma. Tara tells her story: 'I got a marker and a sticker and kept marking all the squares that we thought were good. We cut them out, changed some colours but kept the same warp, which was an off-white warp.' A small trial order was given to the weaver of just the popular sizes of bedspreads, which were a single, a double and a queen size. When this order came in the team 'thought they were fantastic'. The bedspreads were kept in the buyer's room and the first one to pick it up was Joyce Burnard of Ascraft. She loved the 'Rajput' and placed a small order with Fabindia. After returning to Australia Joyce inaugurated the 'Rajput' with a cocktail party and sent out invites with the 'Rajput' printed on the card. The party was a success and she ordered bedspreads in all widths—48", 60", 72" and 104" and in all colours. Her favourite was a beige and white and a green and beige. She ordered several colour combinations and this bedspread sold at Ascraft for almost ten years.

Joyce was one of Fabindia's favourite buyers. She started her business out of her garage when she was over sixty years old and 'did brilliantly'. 'Rajput' was later picked up by Soli Mehta, one of John's oldest buyers in London, who stocked it in his warehouse and supplied it to stores in the UK.

Since Sudarshan was looking after the finances in Fabindia she knew exactly how the money was spent. John used to encourage all weavers associated with the company to buy more looms to expand their unit capacity. Loans given to them were adjusted against their invoices in small instalments. Fabindia gave S.K. Handlooms a large order worth Rs 1 lakh in 1984 which would have entailed buying large lots of yarn. But Abdul Sattar did not have that kind of savings in his account. So John advanced him a cheque for Rs 1 lakh and said 'go buy the yarn and give us the work on time'. Fabindia enjoyed so much goodwill in the market that with that cheque in his hand Sattar could collect both the yarn and the colours without paying a single rupee.

'Yarn is like gold in the open market. Instant cash payments entitle you to discounted prices. Otherwise the rate is much higher and credit is discouraged,' Mr Agarwal from Muradnagar explains. Tara Sahney used to get a yarn report every morning in the office. Like any other commodity the prices varied and Tara kept a chart to mark the prices of four-five yarns every day. The yarns normally used in the fabric sold by Fabindia were 2/20s, 2/40s, 2 singles, 4 singles and 10 singles.

'We had to know the prices in the back of our heads,' Tara says. Detailed costing was done for every product. The fabric would be weighed and it would be determined how much of that weight was in the warp and how much in the weft. Typically the warp was 1/3 the weight of the weft. Those costs would be noted along with the dyeing cost and the cost of labour. 'We used to give a good daily wage,' Tara declares proudly. The supplier then got paid a 20 per cent profit on the total calculated cost. The final selling price of the product was 25 per cent more than the cost paid to the supplier. The pricing process involved the weavers and the suppliers, Fabindia itself and the buyers who were encouraged to look at the cost ledgers lying open during their visits.

Mr Agarwal's association with Fabindia started because of 'Goa'. In 1971 Agarwal used to get orders from a lady in Delhi who was a supplier to Fabindia. He would make the fabric in his unit in Muradnagar and take it to her home in Jangpura. One day she gave him an order for Goa cotton which was a thick fabric with a 2/20 count in the warp. '[I]ts look was of a handloom fabric,' reports Agarwal. Goa cotton used to be sent to the US to be rubberized for the floor and the wall. (The process involved coating the fabric with rubber so as to make it oil and water proof). The lady approved the sample and gave Agarwal the next order for a thousand metres. Each weaver produced 22 m a day and since Agarwal had eight looms at the time, over 1000 metres were woven every week. Agarwal supplied her regularly and was comfortable with the arrangement. But after a few months she started defaulting on his payment. He had over 6000 m of Goa stock in his factory in Muradnagar waiting to be delivered. He made many trips to Delhi to collect his cheque for the last order but the lady made excuses and refused to meet him. Agarwal knew that fabric stocks lying in the lady's house in Jangpura were taken to the client when required. One day he followed the man carrying some fabric out of the house and discovered Fabindia on Mathura Road.

Hesitating to approach the office directly, Agarwal returned to his factory and wrote a letter to Meena Chowdhury on an inland letter form and stapled the sample with it. He told her the whole story and asked for advice. Meena Chowdhury replied that Fabindia would be happy to meet him and that he should bring his entire stock and come to Delhi as soon as possible. Agarwal says that he was so happy with her letter that he read it out to his whole family. Fabindia bought up the entire stock of Goa lying ready with Agarwal and gave him a cheque on the spot. The lady stopped dealing with Fabindia and never contacted Agarwal again. Thereafter, Agarwal became one of Fabindia's regular suppliers, supplying over 1000 m of Goa a week for many years. Then Heavy Goa started and Goa cotton was renamed Light Goa. Light Goa and Heavy Goa were basically the same design, and differed only in the quantity of thread used. Heavy Goa, the more popular fabric, had 36 inches in the reed. Tara explains that the reed is the count of the warp per inch (seen through an eyeglass) and increasing the reed makes the fabric heavier. Light Goa had 24 inches in the reed. But the weft was the same for both–2 Singles. Charu Sharma recalls that in 1983–84 Fabindia was selling 10,000 m of Heavy Goa to Habitat per month.

Bob and Blaikie Worth, good friends of the Bissells for over fifty years, said that the entrance to their apartment in New York was 'wall-papered' with a fabric from Fabindia. It was 'Heavy Goa' that they had bought in the Canton Green Store many years earlier.

Agarwal remembers that 'At peak production I supplied 30,000 m of Goa to Fabindia'. He was paid Rs 10 per metre in the beginning and the rate gradually increased to Rs 22 per metre after which it stopped being produced in the '90s. Agarwal handled four of Fabindia's best-sellers, expanding production to eight units with 130 looms over twenty years. In addition to Goa he supplied the extremely successful Shaila bedcovers, the handloom bed sheets for Fabindia Inc. in Canton and the shop in Delhi, and the base fabric for the Alwar bedspread.

In 1984, Agarwal was persuaded by John to set up two Jacquard looms to make towels. 'Make this a success. If a man bathes he also has to wipe his body. This is a towel. If you start on this it will make your future,' John Bissell told him. Agarwal was initially reluctant since the Jacquard looms were expensive and involved an entirely different technique not familiar to his weavers. But finally he found a master weaver who managed to produce the quality required and he got his first order from Tara Sahney. The Jacquard towels were woven in the same pattern as the Haseena durries. Thirty lengths fitted one loom, viz., thirty towels were woven on one loom at a time. Agarwal was asked to weave ten different colours of towels, each on a different loom, making 300 towels for his first order. Over the years he averaged a turnover of Rs 1 crore as Fabindia's second-largest supplier. Fabindia's towels are still being produced in Muradnagar.

The policy in the office was very strict about payments to suppliers. John would say he 'did not want any credit stock at the end of the month', so supplier's bills were paid as soon as their fabric had been checked and cleared by Production. Since payments were being made regularly to weavers but buyers often resorted to a credit period for paying Fabindia, there was a cash flow crisis during the months when Production was heavy. The order book used to look better than the bank statement and Sudarshan would question the need for handing over yet another loan. On being asked to make an advance cheque of Rs 50,000 to a weaver, Madhok questioned: 'We have just paid him. Why do you want to give him more money?' John Bissell replied: 'Sudarshan, these are not household accounts. We are running a company. You have to think big.'

In the mid '80s, one of the incentives for exporters was that 50 per cent of their profits was tax free. They were allowed to share some of this benefit with their suppliers and show it as an expense in their account books. It was the prerogative of the exporter to distribute the benefit if and as he wanted. In response, John Bissell announced a cash benefit equal to 2 per cent of each supplier's total billings to Fabindia over the preceding year. All the suppliers came in to Fabindia with their invoices which needed to be reconciled with the ledgers before the money was paid. Sudarshan remembers that they were busy with this project for days. Mohammad Yunus from Mehboob Textiles in Naugaon says that their grass sheds were converted into permanent buildings with the profit that John Bissell shared with them in 1988.

There was a time when 75 per cent of the weavers in Naugaon were working for Fabindia. Meena Chowdhury ordered products for the home market and Tara Sahney and Meena Sharma for export. Abdul Sattar states that since 1980 he has worked only for Fabindia and has introduced another twenty people from his extended family into the business. Maulana, Abdul's brother, printed vast quantities of table linen, sets of check tablecloths, mats and napkins for export. He recalls the time yarn prices increased substantially and Tara increased their rates to compensate for the rise. A couple of months later the prices dropped again and John decided to continue paying the higher rate to the weavers because 'Its their time to make some money. They are poor weavers.' Another brother, Nishad, supplied 'Rajput' and Delhi Handspun Cotton. Delhi Handspun was made in over a hundred colours and production is still continuing. Muhamad Yunus from Usha Textiles recites buyers' names and the products that were made for them like a nursery rhyme: 'Kotwara for Canton [Fabindia Inc.], tea towels, tablecloths and napkins to JPD [Jean Paul Denton], Habitat, Zibayish, Chandni Chowk, Bazaar, Gilbert Powerie.'

Kotwara was a base fabric for most of Fabindia's make-ups. It was produced in green, blue, red and yellow. Tara Sahney remembers that once the staff had gone to see a film made by Muzafar Ali, John's good friend. The film was set in Kotwara. So the next fabric approved was named Kotwara. 'Hastina' was a fabric that had its origins in the original cotton durrie, Haseena, and was a good seller in the home market. It was supplied by one of the earliest weavers, Kamaluddin, in Delhi. The warp had a beige-coloured dye which gave it a random pattern. The weft was hand-spun. Hastina was one of the few fabrics in Fabindia made with hand-spun yarn.

Charu Sharma explains that most fabrics were made from mill-spun yarn because fine-count hand-spun broke while weaving. Since durries used thicker hand-spun there was less breakage. Hand-spun yarn was more 'slubby', (tendency to form soft lumps of twisted yarn) and therefore had more character. Mill-spun yarn came in cones from the mill in counts of twenty, forty and sixty, and was really very fine. Understanding yarn counts was crucial to the handling of handloom products. Meena Sharma explains:

You cannot see yarn and tell the count, you have to feel it. 2 singles is one yarn with the thickness value being 2, which is quite thick. 2/20s is one yarn comprising 2 threads of the thickness value being 20, which is relatively thin. The count denotes the amount of cotton that has gone into the spinning of that thread.

The higher the count, the finer the yarn. The Fabindia team was familiar with the composition of each piece of fabric and every durrie that passed through their hands.

The origin of Barsat is one of the best stories of all. Tara Sahney says that the team had developed Hissar, a fabric which they wanted to try in different colours. Kamaluddin had hung the hanks from the roof of his shed and was cooking on the floor. The smoke from his stove burnt the yarn randomly. Unable to waste so much yarn, he wove it and carried the sample to Fabindia. The yarn was a 'lovely, smoky brown colour and I loved it. I showed it to John Bissell and to Meena Chowdhury and they thought it was terrific. We had a buyer in the office and he thought it was terrific.' They gave an order for the first 500 m to the weaver, and that's when they realized that he could not consistently recreate an outcome of an accident. How could he burn so much yarn to the exact colour, thickness and weight of the sample? So they worked on a dye to create the burn-colour effect, and when the fabric was woven it was named Barsat. Tara recalls, 'It was 2/20s in the warp and a handspun weft.'

In the early days direct dyes were used and the colour of the fabric would 'run' when washed and fade too quickly. When the shop customers started complaining, a decision was taken to introduce permanent 'vat' dyes to the weavers. A 'vat' dye is a chemical dye based on hydrochloric acid, and costs four to five times more than a natural dye. Loans were given to weavers to switch to 'vat' dyes and invest in cement tubs.

Dyeing is done in lots and yarn is rinsed after it is dyed. Supervision was required to control consistency in colour and 'fastness' of the dye. Fabindia raised its sales' prices to offset the increase in the cost of the dye. Now the girls in Production started checking every item by testing a small corner of the fabric, bedcover or napkin with the acid to make sure the weavers were not using direct dyes. In 1990 Fabindia got a big order for red tablecloths and napkins for Christmas. When Tara went to Naugaon to check on the progress of the work she found all the ponds in the village had turned red with the dye water. But the napkins produced were not matching the red of the tablecloths. 'Ne'er the two would match,' she says. Of course all such problems were resolved by Fabindia buying up the reject items for sale in the shop, and the weavers getting another order to remake the product for export.

Meena Sharma remembers an order for napkins from her client Cornell Trading in Canada. The company had sent a very small colour-matching pantone chip for reference. It was so small that Meena tried to get another bit from them so that she could give one to the supplier and keep one in the office to compare the final colour. She did not get another reference and handed over the one she had to the weaver. He vanished for weeks. The order got delayed and when the weaver did come in it was to inform her that he had dropped the shade card in the dye-bath and so could not deliver the order.

It is accurate to state that 65 per cent of Fabindia's export sales were on account of the Habitat Group through the '80s. In 1986 Fabindia earned Rs 1.65 crore from Habitat, against a total export revenue of Rs 2.86 crore. In the same year, Fabindia bought Rs 76 lakh worth of rugs and durries from Madhukar Khera's factory in Panipat. That was almost 50 per cent worth of Fabindia's sales to Habitat that year. Bharat Carpet Manufacturers (BCM) were Fabindia's largest suppliers. Madhukar Khera and John Bissell created some of the greatest best-sellers together. Durries were also being woven in Delhi by Mr Banga, and by Vineet Minocha in Chandigarh.

It is likely that durries accounted for at least 50 per cent of Fabindia's revenue at that time. Some of them became icons in the Habitat inventory and have persisted through the years, regardless of corporate buy-offs and brand changes. Madhukar says that the Ajanta durrie introduced to Habitat in 1968 was re-ordered in 2007 after a gap of fifteen years. By then Habitat had been bought over by Ikea and Fabindia had stopped dealing with them. But after John's persuasion BCM eventually continued to supply some of the old favourites directly.

The Ajanta durrie was conceived by Madhukar in an effort to recreate the look of the Berber rug found in Morocco. It was a hand-spun rug in a brown natural colour, and Madhukar had found the right yarn in Mirzapur in 1967. He talks of sitting on the loom every week in 1967–68, personally perfecting the weave while samples and feedback flew back and forth between him and John Bissell in Delhi. The making of the Ajanta durrie initiated the friendship between the two men and ushered in a partnership that supports Fabindia even today. The Ajanta durrie has a hand-spun wool-weft and a cotton warp and has sold well in three colours—natural, brown and grey.

The fascinating evolution of traditional products into international best-sellers is best illustrated by the story of the Haseena cotton durrie made in Ambala by Mr Shyam Sundar. Terence Conran and John had worked on the original Punjab cotton durrie and redesigned it for the world market in 1968. Habitat would order 500–800 pieces of Haseena per colour because it sold at every one of their stores. Haseena was the inspiration for Hastina, a fabric that did very well in the Fabindia shop. The same design was woven as a woollen durrie by Madhukar in 1969. This was called Jaldar. In 1972 Jaldar was converted into upholstery fabric in 50 ft rolls for export. This fabric was exported to Australia in different colour schemes like pink and orange, and turquoise and green.

Saranga was a cotton durrie that remained a favourite for

fifteen to twenty years. This was a traditional geometric pattern that had been simplified and the original bright colours substituted with pastel colours. Saranga would be presented to Jeremy Smith in different colour combinations every year, and he liked them all. Somehow these combinations suited Habitat's clientele and Jeremy would report back from the UK: 'Your durrie won an Oscar!' Saranga was a 'punja durrie' which meant that the weaver pushed the weave down with a type of comb called a 'punja'. The weavers sat on the floor, wove a bit and pushed the weave down, then wove a bit more and pushed it down again. This continued till the durrie was complete. Due to this laborious process the durrie grew very slowly, only six–eight inches per day. Only one durrie was made at a time on the loom and therefore it was an expensive product. Punja weaving was practised only in Agra, Jaipur and Panipat.

Charu remembers that only six pieces of Saranga could be produced in a month, so it was not shown to many buyers at a time. The first buyer was Bijenkorf in Amsterdam and they placed an order for twenty-five to thirty durries. They had six to eight stores and they wanted a couple of durries sent to each store. On receiving the order, there was celebration at Fabindia because the order book was full six months in advance. But then Habitat saw it and also wanted to buy it. After it was featured in the Habitat catalogue the demand was much higher than could be managed at one time, so Fabindia had to work out a strategy for maximizing production.

All three Fabindia durrie suppliers were given the job of making Saranga. Fabindia would call them for a floor-covering meeting at the beginning of every month. To prepare for this meeting the Export department compiled their Habitat orders. Madhu Mathur for the Conran Shop, Neela Sontakay for France, and Charu Sharma for UK. These were then passed on to Tara Sahney who was in charge of Production. The team would meet Madhukar, Mr Banga and Vineet Minocha to allocate production for the month and fix targets. Per colour per loom per day—how many durries could each supplier deliver in that month? Firm commitments were taken on quantity so that customers could be sent a realistic idea of schedules. The Export department ensured that each buyer was allotted some percentage of the order every month. If the total order was for 200 durries and only hundred could be made, these hundred were distributed between the US, France and UK orders to keep everyone happy. Tara Sahney says: 'I had to keep a record of who was going to produce what. We made a huge spreadsheet with all our customer's names and their products. Half my battles with the Export department were on account of these durries.'

Haryana Primitive was another 'punja' durrie that had a history. Madhukar had always been interested in the durries woven by girls in Haryana to carry in their bridal trousseau. When the son of an old Hindi teacher requested Madhukar for a job, Madhukar started him off on this project, working with these girls to see if they could be trained to produce these durries for the commercial market. During the years this durrie was made it was very popular. In a letter to Madhukar John wrote:

> A Canadian buyer who is in town just bought 14 of the Haryana Primitives!!—she has a small operation but great taste. Please tell your old teacher & the ladies who make them that they have been much admired by all + Send More Soon. John.

Tara says that once a whole consignment of 500 Haryana Primitive durries got cancelled for some reason. An expensive durrie to stock without a buyer. Tara asked John if they should be returned to the supplier. But as usual John's solution was to take them off the supplier so that the weaver did not suffer. Fabindia had paid Rs 400 per durrie to the supplier. The durries lay in the Fabindia store, with their value depreciating every year in the books of accounts. The value was down to Rs 125 per durrie a few years later when Martin Wright from Bazaar came to Fabindia looking for a large stock of durries. Tara showed him the 500 pieces of Haryana Primitive, and he bought the lot at the original price. Tara says:

> The 'Haryana Primitive' measures 105 x 180 cm, it has a big diamond in the middle, and is off-white and mustard with the diamond in yellow. I was so happy we finally sold them. You know, whatever people say, it does become personal.

Every durrie has a personal history and there are many. Reading the inventory from the Fabindia books is like calling out a magical travel itinerary—Bikaner, Barmer, Ellora, Kinnaur, Samalkha, Rohtak, Pokhran, Sagar, Jhansi, Karnal—the list goes on. In Madhukar's words:

> It was a great collaboration between Habitat, Fabindia and BCM. When we had a product where the weaver makes decent money, BCM and Fabindia make their normal margin, and Habitat is able to sell at a decent price, then it works.

The success of Fabindia was that it worked every time.

·4·

THE OLD ORDER CHANGES
1990-93

In 1977 John Bissell gave an interview to William Borders of the *New York Times*, where he stated: 'When I began, nobody was coming here [India] to buy. Now there are hundreds of buyers every year from all over the world. This has become an important marketplace.' Needless to say John was one of the earliest catalysts in this process. And then at the end of the interview he concluded, 'I started this business because I was excited about the challenge of getting these products into the world market and because I was simply excited about handloom fabrics. I still am.' ('Connecticut Yankee in Business in India', 26 June 1977)

This enthusiasm characterized Fabindia's work practice and defined John's personal identity for the next twenty years. John's son William talks of his father's strong New England Protestant background, and the ethic of austerity and hard work that equated the idea of privilege with responsibility for bettering the world. Marie, John's sister, said that he 'even considered going into social work' while still in the US. John Stewart Cox, John's cousin, speaks about his 'missionary zeal' and remembers that John was engaged in social work in an Episcopal church in Manhattan during Macy's training programme. He thought John was influenced by 'Gandhi's effort to refloat khadi industries in an effort to keep people in the villages' gainfully employed. After coming to India, John internalized Gandhi's ethic of self-reliance and the significance of khadi within the concept of 'swadeshi'. Many of his letters to his parents in the early years mention the similarity between Gandhi's cause and the philosophy of a new economic order established by E.F. Schumacher in his path-breaking book, *Small Is Beautiful*. 'I have read 'Small is Beautiful' [and] so have some friends—those with the "right" ideas—i.e. views similar to mine.' (John Bissell, 17 April 1978)

Both thinkers espoused the urgent need to minimize personal consumption in order to restrict the endless cycle of economic growth to the detriment of man and the 'finite environment'. A quote from Schumacher echoes the ideology that fashioned Gandhi's ideal path to independence: 'Wisdom demands a new orientation of science and technology towards the organic, the gentle, the non-violent, the elegant and beautiful.' Gandhi's call to Indians to spin and weave their way into a self-reliant village economy was reflected in John Bissell's passion to resurrect handloom industry by successfully marketing its products.

Faith Singh, who founded Anokhi along with her husband John Singh, states it emphatically:

> John Bissell's take on things was very clearly defined by his background in Connecticut. It was that whole value system that he came from and then applied in a clear, non-compromising and most exceptional way to his work in India . . . he was a purist for cotton . . . and was committed to a weaving base with rural artisans.

John's own wardrobe consisted of handloom clothes in cotton and wool. He was always seen in 'a khadi kurta and his trousers were made with Fabindia fabric. He never wore mill spun trousers. His shirt was made of 'shok' or light cotton and in winter he wore a khadi jacket over his shirt', says Amrita Verma. 'It became quite the style, the "JB look"!' says Amrita Verma. So the first lot of garments that sold in Fabindia in 1977 were khadi kurtas, soon to be followed by khadi shirts and cotton pyjamas.

In the previous chapter, Tara Sahney had recounted Fabindia's annual pilgrimage to the Khadi Gram Udyog to buy khadi during discount week (around Gandhi's birthday) in October. Since he was so passionate about khadi John said, 'Let's make our own.' This was a tricky business because the warp and the weft both had to be made with hand-spun cotton, and a single hand-spun yarn broke very easily when tightened on the warp (the length of the weave). This resulted in 'cheating' as the Fabindia team reported, with much of the available khadi using mill-spun yarn in the warp. So John found a solution with the use of a particular kind of *charkha* to spin the yarn. The *amber* charkha required the spinner to pull the yarn into a tighter twist while spinning so that it would come out stronger. Since it needed greater discipline and strength to produce the yarn, it was not the most popular spinning wheel in use. One of the weavers in Naugaon, Mohammad Akhtar, started making khadi for Fabindia in 1981 using the amber charkha. His production unit was called Shabana Handlooms and he specialized in producing khadi exclusively for Fabindia for years. The fabric was named Amber khadi and 'it really took off', says Tara. 'We loved it. All our kurtas were made out of Amber khadi, and our shirts.' The khadi looked best in its natural, off-white shade. And then another weaver, Imtiaz Ahmad, managed to produce a khadi that looked even whiter and brighter. He had dipped the yarn in soda-ash and 'it was beautiful', exclaims Tara. They called it Soda Ash khadi, and soon there were many varieties of weights of khadi coming into the Fabindia store depending on the heaviness (or lightness) of the yarn being used. This 'pure' form of khadi was more expensive since the spinners were paid higher wages for their labour intensive work. Mohammad Yunus of Golden Handlooms started producing Daman khadi (forty-eight inches wide); and then there was Roshan Handlooms, another long-term supplier, who began supplying khadi. Fabindia got the yarn dyed and started selling khadi kurtas and shirts in different colours.

Madhukar Khera remembers that khadi was one fabric the weavers were encouraged to produce in any quantity and bring to Fabindia to sell. And they would get paid even though at the beginning there were no big export orders for the product. The store used some of the material for making kurtas and shirts but the rest was stored. 'We were perhaps the only store that carried such a huge stock of khadi at any given time, because we all liked khadi as a product and as an ideology and we wanted to support the weavers. This was a dying art and Fabindia wanted to keep it going for as long as possible. Sometimes, during a sale, khadi bolts were sold at a discount,' says Tara.

Then an 'extraordinary' clothes designer discovered this fabric and started buying khadi in large quantities from Fabindia. For many years Marie Jean Hunter would sell only khadi clothes in her shop in Australia. She is still remembered by Mohammad Akhtar who said 'John sahib would get us to produce this Amber khadi the whole year and stock it in his godown. Marie Jean madam came once a year, stayed for one week, and bought up the whole stock.' Another buyer, Anokhi (Faith and John Singh's company in Jaipur), ordered striped khadi fabric in twenty colours sometime before 1986. The weavers remember producing 50 m of khadi in each of the twenty colours for Anokhi. Khadi, even more so than the other handloom fabrics, was intrinsically inconsistent in its weave—sometimes it was thicker, sometimes it carried an unscheduled stripe in its length. 'It was hand-spun, after all,' explains Tara, 'but it was successful and we did very well.' For the heavier variety of khadi Fabindia had several clients from Australia and New Zealand, but Marie Jean was the greatest promoter, for 'she encouraged us and she bought a lot'.

By the early '90s khadi had become a fashion statement. In 1989 the first khadi fashion show was presented in Bombay by the Khadi and Village Industries Commission, where eighty-five garments were created for display. In 1990 Ritu Kumar, a brilliant designer and entrepreneur in the revival of traditional

Indian textiles, showed her first khadi collection in the Tree of Life show held at the Crafts Museum in Delhi. Gandhi's 'uniform' symbolizing the freedom movement was now the rage of the elite, politicians and socialites alike.

The business was doing well and Fabindia continued to show a steady growth in revenue, with the home market slowly inching up the scale from 24 per cent in 1989 to 29 per cent of total sales in March 1991. The optimism of the late '80s was reflected in the bonus shares that were offered to Fabindia's shareholders twice, first in 1984 and again in 1987, when domestic sales turned over Rs 1 crore for the first time. By 1989 exports were just under Rs 5 crore and domestic sales had risen to Rs 1.65 crore.

But in the realm of politics things were beginning to fall apart. The prime minister, Rajiv Gandhi, had begun to tumble from one political crisis to another. After the retrograde Muslim Women's Bill introduced to placate the Muslims in the Shah Bano case, Rajiv Gandhi gave in to a demand to allow Hindus to worship in a small shrine in Ayodhya called the Babri Masjid. He then ran into an issue with V.P. Singh when, as the finance minister, Singh started conducting income tax raids on prominent businessmen. Rajiv removed him from finance, made him defence minister and then totally axed him from the cabinet. The ex-finance minister promptly formed another party, the Janata Dal, and allied himself with all anti-Congress elements including the regional parties. By the time the elections were held in 1989 the government was tottering at the edges. Rajiv Gandhi could not hold on to a decisive number of seats and Congress was left in a sad minority. V.P. Singh formed a government with the support of the BJP and the Left from the outside. This was an unmitigated disaster that brought on a headlong collision between the 'socially and economically backward classes' (Mandal Commission) and Advani's frenzied Hindutva 'minority'. Singh was forced to resign. But the era of minority governments would be there to stay.

The economy was in tatters. Public debt was high, an overvalued exchange rate had raised imports and hurt exports and India's foreign exchange reserves were too low to meet its balance of payment deficits. As the country was forced into another general elections in 1991, tragedy struck the Congress party once again. Rajiv Gandhi was killed by a suicide bomber from the Liberation Tigers of Tamil Eelam (LTTE) while he was at an election rally in Sriperumbudur in Tamil Nadu. The Congress found itself going into an election without a member of the Nehru–Gandhi clan at its helm. India was in a crisis.

Though there had been some pro-business policies introduced to encourage private enterprise during the 1980s, it was not till India was on the brink of a foreign exchange disaster (reserves were down to two weeks of imports) that the government took decisive steps towards a fuller liberalization of the economy. P.V. Narasimha Rao, the prime minister in 1991, appointed Manmohan Singh, an apolitical economist, as his finance minister. In Manmohan Singh's own words, '[T]he crisis in the economy is both acute and deep. We have not experienced anything similar in the history of independent India.' (Union Budget, 1991–92) India was forced to embark on serious reforms and greater globalization. Ramchandra Guha lists the changes made by Manmohan Singh with the full support of a desperate government, finally setting India on the path of an open trade regime. In *India after Gandhi: The History of the World's Largest Democracy* he writes: 'The rupee was devalued, quotas removed for imports, tariffs reduced, exports encouraged and foreign direct investment welcomed in. The domestic market was also freed; the license-quota-permit–raj was substantially done away with, and the public sector discouraged from expanding.'

As Fabindia along with thousands of similar companies applauded these decisions, a quiet revolution started transforming the economic strata of Indian society. Steady economic growth gradually led to an expansion in the size of the middle class, the extent and influence of which would have far-reaching consequences for the protagonists of our story within the next ten years.

In the meantime John and Bim's children had grown up. Both William and Monsoon had first attended schools in Delhi and then been sent to boarding schools in Connecticut. This enabled the children to establish close ties with the Bissell clan in the US, particularly with their grandparents Bill and Elinor, and John's sister Marie and her husband and children. William, the older of the two siblings, had left India in 1982 and had the advantage of spending a fair amount of time with his grandparents in Canton before they passed away in April 1984.

In 1986–87 William, then at Wesleyan University, decided to take a gap year and intern in different work environments. He was studying philosophy and political science and would finally major in governance. Not entirely happy with his son's decision to take a year off, John Bissell negotiated with him to spend a part of that year with a couple of young environmentalists he had met recently in India. Anil Agarwal and Sunita Narain had set up the Centre for Science and Environment (CSE) in Delhi to research and document urgent environmental issues facing India. According to William, John said he would support his year in India if he interned at the Centre because he believed there was good work being done there.

In November 1986 William came to Delhi and first went to work with the BBC. Handled almost entirely by the legendary journalist Mark Tully and his colleague Satish Jacob, the small BBC office in Nizamuddin became William's training ground in Indian politics. William says, 'With one ear I would be listening to Mark and with the other ear I would be hearing Satish talk about politicians and elections . . . and in the living room they had the dog, a table-tennis table and very nice Darjeeling tea . . . and I also got to go out on assignment, which was great.' And then William joined the CSE as promised to his father. At the time Anil and Sunita were compiling their annual Citizen's

Report on the State of India's Environment. Rajiv Gandhi had asked them to put together this presentation for Parliament. For William it was an amazing experience to be working in that small office, filling out and filing index cards with details of each grass-roots organization in the country and participating in discussions on tribal rights, mining disasters and deforestation. The Bissells' passion for travelling around India by train stood him in good stead. William knew the geography of India intimately and could locate small towns by their proximity to train stations and weaving centres! Anil Agarwal and Sunita Narain were working to influence government policy by exposing hard-hitting and accurate facts about unrealistic development projects that were sliding marginal groups towards cycles of impoverishment. Their thesis was that people who lived on the fringes of society were disproportionately affected by environmental degradation. Today this fact is *de rigueur* but in 1987 it was anti-establishment and it affected William intensely. He says, '[It] gave me a lot of ideas about what I wanted to do after college.'

By the time William Bissell returned to India after his studies in 1988, Fabindia was a well established and fairly successful business. The company occupied four different shops in the N-block, GK-1 market. There was the flagship store N-14, with the Fabindia offices on the first and second floors. This also housed the popular terrace where winter lunches were enjoyed under a thatched roof by the Fabindia staff, and any other lucky guest— buyer, supplier or friend, who happened to be present when the famous tiffin-carrier was opened. John Bissell's generous home-cooked meals are still remembered by many who shared the winter sun during those days. N-13, the store next to N-14, was rented in 1978, the N-5 ground floor and basement in 1986 when grass mats were introduced from Kerala, and then N-7 was acquired in 1988 for storage. 1988 closed with Fabindia sales well over Rs 5 crore. Floor coverings accounted for Rs 2.6 crore, bedspreads for 1.5 crore, handloom fabrics for almost Rs 80 lakh, and garments for over 10 lakh. The four stores in the GK-1 market were handling good business. By 1990-91 export stock was stored, packed and shipped from a beautiful warehouse designed by Morad Chowdhury, Meena's husband. In 1987 John Bissell, along with Madhukar Khera and Sudarshan Madhok, had bought 1200 sq. yards at D-12/4 Okhla at a Delhi Development Authority (DDA) auction. So far all of Fabindia's businesses were being run from rented property. John had been advised that it was expeditious to pick up land in south Delhi whenever possible. With him, the big problem was that he would only consider a deal that could be executed by cheque, basically with hundred per cent 'white' money. Property transactions in Delhi typically had large components of 'black' money (unaccounted cash). So the only option left was to negotiate for land at DDA auctions where he could pay by cheque.

William remembers that he was very sure about what he wanted to do on his return from the US, and it had nothing to do with Delhi. Idealistic and impulsive he got into a car in August 1988 and drove towards Rajasthan. One evening his car developed a mechanical problem and he had to stop the night at a roadside village. A man at the local tea-stall led him to the palace of a raja located nearby. As it happened Raja Gopal Singh was not only hospitable but also keenly interested in the young man's ideas. 'I told him what I wanted to do and the next morning he said, why don't you make this your home? Do your project here. And so, on the spot, I just made my decision to stay,' says William.

William Bissell would set up an artisan's cooperative right there, 2 km from the village of Bhadrajun, in one of the palaces on Raja Gopal Singh's property. The idea was to set up a collective with leather workers, printers and durrie weavers living in the area. The organization would support them with funds, maintain quality control and introduce them to a wider market. The profits generated by this business would be shared by all the members and would also build a corpus fund to build capacity. 'My idea was to set up a model cooperative, make it a test case, and bring people here to study it so that they could replicate it everywhere else,' says William. He returned to Delhi to tell his father of his new plans and to collect his things so that he could shift to Bhadrajun as soon as possible.

Raja Gopal Singh's palace was a decrepit building and William settled into the first floor converting its long galleries into bedrooms. He was introduced to the sarpanch of a nearby village, Raj Kumar Rodla, who became his good friend and business partner. With Rodla, William visited the villages talking to different sets of artisans about his cooperative. On some days they drove up to 300 km locating villages and craftspeople they could incorporate into the project. In September 1988 William registered the Bhadrajun Artisan's Trust, and became its sole chairman, secretary and treasurer. In the course of that year he visited another association of leather workers and weavers located in Jawaja, just off the Jaipur–Udaipur highway. This was an NGO called the Artists' Alliance and they were being helped by Prakash Tripathi, a dynamic man who was directing them towards a professional association with Fabindia. William was very impressed with Prakash Tripathi and requested him to join his project in Bhadrajun. By 1989 William had his team in place. Raj Kumar Rodla, Prakash Tripathi and William worked out of Bhadrajun trying to organize the different categories of craftspeople into efficient production units that would collectively pool resources to improve quality and enhance output. William's dream was that they would 'all sit together under the great old neem tree in Bhadrajun and take decisions.'

There are many advantages to a collective effort—weavers can buy larger quantities of superior yarn, facilities for dying yarn can be shared, larger looms can be jointly invested in to make customized durries that pay higher rates and most of all, loans can be taken to tide over the lean months between orders and payment. The Bhadrajun Trust supplied infrastructure and training to weavers to weave larger sizes of the flat durries where five of them had to sit together to produce one piece. The concept of a *jhula* (swing) was evolved so that weavers did not have to sit on the durrie while weaving and therefore dirty it. Loans from Fabindia funded this project and so products were sent to Delhi for sale in the stores to pay back the money. William experimented with new products. There were handmade leather *jootis* (open shoes) and goat-hair door mats. He also produced camel-hair durries and presented them at Fabindia. That particular day one of Fabindia's buying agents, Rahul Gupta (from Burlington Agencies, based in Mumbai), was visiting with his Danish buyers. They found the product interesting and decided to support William with his first order. Later they had to find a way to moth proof the durries because they got eaten! William had not had the time to work out their durability.

Amita Prashar Gupta, a photographer working in Tilonia, became one of the first to record the work William was doing in Bhadrajun. She visited the home-based artisans and spent days shooting them at work. Amita recalls William's passionate commitment to the project. She says, 'William had his own vision . . . His whole idea was returning to the roots—to the artisans and products—and make it happen better.'

But even William's enthusiasm could not solve the obstacles that were intrinsic to the nature of the project. To start with the location was a mistake. Bhadrajun was far from the main highway, and Raja Gopal Singh's house was even further away. Very few buses plied down the dusty road. Artisans were scattered in distant villages and found it very difficult to connect to the Trust office. It was tough to maintain quality or deadlines at long distance. There was no public communication at the time. As William mentions, jokingly, there was only one telephone connection in the area and it was at the raja's home. His phone number was 1 and nobody else around had a phone so he could

call only himself! The electricity was erratic, so work was confined
to a few daylight hours when indoors. Then there were problems
of cooperation. The artisans belonged to different castes and
hierarchies within their groups. Often there were tensions within
the same community, whether of leather workers, weavers or the
'jatia kumars'. Goods were never ready on time, and it was
impossible to chase payments without an efficient communication
system. The only reliable buyer was Fabindia because the payment
was collected immediately. So Fabindia became the de facto client,
but it had problems with some of the products. The store staff
struggled with mismatched jooti pairs and irate customers.
Sometimes the left shoe was missing, sometimes the right, and
often the pairs did not match—leather could not always be bought
in large enough quantities. The goat-hair mats left an offensive
smell in the closed store and the flat-woven durries did not have
straight edges since they were home-woven.

As it happened the very nature of the organization became a
handicap to William. Prakash Tripathi states that there have
always been too many government restrictions on trusts to inhibit
the misuse of funds. Trusts cannot trade or share dividends.
Permissions are required for each new activity and files get
delayed for days with the government. In those days banks also
took months to clear outstation cheques. Thrilling as the work
was, the frustrations were overwhelming. With the dilution of his
vision of distributing profits to the artisans, William's concept of
the cooperative was struggling to find meaning.

The Bissells visited Bhadrajun to encourage their son. There
was a lot to be said for a Wesleyan graduate who could be happy
living with such a lack of urban amenities. The ease with which
William interacted with the local community made his parents
proud. Even though people have stated admiringly that John was
too busy communicating with the people of India to learn the
language, there is no doubt that William's fluency in Hindi
worked to his advantage. Here was this young idealist just

returned from the US who was ready to carry his father's vision beyond the now established and successful supplier-buyer interface. Had the cooperatives worked well the member artisans could shape their own future. They would cease to be the marginal group at the bottom of the food chain.

In 1990 William started discussing the problem with his father. The idea of the cooperative was not working. It looked good on paper but had not translated into benefits for the artisans. John, as was his nature, had totally supported the project. As William said, there were two very special things about his father. First, he carried no emotional baggage about the way things should be done and accepted that there were many roads leading to the same goal. And second, once he was convinced about what his children wanted to do, he threw his weight behind it. The idea of converting the trust into a company with shares finally came up. By the end of 1990 the structure of Desert Artisans Handicrafts Pvt. Ltd was finalized, with William as the managing director, Raj Kumar Rodla as the general manager and Prakash Tripathi as the production manager. The paid up capital was Rs 1 lakh. Raj Kumar Rodla had an old family house in Jodhpur which was rented to the company. So Desert Artisans Handicrafts (DAH) came to be established in Rodla House, Jodhpur, in 1991. It would work with weavers, leather workers and fabric printers and introduce new items to Fabindia's range of products for many years.

In the meantime, in late 1989, John Bissell had recruited a young architect to work on a project that would satisfy another life-long interest he had in the heritage properties of India. Ravi Kaimal was first introduced to John in 1988 after he had repaired and upgraded the Samode Palace in Rajasthan for Anokhi's twentieth anniversary. John felt that Ravi could do a similar job on a palace at Ghanerao in time for Fabindia's thirtieth anniversary party. Ravi recalls touring Ghanerao with John, Bim and William and coming to a broad consensus on what could be done quickly.

They needed to have proper plumbing, install toilets and clean up the old façade while preserving its original look. The idea was to 'create a hotel in three months out of a crumbling old castle in the middle of nowhere' so that 150 people from around the world could camp there in batches over a period of two weeks. Ravi took up the daunting task and when he was finished with the project he had to contend with the question 'but what did you do?' since the building looked perfectly preserved but old! 'That is the bane of my life', says Ravi. Since then he has been involved with a number of similar restoration projects for Fabindia. While John found in Ravi a young and eager architect for his building projects, Ravi discovered an incredible mentor in John. A man who trusted people so totally that they inevitably ended up doing better than they thought they could, if only to live up to his belief in them. Ravi says, 'John had a very special quality. He revelled in the fact that people were not perfect, and in spite of their imperfections he trusted them.'

Ravi was invited to attend the celebrations at Ghanerao in March 1990 along with many other Bissell friends and family from India and abroad. Reminiscing about the event William says, 'That was a wonderful party. It got us in an age and a time that was really good.' Fabindia had turned thirty that year. Such events became a Bissell hallmark, supporting and promoting heritage properties by celebrating special occasions within them.

At the event Ranisahib Ghanerao mentioned that there were no schools for girls in the area and that they were actually discouraged from studying. The next thing Ravi knew was that he had got involved in the setting up of a rural school for girls in Rajasthan. During 1990-91 William and Ravi scoured the area for a suitable location for a school and finally found a barren plot of land at Bali, a kilometre from the main road between Udaipur and Jodhpur. The Bhadrajun Artisans Trust purchased the land and Ravi was entrusted with the job of building a school. It was designed in a simple modular way with the possibility of blocks being added at minimum cost as the school grew. Each block consisted of four classrooms, two store rooms and two verandas. The first block came up in 1992 and the school became fully functional in 1993. The Fabindia School at Bali now consists of six blocks, a thousand children and school buses going up to 20 km to pick up girls. It is still entirely funded, partly by Fabindia and partly by friends and organizations in the US who aid education in India.

William was living in Jodhpur after the incorporation of Desert Artisans Handicrafts Pvt. Ltd in 1991. They were still dealing with the same products—jootis, durries and printed yardage but business was much easier from Jodhpur. The city was colourful and lively and on its way to becoming a handicraft centre. Winter would bring visitors to the city—designers, buyers and tourists. Even the artisans found it more convenient to carry their goods a hundred kilometres to Jodhpur than the thirty to Bhadrajun because it was well connected. The move to Jodhpur catapulted Desert Artisans into an exciting process of discovery and production. William Bissell says, 'As soon as we moved business grew in leaps and bounds—some export but mainly through selling to Fabindia.'

Block printing with vegetable dyes was becoming a big thing at the time, and DAH located artisan families who were still using the traditional method of block printing called *ajrakh*. This was an intricate method where the textile was printed on both sides using natural dyes and a technique called resist printing. Resist printing was laborious because certain sections of the fabric were pre-treated to resist penetration by the dye. Repeat printings gave a depth and glow to the colours and the process softened the fabric. Tradition speaks of ajrakh printed fabric being used to swaddle new born infants because of its softness. DAH started sourcing prints from Barmer, Chittor, Ajrakpur and Akola and selling them to Fabindia. Charu Sharma says that the company had become a major supplier of printed fabric in the 1990s for

Fabindia garments. Once sold to Fabindia, the fabric was outsourced to tailoring units set up in Delhi which were independent of Fabindia but producing entirely for them. The demand for these prints was so high that DAH started buying handloom fabric to get it printed, sixty counts (thinner cloth) for summer, and twenty counts (thicker cloth) for winter.

When the growth in Fabindia's garment retail section necessitated a faster supply of printed cloth and handloom fabric was not accessible, power-loom material was used as the base for garments. This fabric would be dyed and then printed. New patterns had started coming from Fabindia where a continuous supply of trainees were experimenting with dynamic new designs. For many years Fabindia and Anokhi were the only two companies in north India where young textile designers could intern or work after their course at the National Institute of Design in Ahmedabad. So through the '90s, product development at Fabindia passed through the creative hands of designers like Bindu Jain, Anshu Nath, Sangeeta Sen Davis, Neeru Kumar and Rakesh Thakore.

Then started the production of fine-count, stone-washed durries. Here the process was complicated and involved many different towns in Rajasthan. Twenty-count yarn was first bought from mills in Hanumangarh. The yarn was then sent to Jaipur to be dyed since the quality of colour fastness required for the stone washed process could only be achieved there. There was a unit in Jaipur that could dye 100–200 kg of yarn at a time. The balls of twenty ply-dyed yarn were then brought back to Jodhpur to be distributed to the weavers who were called in from their respective villages. Weavers would pick up the yarn along with the durrie design and return to their villages. Regular monitoring by DAH ensured that the weavers kept to the design. The woven durrie was then taken to Jaipur to be stone washed, that is, dipped in potassium permanganate and then washed with soap and water and beaten soft by wooden batons. This gave the durrie an antiquated look and over time it became a very popular export item for Fabindia.

William also introduced Jacquard fabrics through weavers in west Uttar Pradesh. The Jacquard is a mechanical loom that simplifies the process of weaving complicated designs such as brocades through the use of a punched mechanism to guide the thread. As Charu Sharma said, 'Instead of a pedal loom where there is just a warp and weft variation of our fabric, this was the first time we had an inlay, like a flower.' Jacquard was being produced in Jaffrabad outside Delhi, and also by Mr Agarwal in Muradnagar. Appliqué bedcovers were brought in by DAH as well. Here white appliqués were cut out and stitched on to white power-loom fabric. Since the base was not handloom the Fabindia ethic demanded that some element of the product should be handcrafted. The same applied to hand-block printing on power-loom textiles.

William spent a great deal of time in Jodhpur that first year, and together with Prakash Tripathi learnt how to handle the business. They learnt for example that vegetable dyes cannot be printed successfully in the monsoon months because the dye does not 'catch'. If woven in winter the yarn sits tight and firm, but during the monsoon moisture loosens the cotton and the weave gets uneven. The team found it difficult to keep production targets for export since even one item could delay the entire shipment out of Fabindia. Prakash Tripathi admits that the DAH office in Jodhpur suffered on account of the vast distances that were 'wound in' to the production of their products: 'The weavers were hundred kilometres away from Jodhpur, and the dyers were 400 km away in Jaipur. Earlier our work was handled by an agent but as volumes grew we opened our own office in Jaipur.' DAH started a printing unit in Osiyan and later an office in Bhuj, in Gujarat. Over the next few years 'we started making [the artisans] shareholders in DAH. They purchased shares at par and saw themselves doing well along with the company. Jooti workers and printers were able to improve their standard of living.' This was William Bissell's first experiment towards his vision of artisan shareholders.

By 1992 DAH 'was an economically viable unit and there wasn't a challenge there any more,' says William. So he turned his interest to converting one of the Fabindia stores into an upmarket version modelled on the Conran shop. N-7 GK-1 had been designed by an architect friend Jyoti Rath as a home store. Here William brought in his Jacquards, the stone-washed durries and terracotta lamps. There was blue-rimmed Khurja pottery designed by Alex Davies and pottery from Minni and Mary Singh in Himachal. (Many homes in Delhi that were furnished with Fabindia products in the early '90s still carry remnants of that pottery). Mala Malhotra from the Fabindia office and William worked on this store together, filling it with sophisticated designer crafts for the home. Mala had a good sense of merchandising and strong administrative skills. It was 'an experiment to say that Fabindia was moving up-market,' says Charu Sharma. The store was opened in 1992 and did very well. For the first time William realized that he enjoyed the business of meeting people at the shop. 'At Fabindia you are always meeting interesting people,' he says, echoing his father.

By that time William was spending considerable time in the office in Delhi. But these two years between 1989 and 1991 had taken their toll on Fabindia. William's youthful enthusiasm and bright new ideas had not gone down very well with the firmly entrenched handloom ethos that had served Fabindia so well for over the past thirty years. Some of the new prints were based on power-loom textiles. From Meena Chowdhury's perspective the strict discipline of dealing purely with handloom was getting diluted. There were new products coming in to the store that had not passed the time-honoured cynosure of the Fabindia team. William Bissell's new company had mastered a technique that had been selling successfully under another well-known brand for

Ikat is created using a resist dyeing process. That requires predetermined sections of the yarn to be tied before dyeing. The technique produces fabric with a unique 'feathered' look to the motifs that emerge on the loom.

The Haseena durrie was redesigned from the original Punjab durrie by John Bissell and Terence Conran in 1968.

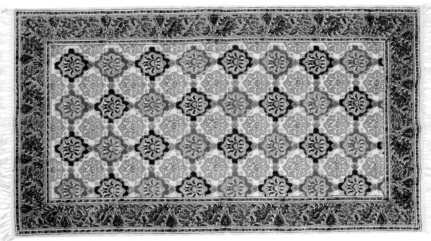

The Kalamkari cotton (jaal) durrie.

The Sitara durrie.

fabindia now at
margao

goa

3 March, 2010

Shop # 2, 3 & 4, Barreto Enclave, Near Ravindra Bhavan,
Borda-Fatorda Road, PO Fatorda, Salcette, Margao, Goa,
Ph: 0832- 3260779, Timings: 10 am- 8 pm, Open all days

50 years of fabindia

Fabindia promotional poster for the Margao store in south Goa.

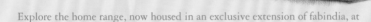

the grandeur of a magnificent building, the richness
& variety of handloom, products crafted with skill
handed down from generation to generation...

fabindia

now extends
the dimensions of heritage
at Kala Ghoda

6th October, '06, 7:00 pm onwards

Explore the home range, now housed in an exclusive extension of fabindia, at

Jeroo Building, 137, M.G. Road, Kala Ghoda, Mumbai, Ph: 22626539, 40
Timings: 10:00 am to 7:45 pm; Open all days

Fabindia as a heritage destination. Jeroo Building, Mumbai.

fabindia - kala ghoda

the grandeur of a
magnificent heritage building
housing the breath-taking
richness & variety of Indian
handloom

in glorious colours and a
spell-binding array of weaves,
textures, styles

and products crafted with
care and skill handed down
from generation to generation

giving traditional skills a
contemporary context

along with that perfect cup of coffee...
yes, sometimes elements do conspire
to create a truly memorable experience!

fabindia

Jeroo Building, 137, M. G. Road, Kala Ghoda, Mumbai, Ph: 022 - 22626539, 40
Timings: 10:00 am to 7:45 pm, Open all days

The largest Fabindia store in India. Kala Ghoda, Mumbai, 2004.

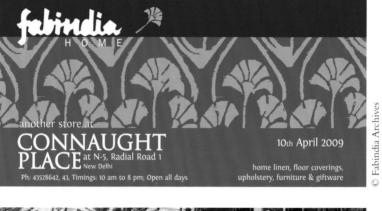

fabindia
H·O·M·E

another store at
CONNAUGHT
PLACE at N-5, Radial Road 1
New Delhi
Ph: 43528642, 43, Timings: 10 am to 8 pm; Open all days

10th April 2009

home linen, floor coverings,
upholstery, furniture & giftware

fabindia
handwoven
kilim dhurries

Central Hall, Above Shop No. 20 & 21, Khan Market,
New Delhi; Ph: 43683100, 114, 120 ■10, Local Shopping Centre,
Nelson Mandela Road, Vasant Kunj, Delhi; Ph: 46041700

5 - 6 December 2009
10 am to 8 pm

classic & contemporary **saris**

An exclusive store of Fabindia saris at Koregaon Park

fabindia
A-4, Ashiyana Park, North Main Road, Koregaon Park, Pune,
Ph: 40024954, 55, Timings: 10:30 am to 8:30 pm; Open all days

Craft techniques and weaves used in posters to announce store openings
and promotions.

some years. Before him Fabindia had steered clear of products that were being supplied by competitors. That had been easy to do in the beginning because there was nobody else in the field when John Bissell started his business. Since then many other entrepreneurs had seized the opportunity to develop and market Indian craftsmanship. This was inevitable and unavoidable. William was merely exploring available opportunities with his artisans. For Meena, it went against the Fabindia ethic.

For years she had nurtured Fabindia under her uncontested and efficient wing. While John Bissell was travelling the world and pulling in suppliers and buyers, Meena was sitting in the office and connecting the threads. She had set up the system and became its greatest advocate. The fabric of her life was woven into a concept that John and she had developed together. This had become the *raison d'etre* of the business—that Fabindia did not need to become greater than the sum of its investment in handloom and the artisans that created it. John had reiterated that ethic so many times over the years that the whole Fabindia effort was coloured by it. The consequence of such a commitment was that business could only grow slowly but the philosophy turned buyers and suppliers into joint shareholders of a shared mission.

The supply of handloom fabric was restricted to the number of pieces a weaver could produce in a day. Production was always increased gradually, and so too the looms, from two to four to six, very often with funds advanced from Fabindia. Charu Sharma says that Fabindia was very clear about this. 'Every time a new supplier was introduced it was because a sufficient need was felt—otherwise orders were distributed among the regular suppliers.' This was the reason large orders from new buyers were generally not entertained by Fabindia and would be passed on directly to other exporters. 'Buyers used to ask for container loads but we could not supply them,' Charu continues. Fabindia's largest customer Habitat 'took whatever our capacity was to produce, and we also kept our capacity to what they required'. John Bissell was not interested in big growth or large investments. Profit margins were therefore low. Sudarshan Madhok repeats John's words, 'Have you seen the number of people in the shop? I just love to see people going for this handloom trend.'

But by 1985 John had started seeing a disturbing sign in the US market with reference to Conran and the Habitat stores. 'Retail is so competitive here . . . I have sort of a strong sense in my bones that we are seeing the beginning of the end . . . at least of the US operation,' he writes in a letter to Madhukar Khera, and then goes on to describe the recently opened IKEA showroom. It was '270,000 square feet with the advertising blitz that goes with it . . . They have engaged in some very questionable practices . . . i.e., making prices very low on some items and then carrying them in very limited quantities.' Ikea was a Swedish home products company that had confined itself to the Netherlands till the '60s but had moved into the Europe and US markets very aggressively by the '80s.

John could see the writing on the wall, seven years before it actually happened. The comfort of the personalized client–supplier relationship that characterized Fabindia's equation with Habitat had come under threat from a new world order that traded in large volumes and low prices, rather than specialized products painfully created by hand, with long delivery schedules. Jeremy Smith wrote an urgent letter to John on 3 July 1989: 'Sales are very disappointing at the moment . . . With severe limitations on spending it is vital that we know what our commitments are week by week; we have a substantial number of orders well overdue . . . Last year Fabindia supplied both number one and number three of the top performers by range in the floor covering department . . . and six out of the top ten. It is therefore obvious that Fabindia is an extremely important supplier and can be extremely influential in helping us to control the present difficulties.' Smith suggested that Fabindia 'carry eight weeks plus stock per line' to tide over delivery schedule delays. But Fabindia was already stretched for delivery of existing orders. 'Since orders were much in excess of what we could produce, we had to allocate looms', says Charu. The orders for the Saranga and Haseena durries would run into 500–800 pieces, and between them the four durrie suppliers, Madhukar Khera, Mr Banga, Vineet Minocha and Shyam Sundar, would complete the order in several months. Such was the nature of handloom production. 'We could do this to Habitat because they had a running order with us and there were no penalties,' Charu Sharma concludes.

Terence Conran had had a dream run for over twenty years after opening his first Habitat shop in Chelsea in 1964. Started with a view to market his own range of furniture, Conran's business grew into a worldwide chain selling household goods and furniture in contemporary designs. A brilliant visionary in retail Conran recognized the worth of John Bissell's commitment to Indian handloom, and from 1967 the friendship between the two men carried Fabindia products to the world through stores in the US, UK and France.

The following are extracts from two memos sent by John Bissell on 25 February 1998. They record the respect that the two associates had for each other.

Dear Terence,
My only disappointment in a very full, happy and now prosperous life has been that William never really knew you. He now runs Fabindia—and wants to open more shops . . . William asked me why I referred to you as Guru.

And then to William:

When we started Fabindia in 1960/61 we did very little sale. 4 years later we were doing fine—mostly due to TOC [Terence Conran] and Jeremy. We have gone ahead since then—never compromising on quality or design. TOC had the best reputation as a merchant in the West—and Habitat got known by everyone ... [Conran] bought more from us every year until Habitat UK was sold to IKEA. I will never forget TOC and Jeremy—what a team ... He is brilliant and I am proud to call him Guru. Much love from Papa.

Flush with success, Conran started empire building in the mid-'80s buying over other companies in the UK including Heels, Mothercare and British Home Stores to form a conglomerate called the Storehouse Group. Not content with retail Conran then leveraged the balance sheets of these companies to get into disastrous investment in real estate development. By 1989–90 he ran out of funds and had to sell his stake in the Storehouse Group to investors. He resigned as owner of the Conran shops in the US and Habitat in Europe. As Madhukar aptly says, by 1990 Habitat was run by chartered accountants and financers who turned the company from a designer-envisioned, product-oriented business to a sales and marketing company. When Jeremy wrote that letter to John in 1989 Conran was on his way out and Habitat was being squeezed to maximize profit. In this scenario Fabindia's hand-weaving delivery schedules were way out of line and delays were proving costly. After Terence Conran sold his shares the new management dismissed their designer Jeremy Smith and appointed an agent in Delhi to deal with Habitat orders. The call from the agent, Sunil Sethi, in early 1991, caught Fabindia by surprise. Sunil's business partner, Kaiser Roca, was known to the Fabindia team. He bought merchandise on behalf of the large department stores Macy's and Bloomingdales and John Bissell had declined to supply them. He was not interested in dealing either with the large volumes those stores demanded or the low prices that would consequently be negotiated. Sunil's company was called Alliance Merchandising and he had been deputed to check the shipment that was on its way to Habitat from Fabindia. In the history of the association between the two companies nobody had ever checked a shipment after Fabindia had packed and signed it off. This time too there had been no intimation about the issue, and the shipment was half-loaded on the ship in Bombay when Sunil Sethi called. Tara Sahney remembers that John Bissell came out of his room, his face red with anger, and said, 'Please ring up the forwarding agent and tell him to take the entire shipment off the boat, and bring it back to Delhi.' The cargo returned to the Fabindia warehouse and further orders were stopped till Habitat clarified its position. After that for the next two years Alliance inspected the merchandise before it was shipped. In 1992 the management of IKEA bought over Habitat and the great brand equity built up by Terence Conran became history. In the mid-'90s Jeremy Smith started a buying house called the Indian Collection and continued to work with Fabindia.

Fabindia was at a very significant moment in its history. Exports were continuing to do well (notwithstanding the glitches with Habitat) but more significantly, domestic sales were now over Rs 2 crore. Meena Chowdhury gives an account of how she used to keep track of daily home market sales to ensure that stocks never ran out. There was a large chart on her office wall which was updated every day so that at the end of the month she could tell which items were selling really well and which were not. Stocks were ordered regularly on the basis of this chart, so there was never a large gap between the product selling out and its replenishment. If a product had 'oversold', a term used for a faster than normal sell-out, Meena would immediately farm it out to more than one weaver/supplier to ensure that more of it was produced next time. Those charts became valuable records of Fabindia sales figures over the years.

The evolution of the home market translated into an increase in garment sales at Fabindia. In addition to the basic plain and printed handloom shirts, kurtas and pyjamas, the line of merchandise now also included women's wear made from the colourful hand-block prints being supplied by Desert Artisans Handicrafts. Prakash Tripathi says that instead of waiting for orders, 'we had begun to understand which prints were doing well so we produced that fabric in advance. We learned that the market requires lighter fabrics and colour for the summer and heavier, darker prints for the winter, so we planned accordingly.' By this time both handloom and power-loom materials were being used for printing fabric. But for Meena Chowdhury handloom constituted Fabindia's identity and she would not compromise on that cause. 'It was not that John was a purist but Fabindia stood for something and for me that was very precious,' she says. According to her Fabindia had survived for so long because it had stuck to handloom. At the time John Bissell never commented on this subtle shift in ideology. Perhaps he foresaw the changing nature of the market and realized that Fabindia needed to move on. Or seeing that the honeymoon with Habitat was coming to an end he felt that his business needed some other market to survive. Or just that William was trying to learn the business on his own and John was happy to encourage him.

Confused by the profusion of ideas and products that were pouring out of the perceived inheritor of the Fabindia heirloom, Meena Chowdhury retired from active work in the autumn of 1991. Asked by an uncle about her reasons for leaving when she was still young and capable she replied, 'I would like to leave when I am right on top. I don't want to leave when I cannot continue.'

The day she walked into John Bissell's office and requested that she be allowed to leave may have been the worst of her life, and it certainly took John by surprise. Meena says he absolutely froze for a few minutes and then said, 'I am very hurt.' She explained that it seemed the most practical thing to do and that it was better to clear the stage than allow problems to fester and hurt the company. She says John hung his head and asked her when she wanted to go, and they settled on a date some months in the future. When the time came John requested her to continue an informal association with Fabindia by coming in once or twice a month to meet him. This would keep her in touch with what was happening in the office and enable them to discuss work issues as they had done since Fabindia began. The arrangement continued through the next two years. Meena says:

It was a couple of hours normally, on a week day, after lunch. During the meetings he would relate all the month's happenings including which big order had come in and we would talk generally about suppliers and staff. That way I also knew what was happening and I think we both enjoyed [the meetings] . . . But I tried very hard not to interfere with any kind of work that was going on.

Charu Sharma had taken over administration after Meena had left and she was working very hard to keep the office together. But nobody could replace Meena and the role she had played. 'It was very difficult for anyone to fill Meena's shoes because they were really big shoes,' says William. Meena operated in a way that no modern management manual talks about. She managed by the power of moral persuasion. Holding herself to a certain standard she expected the same from all the staff. She had the ability to make people feel embarrassed about raising issues that were not appropriate to office harmony and routine. It was a very rare ability and everybody respected her immensely. She had a very clear sense of what was right and wrong, and having earned that mandate from John Bissell, she applied it unilaterally in the office. John never interfered with the day-to-day business of running Fabindia, or with administration or personnel. He left it to Meena and she took care of everything. She had everybody profiled and knew how to get them to work to their optimal. In a good year John would say, 'let's do something wonderful for the staff', and she would work out how to do it. That was their relationship.

From her point of view Meena says that she felt she was very often in limbo with reference to Fabindia. John Bissell was a very friendly, open person, but he was undoubtedly the boss, 'way above everybody else'. In the hierarchy Meena came next. Holding the reins she could decide for everyone else, but nobody decided for her. John did not handle administrative matters and it never occurred to him to interfere. Therefore absurd situations arose where salaries were raised every year by Meena for the entire staff, but her moral rigidity came in the way of dealing with her own. Consequently it did not increase for years. But that it did not lead to any rancour in her is a reflection of her commitment to John Bissell's ideology and complete absorption into Fabindia. She jokingly says:

> My own position was ambiguous. I didn't know what I was. I used to joke about it all the time ... If anyone asked me what I was in Fabindia, I would say I am the chief 'karamchari'. Because that was the best way I could describe it.

In 1993 when the issue of salaries blew up a storm in Fabindia John was not equipped to handle it. He had never dealt with it and, as William says, it 'was not part of his mental make-up'. When Meena Chowdhury was in charge of administration, people were too much in awe of her to complain about anything. Meena says that when questioned she always had a satisfactory answer. She would explain the reason the salary had not been raised and convince them that the decision had been fairly taken. Whether the staff agreed with this or not the fact was that people never publicly displayed their dissatisfaction. In 1993 Fabindia faced as serious a revolt as was possible in such a small company. Some of the senior staff went to John and argued that they had been dealt with unfairly and would not accept the terms they were being offered that year. John had never faced anything like this before and later told Meena that he was shattered and that was the worst day of his life.

He had his full share of problems that year. In April 1993 a telex came from Habitat stating that one of their orders was running late and that this was not acceptable to the new management. As William says, 'Habitat orders traditionally ran late at Fabindia. This had been happening for so long that there was a joke about it and it had not mattered all these many years.' But this time it was different. A few weeks later Barbara Dickman visited John Bissell in Delhi. She was part of a team that had been called in to put Habitat back on its feet. With a mandate to cut costs the lady was on a mission to connect Habitat directly to the suppliers (via an agent) thereby removing merchandisers such as Fabindia. William walked into the meeting and was appalled at the aggressiveness displayed. 'You are part of the past and the past we know is wrong. We don't want any intermediaries. We need to go straight to the source. We need to buy sharp. You are the problem, we are the solution. We have an amazing team,' she was saying to John, referring to Sunil Sethi and Alliance Merchandising Corporation, 'and we represent a new leadership'. They had it all worked out and Fabindia was in the way, so they had gone through the motions and the pretext of a late order to close the relationship. John tried to suggest that it was not easy to deal with the complexities of India's rural supplier base, but they were not listening. As William said so succinctly, 'Fabindia was an inconvenience from the past, a historic relic that had to be pushed off.' After a few cursory meetings with this new team listening to their unrealistic terms, John Bissell decided that Fabindia would exit the stage. That ended a historic relationship between the two companies.

William learnt a lesson that day. He was determined never to get into a similar space. That twenty-eight years of a committed business association could be dismissed so easily was a revelation. In this partnership between the producer, the exporter, the importer/wholesaler and the retailer, the weakest link was in the middle. The exporter would be the first to be dropped in a tightening circuit, and ultimately when the retailer got to the supplier, even the importer was dispensable. Fabindia's years of investment in sourcing and developing the product were inconsequential to the new management team at Habitat. In his zeal to promote the product John had connected importers directly to his suppliers on several occasions. Madhukar Khera, loyal to his old friend, discontinued exporting durries from BCM to Habitat after John closed his account with them. But soon Sunil Sethi requested John to persuade Madhukar to continue the supply of woollen durries to Habitat, in particular a durrie named Rohtak Wool. Thus the BCM–Habitat association continued and goes on till today, with three to five different types of durries being sold to them every year. Since Habitat had been bought over by IKEA in 1992, BCM now exports directly to IKEA. In 2007 a bestseller was reordered by Habitat and introduced into the market after a gap of thirty years. This was Ajanta, the original woollen durrie created jointly by Madhukar Khera and John Bissell in 1968.

William Bissell recounts an incident in early 1993 that left him with an enduring philosophy. While travelling in Australia he had stood on a beach with an experienced surfer and asked him what skills were required to become good at this sport. The man said that you need to learn how to surf of course, but more importantly you need to know where the next wave is coming from. 'You need to be skilful enough to ride the wave but you must be at the right place at the right time to successfully catch the wave,' said the surfer. These words left a deep impression on William and 'a penny dropped in my head', but he didn't know what the penny was at that time. Everybody was certain that William would join his father's business full time but he was still uncertain in May 1993. He wanted to do something but wasn't sure what it could be. He felt he was 'in holding pattern', dividing his time between his company DAH in Jodhpur, the N-7 store in the GK-1 market and the Fabindia School in Rajasthan.

1992-93 had been another good year with Fabindia sales turning over more than Rs 12 crore, with a post-tax profit of Rs I crore. Export sales were Rs 8 crore and domestic sales Rs 4.24 crore. The interesting detail was that the home market was now contributing 35 per cent of the total revenue having grown at a rate of 40 per cent during 1992-93.

On 22 March 1993 Mr Agarwal from Muradnagar (supplier of some of Fabindia's most successful fabrics since 1972) dropped in to Fabindia to wish John Bissell on his sixty-second birthday. He was invited to stay on for tiffin-lunch as was the custom. John told him that he was looking forward to attending his daughter Monsoon's graduation from Bryn Mawr that year. John had been totally focused on his two children furthering the Bissell legacy of graduating from reputed New England colleges. Elinor Latane Bissell, John's mother, had won an award in 1926 for high honours in History and Music when she graduated from Bryn Mawr College in Connecticut. Monsoon describes her grandmother as 'an entrepreneur, fiercely connected to people and a huge networker who spent many years in public service.' When they passed away within three days of each other in April 1984, Elinor and her husband Bill Bissell were described in the 19 April 1984 issue of the Farmington Valley Herald as 'pillars of their community ... exceptionally gifted individuals who incorporate[d] public service as an integral part of their lifestyles.' Monsoon was still in school in Connecticut when her grandparents died, but she stayed on in the US to graduate from the same college as her grandmother.

Monsoon's story of her first notion of Fabindia is very amusing. She recounts an incident in Modern School where she was studying when she was about six years old. The class teacher was asking each student in turn to describe where his/her parents worked. While Monsoon was waiting her turn she realized that the answers were following a pattern that did not apply to her. Without exception the children were reporting that their fathers were in business and that their mothers were housewives. Not wanting to stand out as the odd ball she lied when her turn came. She said that her father worked with the World Bank and that her mother was a housewife. When she came home and told the family there was some mirth and much discussion. She said that she was not sure what her father did, except that he ran a '*dukan*' and that it was not 'cool'. On the other hand her mother seemed to have an important job because you had to make an appointment to meet her while at work. So she had switched around her parents' jobs to be as normal as everyone else. As it was Monsoon always felt that she had to constantly negotiate her cultural identity—between the American and the Indian, the white Anglo-Saxon Protestant (WASP) from New England and the Punjabi!

'My earliest memory of Fabindia was a playground,' she says. William, older by three years, and Monsoon, used to go to Fabindia after school to be taken swimming by their father. They used to hide in the bales, climbing mountains of cloth and slipping underneath folds of fabric. 'It was fabulous,' she says, 'and that is one of the smells of my childhood, of going into that room full of durries, the damp, musty smell of a basement filled with wool and cotton.'

Though 'Fabindia is in my blood', says Monsoon, John made sure that his children never felt any sense of entitlement or ownership towards the business. They were taught to never expect differential treatment and to always pay for any item they took off the shelves in the store. These were values firmly instilled into them by their father—American values, Monsoon feels, of separating the private from the professional. 'Everything in life is not a right, it is a privilege,' she says. Fabindia stood for a commitment to a value system because that was John's philosophy and 'he walked the talk'. In 1988-89 Monsoon took a year off from her studies and wanted to work with Fabindia. John told her to report to Meena Chowdhury. Monsoon had been scared of Meena as a child and could not believe her father would make her do that. But she did and Meena sent her off to fold clothes along with Kirti and Seema who worked in the front of the store. 'I spent weeks just sitting there folding clothes,' she says, while friends of the Bissells' would come in to shop and get indignant about the job she was doing in her father's store! According to Monsoon, John never spoke to her in the store nor asked her to have lunch with him all the time she worked with Fabindia. She brought her own lunch from home and ate with the ladies every day. She says she was so scared of Meena that she found it difficult to swallow her food in front of her. 'She had this way— with the most minimum of words you knew what was right and what was wrong!' After a while Monsoon was upgraded to making bills. After spending four months at Fabindia she realized that she was not interested in merchandising, so clearly this was not her vocation in life.

Soon after that Monsoon returned to the US and joined Bryn Mawr as an undergraduate, treading in her grandmother's footsteps of over half a century ago. 'For a man of decidedly simple tastes, John Bissell possessed an extravagant love of the florid deed,' says John Stewart Cox, referring to the happiness expressed by John when he visited the US for Monsoon's commencement ceremony at Bryn Mawr in May 1993. John was accompanied by the extensive family from Delhi. It was going to be an occasion and in true Bissell style, friends had been invited to a large party at their home on Old Canton Road, Connecticut. Bim relives a lovely memory of John expressing his joy at Monsoon's commencement. Just before the graduation in the school she remembers that John 'ran down into the quadrangle at dawn and did a dance all by himself to celebrate the fact that his daughter had passed.'

On 21 May, after Monsoon's graduation, the family drove back to Connecticut stopping by a cousin's home for a leisurely lunch. Isabelle and John English had a lovely house on a hill overlooking Long Island Sound. Meena (Bim's sister) recalls that it was a beautiful day, warm and sunny with a refreshing breeze, and the family stayed the whole afternoon. After tea Monsoon returned to Canton with her grandmother Sita, and William left with his friend to show her his old university, Wesleyan, before driving back to Canton. John, Bim and Meena stayed on with their hosts for at least an hour more. Since the drive back to Canton was not too long and they were not in a hurry, Bim decided to stop at a shopping mall on the way to pick up some things for the house. Once they were back on the road after visiting the mall John announced that he was not feeling well, swerved the car off to the side of the road and passed out.

This is Meena's account of the events that followed. They tried to revive John but he had collapsed. Meena jumped out for help. She stopped the next car on the road. Luckily there was a paramedic in that car and he was carrying a cellular phone. He called for medical help. They thought John could have been suffering from a severe case of food poisoning. Within ten minutes the ambulance arrived, John was given oxygen and rushed off to the Middlesex Hospital with Bim by his side. In the meantime Meena had made a call from the same phone to Monsoon in Canton and told her that her father was unwell and that they were going to the hospital in Middletown. She told her to get hold of William and come to the hospital. There were no mobiles in those days and William must have just driven past Middletown on his way to Canton when his father was being taken there. Monsoon was standing outside their home when William arrived and she told him that something terrible had happened to John. Together they drove back to Middletown and reached the hospital at 8 p.m. John had been taken in to the emergency room and within the hour the resident neurologist confirmed Bim's worst fears. John had suffered a stroke, or a brain bleed as they called it in the US. He was haemorrhaging. The doctor said he had to be taken to the Hartford Hospital where there was a specialized neurological department. A helicopter was already on its way to fly him there. William says the doctor told them the situation was critical and that they should expect the worst. He was handed his father's things and told to rush to Hartford immediately. His last memory was of the helicopter taking off from the roof of the hospital as he walked to the parking lot.

It took them forty minutes to drive to Hartford Hospital; the helicopter must have made it in five. William, Bim, Monsoon and Meena reached there at about 9.30 p.m. John's sister Marie and her husband Tim were already there. A health worker informed them that a top-level neurological team had been pulled together and John was going to be taken in for surgery at 10 p.m. John must have had his stroke at about 6.45 p.m. and barely three hours later he was in the operating theatre. William remembers that the head of the surgical team was Dr Charlie Poletti and that the operation went on for hours. John was shifted to the ICU after 2 a.m. that night and he stayed there for three weeks. He was kept sedated most of the time and made a partial recovery though he could not follow commands, swallow or talk. He started to lose weight. The family camped in the waiting room. The doctors were waiting for him to stabilize before sending him to a rehabilitation centre. John's brain had suffered 'significant intensive damage' and it needed a great deal of help to get him back. William was told that in such cases the maximum recovery takes place in the first month. After that some improvement could be expected between the next three to six months, and then it plateaus.

This is William's account of those months:

> I don't remember the next six months; from May to October my memory is very sketchy. Mostly of going to the hospital and coming back repeatedly. Once John recovered it was clear that he may remain severely vegetative. But we pushed ahead. He was moved to a room at the Hartford Hospital. We saw that things had started happening in his

head. He began to follow simple commands—close your eyes, lift a leg, he started recognizing people. He was moved to a good rehabilitation hospital in Wallingford near New Haven. A lot of John's family lived close around there. Gaylord was in a lovely campus and we rented a small cottage there. Bim and I took turns. Monsoon had gone to Kerala by now. She had accepted an assignment to work in the Corpus Christy School run by Mrs Mary Roy (Arundhati Roy's mother). Monsoon was shattered and this was her way of dealing with it.

Meanwhile back in Delhi Meena Chowdhury had received a call from one of the ladies in the Fabindia store. Chitra Chopra's daughter was working at the World Bank in Washington and she had heard that something had happened to John Bissell. Meena called Canton immediately and spoke to Bim on the phone, who informed her that John had had a stroke and was unconscious. At that moment, while on the phone, Meena took a decision. She said to Bim, 'When John gains consciousness tell him that I will look after Fabindia and he is not to worry about it at all.' That evening she told her husband what had happened and said, 'I have told them I will look after Fabindia.' She thought she would handle the company for a few months while John recovered. She didn't know that those 'few months' would add another ten years to her association with Fabindia. The next day she went back to the office and called the staff together to let them know what had happened. Soon a fax was sent to Fabindia Inc. addressed to John and signed by the Fabindia team, and Madhukar Khera from Panipat.

The fax is dated 26 May 1993 and it reads:

DEAR JALEBI, ALL OF US ARE PRAYING FOR YOUR SPEEDY RECOVERY—LOOK FORWARD TO YOUR RETURN. PENDING ORDERS FOUR CRORE—MAY EXPORT FIGURE 80 LAKH APPROX. FONDEST REGARDS.

The girls must have been referring to John Latane Bissell, or JLB, as Jalebi because of John's fondness for the Indian sweet of the same name.

On 3 June 1993 another fax was sent to John with even more details of business at Fabindia. Orders had been received from two of their bigger buyers, Tomo and Dulton from Japan, and three other buyers were expected later that year. After that there were the final sales figures for the month.

EXPORT FIGURE FOR MAY IS 85.83 AND HOME MARKET FIGURES ARE–N-14: 23.87, N-5:7.04 AND N-7:11.61.

The message continued telling him that his friends were calling in every day and everybody wished him a speedy recovery. This fax was signed by twenty-three people. Extraordinary care and support from the Fabindia team in Delhi is apparent in yet another fax written to William in the US wishing him on his birthday on 10 June 1993. This is handwritten by Meena Chowdhury and mentions that so many people have sent their good wishes and prayers for John that 'he cannot but get better and come home perfectly well.'

Monsoon talks about Meena Chowdhury's response:

Look what MC did. She came back when he had his stroke. That was really something. For us it was like someone had put a hand under us to support us. We had gone from everything to nothing in one day. The day John heard that Meena was back, when he could be coherent enough to understand it, he was like, we are going to be okay, we are in safe hands. Think of how awful it would have been for my father to sit there recovering and worrying about how to make things better for the people back home.

Meena's sense of loyalty and commitment affected everyone in the office. The staff got together and dedicated themselves to work. They felt that they should make a special effort now that John was so unwell.

Meena says:

> I have to say that there was a feeling that 'Mrs Chowdhury is back!' and we are all together again. I think that because I called them in and said we have to do this for John, everybody responded. And what a response! Nobody said there is no boss so I'll leave early or come late or anything. The girls worked tremendously hard. The systems had been set in place earlier and exports did not suffer at all. There was an export room and clients would be shown the products. Orders were taken, prices fixed, delivery dates discussed—the customer was taken care of completely. Tara was head of the export department and she worked really hard. There was a tremendous feeling of energy in the office at that time.

William comments: 'Those were Meena's finest hours. She really drove the team and got the shipments out. There was a huge effort there. Everybody worked really hard to put their differences aside and pull together. Export sales that year were record breaking.'

As news spread of John, his friends and suppliers started dropping in to Fabindia wanting to send prayers, charms, cards and wishes. William says that hundreds of people wrote to John 'and we would get those aerograms arriving all the time from small places all over the country. So many people wrote to me too and I didn't even know them.' It was then that he realized what his father had done for all those years at Fabindia. While setting up the business John had 'spent most of his time making things happen for other people.'

The collection of cards and letters that has since been archived includes postmarks that had built Fabindia's business around the world—Joyce Bernard from Ascraft, Australia; Terence Conran and Jeremy Smith from the UK; Yves Cambier from France; Begonia from Becara, Spain; Hiroko from Japan; Jean Paul Denton from Switzerland. Then there was Calico House, Design Imports, Zibayish, Bazaar, Chandni Chowk, Malabar Imports— the names spill out of the cards in a profusion of global destinations. There were suppliers from all over India and of course, many friends. John Bissell had supported causes, funded projects, helped many entrepreneurs. And all those people wrote to him, reminding him of the great times they had shared and the good deeds he had done, as though the memories would jostle his mind and aid his recovery.

William says their home in Canton became a repository of love and good wishes and visitors. Lucy (an old family retainer) who had travelled with them from India to attend Monsoon's graduation, cooked all the meals, received the phone calls and cared for the anxious family through those months of crisis. Many people who were close to the Bissells made a trip to Canton to lend their support.

During the first month at Gaylord, John Bissell made rapid progress. The rehabilitation centre offered physiotherapy, exercises and medical care under a team of doctors called physiatrists. Bim and William lived on the premises and the rest of the Bissell clan visited often since their homes were not far from Wallingford. And then John had another accident. As his brain cleared he began to comprehend the extent of his disability. The frustration of his predicament would cause intense anger and he would fly into violent rages jeopardizing his physical condition. Notwithstanding these problems he was doing quite well. As William says, 'We were pushing him really hard because the doctors had said that this condition will not improve beyond what is achieved in those first three to six months.' John had been assigned a special wheelchair with ballasts and a seatbelt so he would not fall out. Anger was a known and expected symptom of intense brain damage and the centre knew how to handle it.

However one particular evening John seemed to have been left alone for a few minutes and he must have leaned forward to move the chair. The heavy wheelchair toppled over and John landed head down on the floor. The fall caused another severe head injury. This was a real tragedy because the second injury almost negated the progress John had made during that first month. This time recovery was much slower and John was eventually brought home to Canton. It was a very difficult time for the family. John still could not swallow or speak and the prognosis was that he might never recover his faculties. In Canton he had intensive physiotherapy, occupational therapy and exercise classes. He had started communicating a little and was learning how to use his fingers to write. There was no more to be gained from the medical system in the US and John wanted to return home. The Bissells decided it would be easier to set up the support structure in Delhi and brought John Bissell back to India in October 1993.

.5.

GIVING WAY TO THE NEW
1993–2000

William says it was a good decision to bring John back. There was a large family living at home in Friends Colony and friends dropped in all the time. John was never alone. He would sit in his wheelchair in the veranda of their house and receive visitors through the day. Everybody wanted to read to him and chat with him. A full-time nurse was hired and a physiotherapist assigned to help him with his exercises. With his Bajaj Tempo Trax and his driver Puran, John was quite mobile. He still couldn't walk, speak or eat, and one eye was damaged so he wore a patch over one eye 'pirate like, except that the patches were made of handloom ikat fabric to match his shirt or his kurta', says Bim. From all reports John recovered most of his mental faculty over the years but his inability to communicate easily frustrated him continuously. Coming to terms with his handicap must have taken all his strength. Under the circumstances he could not have led a more complete life than his family organized for him in India.

The first time he came to Fabindia after his return to Delhi the N-block market came to a halt, remembers Meena Chowdhury. People came out of every shop to meet him, including the mochi and the paanwala. They all stood there stunned at his physical state. A ramp had been placed for him to get up to the N-14 shop. Meena narrates:

We all rushed out when the wheelchair was coming in. We gathered around him. My goodness, there were people who stood in corners and cried. To see John Bissell like that was incomprehensible. He had no control at all. His eyes didn't change; there was no expression, no smile. But you could see that he was excited. He tried to talk and a shriek came out. He tried very hard to call my name, and then he called 'Swati'. It came out like a shout but you could understand. He wanted to go to the Finance section. He wanted everyone to be called down to see him, Madhu, Neela. From that day on he wanted to do this every day. It gave him comfort. This was his life.

Whenever he came everyone would drop everything and collect around him. He would sit in the middle of the shop and keep trying to ask questions. The strange sounds used to scare customers and their children initially. But soon people got used to him. 'He used to sit on that shop floor—this white man in a black wheelchair, screaming,' says Bim. Customers who recognized him came up and said, 'Hi John!' and carried on with their shopping. This went on for a month. John's visits became the focal point of the day and disrupted the entire office because the staff would drop everything and want to stay with him. So Meena had to restrain the staff and explain gently to her boss, 'John, there's a lot of work for them to do so I've asked them to go back to their desks.'

After the Bissells returned to Delhi William moved into the Fabindia office on the second floor of the N-14, GK-1 building. He had to look after Fabindia. Whatever else he may have been interested in doing, now he had no options left. John's disability was too severe for him to handle his work as before. William's advantage was that since Meena was back she was taking care of the entire functioning of the company. John Bissell had been the managing director of Fabindia since 1976. In 1992 the other directors were Lt Gen. Sibal, Meena Chowdhury and Madhukar

Khera. In late 1993 William Bissell became a director and continued the projects that John had started before his stroke. In 1992 Fabindia had bought a plot of land in Vasant Kunj at a DDA auction. Ravi Kaimal was commissioned to design a three-storey building to house a store. The idea was that since Delhi was expanding rapidly, a large store would cater to the residential areas developing south of the existing South Delhi constituency. Building work had started and John Bissell visited the site often watching it come together from the confines of his wheelchair. He was excited by the prospect of Fabindia's first location outside Greater Kailash. The store opened in 1994. 'We had a huge inventory in that store,' says Charu, with four floors stocked with Fabindia merchandise. Mala Malhotra, who was responsible for the success of the N-7 shop, was sent there as manager. It took a couple of years for the sales to pick up. Meanwhile the GK stores were doing great business, and exports also peaked in 1993-94. John sent out a letter to the directors and staff in April 1994:

> Please note; hmkt [home market] sales about 5 crore, export about 10 crore. Makes sales about 15 crore—it has never been so good [in] previous years . . . Your company has never done so well and probably won't do this well again . . . Profit 148 lakh after taxes and bonus—terrific . . . great job by all men and women—Thanks.
>
> John Bissell

The tremendous effort made by the Fabindia team in the face of John's tragedy had resulted in greater production and sales targets. Charu says, 'At the time we closed shop with Habitat we were lucky enough to have a lot of other buyers who had been "kept hungry" since we could not increase production enough to satisfy all.' That year Fabindia had supplied largely to Chandni Chowk, UK; Ascraft Fabrics, Australia; Gilbert Poweri, New Zealand; J.P. Denton, Switzerland; Coin, Italy; and Malabar,

Australia. There was also the Conran Shop in London and Fabindia Inc. buying for the US market.

Also, and most importantly, liberalization—even in relatively small doses—had created a phenomenal milieu for enterprise, greater jobs and higher per capita disposable incomes. India took off on a very different growth rate. Writing about the late '90s Ramchandra Guha says that excluding all those earning less than Rs 140,000 per year (at 1998-99 prices), the middle class could consist of fifty-five million Indians—a very substantial market for those offering services and products! This was going to impact Fabindia hugely.

Already by late 1995 retail had become an overwhelming business and the GK store was booming. Garments became popular and Fabindia provided clothes off the shelves—quality ready-to-wear at competitive prices. Working closely with designers Fabindia added new ranges of women's clothing—short shirts and kurtas over trousers—styles for the modern woman. 'There may have been about 2000 people working on our products at that time—new suppliers, new products, new ideas,' says William. Exports were still doing well but 'the sun was setting on that business model . . . we had the afterglow of a very lovely high noon.'

Meena Chowdhury's office was on the first floor and William's on the second floor in N-14 GK-1. Meena admitted that the young man was working very hard. He had initiated the process of computerization in Fabindia and was studying the finances of the company. William says Meena and he 'had a lot of discussions on various issues and she was always the cautious one.' According to him Meena and he shared a great working association:

> The reason is that I used to be an eternal optimist, looking at the best possible outcome, and MC always looked at the worst possible outcome. The reality used to be somewhere in between the two. If there had been two like her we

would have ended up doing nothing . . . if there had been two like me we would have collapsed all over the place.

He adds, 'JB and she were in the same frame.'

William felt that there was no future in exports. To 'work like a dog and produce something under someone else's label', was not the way he wanted to run his business. Fabindia's long-time Swiss buyer, John Paul Denton, had also moved in to the suppliers directly and cut Fabindia off. Rahul Gupta says that his company, Burlington's, had been attending the trade fairs in Delhi and they had seen that suppliers-turned-exporters were meeting clients directly. 'Merchant exporters like Fabindia were being cut out of the loop,' says Rahul. The writing was on the wall and everybody had 'to move one step ahead before the events overtook' them. Between technology and international fairs major structural changes were taking place in the business model. Wireless communication had opened the air for faster supplier-to-buyer interactions. Tourism infrastructure had improved, and small towns had become habitable for foreign guests. Buyers could travel directly to their suppliers. And trade fairs brought the suppliers to the cities to meet the buyers. There was no space for the merchant exporter any more.

Madhukar remembers that Fabindia tried different strategies to revive exports in those years. Sometime in the early '90s Fabindia attended an international fair called the Japan Tex. Charu Sharma, Madhu Mathur, Madhukar Khera and Jagdish Banga (Madhukar's brother-in-law and also a Fabindia supplier) travelled to Japan. They carried an artwork (collage) designed and made by Anshu Nath, a designer who occasionally worked with Fabindia. This was in the form of an enormous wave, 3m x 30m, or ten lengths of 1m x 3m of different durrie patterns stitched together. The 'wave' (sample) was displayed in the Fabindia stall and attracted a lot of attention. The team came away with a large number of queries and some reasonable orders. John had been very keen that Fabindia attend this fair and it turned out to be a 'hugely important exercise', says Madhukar. But the scale of business that such fairs generated was beyond the capacity or interest of Fabindia. For example, a customer was ready to give them an order to supply ten different fabrics of 500 m each. When they informed him of their varying prices per fabric, he gave them a simple formula—add up all the rates and divide by 10, so that they could give him one price! This was merely a trial order and they could expect bigger business. Once back in India they thought they would give it their best shot. But, as Madhukar says, in the stipulated three to four months for delivery, they had not produced even 50 per cent of the order. And so they found themselves selling off the 100-200 pieces of the order as it arrived from the weavers to recover costs. Fabindia was simply not organized enough to deal with such large quantities.

As John's friend Raj Kathuria of Globe Enterprises says, 'John preferred to sell 1000 m of fabric to twenty people than 20,000 m to one. He didn't want to go big.' Anyone who came to Fabindia wanting 5000 m of some fabric would be directed to Raj Kathuria. John would tell the customer, 'Wait a minute', and grab the phone and say, 'Raj, I'm sending so and so to you. He wants 5000 m and I cannot supply more than 1000 m, so please help him.'

Charu analyses the combination of events that led to the decline of exports at Fabindia. As the markets expanded for imports of Indian products, buyers looked for quantity and the price points became crucial. Importers arrived in India to source fabric in bulk. Fabindia could not increase production to accommodate demand since they were still dealing with handloom products that were labour intensive and time consuming. According to Charu some buyers also moved on to products other than handloom, so Fabindia was not relevant to their business any more. In the '60s and '70s Fabindia had evolved as a facilitator between the weavers and niche buyers who needed a merchandiser for their varied demands. They charged a fee for this service. But this seemed unnecessary for wholesale buyers especially when they could visit the supplier directly. Fabindia had also been useful to retailers who visited the store and picked up the few pieces they would sell in their own shops back home. Since Fabindia always carried a huge inventory there was enough merchandise to supply walk-in first-time buyers from abroad. That was one of the main advantages of the store which sold Fabindia export surplus as well as its regular stock of products to the home market. The team at Fabindia is convinced that John's efforts at directing buyers to suppliers was one of the reasons that cost them the export business. Charu Sharma says, 'Buyers were directed to suppliers consistently through the years, so they had a great chance to find their own vendors and develop a relationship.'

Returning to his lesson from the Australian surfer, William was quite sure that:

> The export wave had crested by then. It would still go on for a while and end upon the beach. You cannot get on to a wave when it's on top, you have to be in position earlier. I knew exactly in that moment that we should go into retail. That would be our wave. And we should build a brand name and if we export it should be under our brand name.

By the end of the 1994–95 financial year it was very clear that the percentage of export in the year's total sales pattern had decreased. By now the home market accounted for more than 40 per cent of the turnover. In four years the Fabindia stores had doubled their revenue. But what was to follow the next year was even more interesting. The balance sheet for 1995–96 throws up the following figures: Export sales 8.45 crore. Domestic sales 9.31 crore. That year Fabindia's retail growth exceeded its exports. The opening of the Vasant Kunj store was the turning point. In 1995 Vasant Kunj was contributing only 10 per cent of Fabindia's domestic retail revenue, but by 1996 the percentage had risen to 20. By this time William decided that he would 'push retail to the best of my ability.'

This became a point of conflict between William and his father. John Bissell seemed to have been quite content to confine his business to the four stores within the GK-1 market, and to the export business that had led Fabindia's entry into the world. Talking about the transition years between 1993 and 1998 Monsoon says:

> I think between him [William] and my father there was a struggle to shift the mantle. William's ways of doing things, his ideas, were not my father's. If my father had wanted to build a huge company he would have built a huge company. It was not his intention.

She remembered Meena telling her that Fabindia was 90 per cent emotion and 10 per cent everything else. Charu Sharma quotes John's words, 'I have made enough and I don't want to make more.' According to Rahul Gupta John did not approve of William's plan to push retail and following John's ideology, Meena Chowdhury was also 'dead against it'. However Laila Tyabji says that John felt very good about the Vasant Kunj shop doing well. He had told her that he had not been keen at the beginning but 'William has done it and I am proud that he is doing well.' In fact John shifted his personal office space into the Vasant Kunj store in 1995. 'So far Vasant Kunj is all fun—I go each morning but take Thursday off and stay at home' wrote John in an email dated 26 Oct 1995. This ambiguity haunted the atmosphere in Fabindia through the mid-'90s. While Meena recognized that William had not only coped with John's illness but was now working hard to understand the business, she was also aware of John's frustration at the direction Fabindia was taking and his inability to deal with it actively.

Over those years John made slow but steady progress. 'He

surprised us every few months with a bit of an uplift,' says William. He struggled to write, pushing himself relentlessly. Ravi Kaimal had made him a chart with alphabets and basic words written out like a spelling board, so that he could point them out while having a conversation. There were different charts for the home and for the office, with names and words that were specific to each place. Later John started using a computer with enlarged lettering, slowly at first and then getting faster and faster till he was 'hammering out the words'. Eventually he even managed to take a few steps with a walker and go out for a walk in the colony with his two helpers, Ramesh and Kalyan.

Bim Bissell said in 2008:

> He made it work for himself after 1993. He did not want to be a vegetable. He wanted to have a life. Of course we were pushing him and made sure that he could do whatever he wanted. We treated him like he was normal and everything in life would go on as he wanted.

Notwithstanding all the care John was obviously not feeling normal. Sensitive to the fact that he was perceived as being unwell he reacted strongly when not taken seriously. In 1994 he sent an email to Madhukar complaining about being left out of official correspondence: '[N]o one has sent a fax without showing it to me before—unless I was away—[and] I was in office everyday. . .!'

John Bissell tried to maintain as normal a work routine as possible. He sent an email record of his weekly schedule to Bim in April 1995. It was a fairly hectic programme and it brought him to at least one of his stores on Mondays, Wednesdays, Thursdays and Fridays. On Tuesdays he attended the director's meeting at GK-1 and Saturday was his special day in the flagship store.

William Bissell says:

> He used to come on Saturdays to GK-1 to see the crowds as he called it. He sat in the store and watched what

people were buying. If someone chatted with him he'd get all excited. He was still very passionate about the product and what we were doing. What was nice for me was that he was happy.

Many years earlier John and Madhukar had started the tradition of Tuesday review meetings at Fabindia. These meetings were carried on even after 1993, and involved John, Madhukar, William, Meena and any other member of the staff who was needed to discuss the issue at hand. To accommodate John's wheelchair they were held on the ground floor of N-13, GK-1, at the oval table, a space that had been used for export meetings with buyers. Madhukar says that after John's stroke these meetings became more formal and structured since the company needed to reorganize to adjust to the changing situation. John was not well enough to handle the company independently, William was still finding his feet, and Fabindia was moving in a direction different from the comfort zone of export. John would work out the agenda for the meeting, and depending on the issue ask specific people to attend. The person involved would make a presentation on the subject—either Charu, Tara, Madhu or someone from Finance. Madhukar remembers meetings where the plan to open Fabindia stores outside Delhi was discussed. Other times products, suppliers and new merchandise were brought to the table. Madhukar says, 'Certainly he [John] was guiding those meetings. After the decisions were taken he was not always in on the implementation. We would not bother him . . .' Sometimes John would get upset and lose his temper and apologize later. He often felt that people in the office were not paying attention to him. Meena says he had started writing letters on the computer, trying to give instructions: 'Sometimes they were clear and at times just not feasible . . . He seemed to be able to deal with day-to-day issues but not the larger picture.'

From inception Fabindia had reflected John Bissell's personality and presented itself as a forum for warm, caring, open-hearted interactions for a wonderful cause. As Laila Tyabji puts it, 'This combination of doing something with and for people while producing something beautiful' was the ideology she shared with John Bissell. The three groups of people who came together at Fabindia were the suppliers, the buyers and the Fabindia team who orchestrated this interaction. The same ethic informed all three and created the 'JLB phenomena'.

Monsoon describes it very well when she says that her father lived with the 'fulfilment that comes from walking around in the world thinking it's a good place.' He believed

> [T]hat if I work hard enough, if my motivations are clear and my heart is open, I can make things happen ... the idea that it's not just good enough to make people feel good about their craft. They have to be able to get a return on it. You make it economically viable and then the craft survives and the people survive. But you have to care about it over and above the money ...

And so John kept his account books open and transparent to buyers and suppliers. The Fabindia balance sheet was sent out every year to many of John's associates—anybody he thought may be interested enough to learn something from it. John and Faith Singh from Anokhi, Shyam Ahuja who was selling stone-washed, handwoven durries in the same market, Laila Tyabji from Dastkar, the Burlingtons' Guptas—they all received the balance sheet. Fabindia products were priced so rationally that rates did not need to be negotiated and everybody shared that knowledge. John once mentioned to one of his friends that the recipients of the Fabindia balance sheet never reciprocated by sharing their own!

Raj Kathuria, John's exporter friend, says that in the success of his own company (Globe Enterprises) 'there is the great hand of a great man and that is John Bissell ... This type of human species is very rare.' In the early '70s John had sent Raj to Fabindia's buyers in Germany and Switzerland to help him set up his company. As we have seen a few years later John was handing over several large orders to him. 'He was such a satisfied man. He would send his balance sheets to me. Can you imagine such a thing?!' Raj Kathuria exclaims.

Tara Sahney says she was shocked when she heard that Jean Paul Denton's durrie order would be handled directly by BCM. Charu smiles now when she states that John Bissell was so keen to promote the product that he helped set up many people to become exporters. John introduced Suraya Hassan of Deccan Exports to Jeremy Smith from Habitat. Rita Paul, Meera Singh Akoi, Madhukar Khera, Jagdish Banga were all encouraged to export directly to Connecticut or Conran in the US. At that time 'we used to be sitting there and getting upset. We were angry and didn't know why he was passing orders on . . .,' says Charu. John would ask his staff to make itineraries for buyers to go and meet suppliers around India. Charu repeats John's words to his clients:

'You must go . . . to Mr Prasad at Travancore Mats & Matting . . . to Anokhi in Jaipur . . .' We planned the trips, organized the train tickets, and somebody was sent along as well to take the buyers around. The buyer went back from India with a fabulous experience wanting to come back over and over again. New persons came into exports and the buyers slipped out of our hands. We didn't even know who all we had introduced them to. We had not just done it openly, we had encouraged it!

Laila Tyabji remembers that John sent his favourite buyer Hiroko to Dastkar to buy products for her shops in Japan. Since Dastkar did not have an export license John decided that Fabindia would export Hiroko's shipment at their own cost. And when Dastkar finally got a license John sent them the Fabindia packers, the Maliks. According to Charu, 'The Fabindia ladies were upset with all this because they saw the Dastkar shop as competition. I mean he was just so incredible!'

The girls working at Fabindia under the influence of John's persona believed that the ideal was possible and therefore tried to make it happen. Each one felt that she was an intrinsic part of a 'family' that was managing a business. It was a supremely successful management strategy that endowed every member of the team with the confidence needed to take the company forward. As Monsoon says, 'I think that what Fabindia represented in those days was what he [John] was. The way he was with each and every person and the way he was with the company was one and the same thing.' There are so many John stories that constitute the JLB phenomena that they are impossible to relate one at a time. Every person known to John Bissell has at least one.

Salaries were conservative but the girls 'had so much fun' that they wanted to work there. 'At that time we were all like one family including our husbands and kids. Everybody was part of it,' says Charu. John was 'dead against hi-tech and I had to persuade him to buy a fax machine. He said it was as expensive as a Maruti car, so I said let's start with one tyre . . . We had an old intercom, the Tinkle Bell one-way system, where you beep the floor and speak your message.' But John did not like using it. He said these things 'came in the way of communication'. He preferred to walk down the stairs to speak to someone. His Kolhapuri chappals made a noise on the steps and he did it purposely so that people knew he was coming and would get back to work in case they were doing something else. He did not want to catch them unawares and embarrass them. Tara Sahney remembers him standing at the stairs every morning looking at his watch clocking the girls coming in. John liked punctuality and would say 'You are late' when someone was not on time, as invariably happened with her. 'Sorry Mr Bissell,' she would say. Sudarshan Madhok on the other hand would snap back at him,

'What are you looking at your watch for? I've come, haven't I?' But he never reprimanded her because she had recently lost her husband and was trying to pull her life together.

Meena Sharma has an amusing story about John's partiality for the words, 'Yes, Mr Bissell.' One afternoon Madhu Mathur came in to Tara's and Meena's room excited about an order that had just arrived by fax. 'Mr Bissell, we've just got an order!' Every time an order arrived the only thing John wanted to hear was when it would have to be delivered. John's room was adjoining and his door was always open. He leaned back on his chair, looked over his spectacles at Tara, and called out, 'Taara!' Tara, who had her back to him while working at her desk, said, 'Yes, Mr Bissell.' She had of course heard Madhu who was standing right next to her. John said, 'We have an order.' 'Oh, how nice Mr Bissell!' said Tara. John went on to ask, 'When can you ship it, Tara?' The order had just come in so nothing had been done about it. Tara said, 'When do you want it, Mr Bissell?' John said, 'Yesterday, Tara.' And Tara replied, 'It's on the boat, Mr Bissell.' And everybody laughed including John.

There were many happy occasions when a particularly good order was received, or when sales crossed a landmark figure. John would order ice cream for the girls, or give a bonus of Rs 2000 to each of them. Madhu relates an incident in the early '80s when she had recently joined and John was presenting flasks to the girls because Fabindia had done very well over the last six months. The question came up regarding the gift for Madhu since she had just joined. John's answer was that Madhu had been lucky for them—her arrival had coincided with a good year at business so she too deserved a present. The girls remember getting gifts on many occasions and for different reasons. There is a famous story about watermelons. John once bought up a cartload of watermelons from a street vendor just because he felt sorry for him standing in the sun on a hot summer day. Then there was the incident of a tempo carrying pressure cookers that was intercepted by John and a good price negotiated for the entire staff. When Chocolate Wheel, a confectionary in Jor Bagh, was opened John made sure that cookies were bought fresh from the oven to distribute among the girls for their morning coffee. Some days they would walk into the office to find a slice of banana bread sitting on their desks from Preeti, a friend in New Friends Colony. To encourage the women's cooperative Women's India Trust (WIT) in Maharashtra John Bissell sometimes bought their jams and gave them to the girls as well.

Tara remembers the first Self Employed Women's Association (SEWA) exhibition at the Blind School in Delhi in 1981-82. Tara told John that she had visited the exhibition but had not bought anything because she could not afford Rs 500 for a sari. The next morning as the girls came in to work they were sent off with Rs 500 each, from the office petty cash account, to SEWA to buy themselves what they wanted. 'We were twenty of us and we went in and cleaned up the exhibition and I think that's how SEWA got its first boost,' says Tara Sahney. The same story was repeated with Richard and Sally Holkar's NGO REWA (a society established to encourage the production of handloom in Madhya Pradesh, especially Maheshwari saris). They had held an exhibition of Maheshwaris and were left with a lot of unsold stock at the end. John bought the entire lot and placed it in Fabindia to sell. They didn't do well there either and so the girls found themselves walking in one morning to a sale of Maheshwaris with each sari priced at Rs 80 only for them.

All this defines a personality that finds greater value in contribution than in consumption. 'You don't just exist, you have to be involved. And you live a life where you are making things better,' says Monsoon about her father's values.

Between 1996 and 1998 John Bissell travelled to meet his friends scattered around India. He was much better, able to feed himself, walk a little with help and speak enough to be understood. He had not lost his sense of humour. 'I cannot talk very much, but this is no disadvantage in Delhi as there are lots around who like to talk,' he stated in an email. He visited Mr Agarwal's weaving centre in Muradnagar and often drove to Panipat to spend time with his friend Madhukar Khera at Bharat Carpet Manufacturers.

Writing to Madhukar's father, Anand Sagar on 2 December 1994 John Bissell says:

> There have been numerous associations during my time at Fabindia, but none with whom I have enjoyed myself as much [as] with your entire family and especially Madhukar. He is truly my best friend in the world, and never have I had such a completely close and open business relationship. Every moment since we met through the good offices of Amrit Lal Batra has been a joy and a treasure to me.

He often spent the day at his friend Krishna (Pogey) and Ritu Menon's farm in Sultanpur. Pogey Menon says:

> John became a regular visitor and started visiting that farmhouse more than we did. He would take off and just spend the day there. He had bought a couple of beds saying he needed to lie down in the day sometimes. He started planting trees and in winter he would carry wood for the fireplace we had built there. He just loved the place and made it his own. Those trees are thriving and each time we go to the farm we refer to them as John's trees.

Suraiya Hassan in Hyderabad refers to John as Bissell Sahib. John and Suraiya had developed durries for Habitat together, sitting with weavers, changing colours and patterns and naming the products before sending them out. The Kanchanpally durrie sold first at Fabindia, as did the ikat and kalamkari fabrics for Fabindia bedspreads and garments. Suraiya recalls that when John first visited these villages the weavers had no electricity. He gave them an advance to install electricity so they could work better. The advance would arrive before the order from Fabindia. John Sahib always said that these craftsmen had no access to credit to buy their yarn and dye so they had to be taken care of before they could deliver the product. John visited Suraiya twice after his stroke, the first time in his wheelchair when he stayed at her home for two weeks. He had always loved her sprawling farm where she grew rice and wheat, vegetables and sweet-smelling fruit and jasmine trees. Suraiya kept buffalos and cows and milked them personally every day. John would sit in the beautiful garden with its lotus pond, surrounded by hundreds of trees and creepers with bright flowers. 'We went to Hyderabad to stay with Suraiya for 8 days—[it was] terrific . . .' writes John Bissell in a mail, referring to a trip in December 1997.

Then there were the Prasads in Kerala. V.R. Prasad ran the family-owned Travancore Mats and Matting Company started by his maternal grandfather in 1917 in a village called Chertalla. The Prasads were a large family and very close to John. Chertalla was a prosperous small town reputed for hosting the largest exporter of coir products in India and for specialized medical facilities run by the Prasads. The family had started the first hospital in the town with an X-ray facility in the '50s, so the hospital was called the X-ray Hospital and the bus stop the X-ray junction. Jeremy Smith had introduced John to the Prasads in the early '70s and thereafter a lifelong friendship began. Remembering him V.R. Prasad says:

What America gave to India is John Bissell. He is a Gandhian . . . what a simple person! He wore a kurta and trousers . . . and mingled with the people. He liked to walk. He would get up early and start walking. He didn't know in which direction he went, he just walked . . . Sometimes he came back on his own, sometimes he would get lost and we would see someone bringing him back. That was John.

Fabindia had done some business with the Prasads but it was very small compared to the large export orders they handled. 'You cannot say it is business,' says Prasad, 'he would say, let me have some 100 pieces and for him we did it. Because for him we would do anything.' They sold grass mats to John, the square ones that were stitched together to form the floor covering that became an essential part of the 'Fabindia look'. In 1996-97 John was visiting the Prasads with Bim and his nurse when he had another stroke. He was admitted to their hospital and given the best possible medical care by their family of doctors. Since this was his second stroke, the situation was serious and his doctors in Delhi advised that he be airlifted back to Delhi immediately. William arrived to make arrangements with an airline to transport his father back to his own medical team. When John realized that he was being shifted he said flatly. 'No, I will not go. If I die, I want to die here. I get the best treatment here with my friends.' Of course he did return to Delhi and survived the stroke. The Prasads and the Bissells have remained very good friends. According to V.R. Prasad, 'There is no point saying we are close because we are close, you know. It's a very super relationship.'

Saurabh Mehta, a close friend and advisor to William, first met John Bissell in 1995 when they were visiting Anokhi in Jaipur. William had accompanied his father to John and Faith's house, a place that was always like a home for John Bissell. He went there several times after his stroke. Saurabh says that:

> What struck me about William was the way he looked after his father who was in a wheelchair. The fact that William included his father in the conversation really touched me. I don't know if his father was hearing or understanding or anything but William treated him like he was very much a part of the discussion.

Saurabh Mehta later established a business interest with Fabindia, and has continued to support William's plans as a shareholder and mentor.

In 1995 when William was introduced to Kiran Chainani by their mutual friend Rahul Gupta to help him find property in Bangalore for Fabindia, he hit the jackpot. Not only was Kiran a hard-working professional, her family had known Bim's family for generations and she was passionate about Fabindia. Growing up in Delhi in the '80s Kiran, like many other young people in Delhi of the time, had a proprietary feeling about Fabindia. It was 'her store, everybody she knew lived in those clothes, and if you were a Fabindia person you were alright' and so on. Kiran jumped into the project and together William and she initiated the first wave of Fabindia's flight towards a national identity. They both agreed that the Fabindia stores they would set up outside Delhi would be more than just shops selling merchandise. They would be destinations. This idea had originated years ago with the GK-1 store being treated as a destination by Indian celebrities in the 80's who had stated that they came to Delhi only to shop at Fabindia. So when Charles and Monika Correa's home came up for sale in Bangalore, William picked it up immediately. It was exactly the place Kiran had visualized for Fabindia—an old Bangalore home with Mangalore roof tiles, a courtyard at the centre, a garden at the back for a little café—and, most wonderfully, it had been designed by Charles Correa himself.

Even John, who had sounded his disapproval to Madhukar Khera in a note written on the computer on 27 February 1995, 'We are a North Indian firm and I think should remain so for at least the time being . . . so I am not in favour of Bangalore . . .' had changed his tone in a letter dated 25 April 1995: 'I have told WNB to go ahead with the Correa place in Bangalore—location good—4 km from Centre.'

John Bissell and the Correas had had a long history of friendship. There is a letter sent by John to Madhukar in 1970

204 / The Fabric of Our Lives

requesting him to procure a number of different coloured dyed yarns for a friend who wove tapestries by hand. The friend was Monika Correa and it was in one of the rooms in that house in Koramangla that she worked. When the sale of the house came up John was happy to buy a house designed by his friend and Charles was delighted that his home was in good hands and would be utilized to promote handloom.

Ravi Kaimal, Fabindia's long-term architect friend, was commissioned to convert the house into a store, as usual without changing the structure. Ravi would have to deal with yet another 'But what did you do?' question when he had finished. This Koramangla property was the beginning of a triangle of interaction between the three protagonists of this phase in the life of Fabindia. For the next few years William, Kiran and Ravi worked together, sometimes from three different cities, coordinating the setting up of Fabindia stores in the Indian metros. Kiran says that the projects ran smoothly because they felt so passionately about Fabindia and were all on the same 'page', even though the original Delhi team was apprehensive of the viability of these stores. They felt that the outstation shops would dilute the equity of the flagship store in GK-1 in Delhi. Ravi was comfortable working on these projects because of the level of transparency and trust that he and William shared. Once the budgets had been decided William did not look over his shoulder and allowed Ravi to find his own solutions to problems. William was delighted that he had a team of professionals who understood the basic tenets of the Fabindia 'look' well enough to work it into the restoration of these properties.

This was the first step in the expansion plan and schedules were easy. Ravi had time to conceptualize modifications which would retain the façade of the house in Bangalore, while creating additional space for storage. His Delhi contractor camped at the site for months, building the wooden shelves that are the hallmark of a Fabindia store.

Garments are placed on shelves in different categories of style, colour and size, and customers are encouraged to pull them out for trial. Typically, unsold clothes are left in the middle of the room on a table where they are refolded and then placed back on the shelves by staff specially hired for this job. This is a Fabindia tradition that is followed even today in stores all over the country, and provides familial comfort to travelling, loyal customers!

In the meantime Kiran sought the help of another friend in Bangalore, Priya Rao, who was a quintessential Bangalore girl, for a database of all the goods, services and people available in the city. Kiran's contract with Fabindia stipulated that she had to set up the interiors, find and train staff, and put together the accounting systems for the Fabindia store. 'To get the store up and running,' as she says. Kiran made up charts, budgets and schedules, and along with William recruited staff and visited the N-14, GK-1 store to familiarize herself with procedures and order merchandise from the main office. Tailoring units had to be located in Bangalore to fabricate garments from the fabrics and patterns that would come from Delhi. In those early days export orders were slowing down at Fabindia and there was a great deal of surplus fabric that was sent to Bangalore to sell. In January 1996 William hired Priya Rao as the first manager of the store, and on 25 February 1996 Fabindia Bangalore opened its doors to the public.

The opening was a great success. Between them Kiran and Priya had invited the whole city. There were the 'page 3' IT professionals, the scientific community, top business families, professional designers and artists—'at least 150 people in the store and the garden'. The guests enjoyed the coffee and cakes that launched the little cafe in the garden and they all shopped at the store. Kiran says that they were not equipped for the number of people who bought from Fabindia that day. The store was not computerized and bills had to be made by hand. The queue of customers waiting patiently at the cash counter extended 'from the men's wear to the women's wear through the linen and everything.' The store turned over more than Rs 1 lakh of business in that one day. In its first year of business, 1996–97, the store brought in a total revenue of Rs 1.6 crore. Ten years later in 2008–09 the Koramangla store was turning over Rs 1 crore a month. It is still one of the top five Fabindia stores in India.

At the beginning there were many teething problems. There was no precedence for selling to the domestic market outside Delhi. The systems in place in Fabindia had been built up by a team that had evolved along with the business. They had dealt with only one city, one culture and a specific climate pattern. Bangalore was to the south of India, the weather and the people were different and the demand was unknown. Kiran had no prior experience in merchandising and Meena Chowdhury, handling the 'central buying' as it was termed, made no distinction between the Delhi and the Bangalore stores. So the first time Kiran picked up 'stuff that just didn't sell'. Export surplus fabric and upholstery in dark colours produced for the international market ended up in Koramangla. But customers wanted lighter shades of beige and white and natural. Mistakes were made and lessons learned. Newly hired assistant managers in the Bangalore store handed over thick fabric to the tailoring units to make garments. They did not realize that this was export surplus upholstery fabric that had been sent from Delhi. But customers, especially women, were so desperate for readymade clothes that Priya says 'garments just flew off the shelves'. Ladies kurtas designed in Delhi were too long for Bangalore so they had to be shortened by two inches. One consignment from Delhi was overstocked with khadi dupattas that were too heavy for Bangalore so they were converted to kurtas. Priya says some categories like women's kurtas and shirts with Chinese collars did really well. Men's kurtas on the other hand did not. The men in the south did not seem to appreciate the idea of the same fabric being used in multiple products—a curtain, a lampshade and a kurta. The staff were taught how to take fabric into stock, sign it out when it was issued to the tailors and sign in the merchandise when it was ready. The big problem was listing each sale of the day after collating bills, removing sold items from the store inventory by hand and keeping track of the balance merchandise. But by the time the office processes had been computerized in 1997, Priya knew what to do. Kiran says she 'was a phenomenal manager' and between them they started the concept of coffee mornings once a month in Fabindia Bangalore. Over coffee and cakes invitees (the who's who of the city) would be treated to a Bharat Thakur's workshop on yoga or Sally Holkar's exhibition of Maheshwari saris or Sangeeta Sen's demonstration on Fabindia designs. This introduced new people to the store and therefore more clients to the Fabindia database.

By August 1996 William had told Kiran Chainani that he knew someone who was offering property for a Fabindia store in Madras.

A year earlier Saurabh Mehta had spoken to William about a building he owned in Madras when they had met at Anokhi. The building had been a part of the Ilford Co. properties from 1915. Saurabh bought out the company in 1977 since he was already a distributor for Hindustan Photo Films and Ilford Black and White Film would add value to his business. Ilford had a large facility for storing medical X-ray films in Madras. The building was called Ilford House and had not been fully utilized for twenty years. Saurabh was happy to establish an association with Fabindia and contract Ilford House to them against a percentage of commission. Kiran describes her first visit to the property: 'The approach was horrendous, narrow and one-way, with difficult access. It was a crumbly building, but when we walked in we liked it immediately!' It had a central room with a high ceiling, wooden rafters and two side rooms, 'like being in a church'. The building had served as a warehouse, a cold storage, a laboratory and a commercial office for the film company. 'It looked like it had been abandoned in 1950 with papers, old photos and typewriters lying around,' says Kiran. Ravi Kaimal was called in to rebuild it so that it looked as close to the original as possible. William wanted to keep the original character and history of the building intact so that it would become the next Fabindia destination store. Saurabh Mehta contributed the funds for the restoration, Ravi Kaimal called in carpenters from Delhi who worked night and day for four months, and Kiran coordinated the project flying in to Madras regularly from Bangalore. Ravi put in red-oxide terracotta floors, treated the exterior with local stone and plaster to match it with the renowned colonial Indo-Saracenic buildings of Madras, and built big racks for fabric rolls to hang from the ceiling to the floor, wall to wall like a grand display in the central hall. They hung up the archival photo prints they had found there and kept the old AC units hanging from the ceiling. When Ravi Kaimal completed the restoration Ilford House looked like it must have when it was built in the early twentieth century.

Fabindia Madras opened on 20 August 1997. John and Bim flew down for the opening and lit the lamp at a small cultural ceremony. Ravi was not able to attend the opening but later he was asked, 'So what exactly did you do in the building?' There was nothing to show except photographs of how badly damaged it was before they started restoring the building. Ravi says that it was a treat working with Kiran Chainani. 'She was terrific, has fantastic people skills and gets things done very professionally.' Saurabh Mehta was very happy with the renovation of his property and says that 'Ravi and Kiran put up a fantastic facility.'

This time Kiran knew how to set up the business of Fabindia in Madras. She recruited a manager who had a background in merchandising for the export market. And she devised a training programme for the staff to explain the products and detail their usage. It was important for them to know what each item was used for when dealing with customers. Madras had a long history of garment export and it was not difficult to set up tailoring units for fabrication. Merchandise for the store was still ordered from the 'central' office in GK-1 in Delhi and Meena Chowdhury maintained the monthly stock position of every Fabindia store. Meena says that when she devised the chart procedure for updating and keeping track of stock position she had only one store to think about. She would study the stock position daily and meet with Sudarshan Madhok occasionally to discuss the Fabindia bank status. Between them they worked out how much money was available for ordering new stock from the weaver. Since Fabindia paid the supplier immediately when the product was delivered, orders were made with a clear understanding of the financial position. By 1997–98 Meena was ordering for four stores. 'Then it became this one for GK, and this one for VK, and this is for Bangalore, and this is for Madras.' So every month a report would come to her from all the managers—Mala Malhotra of Vasant Kunj, Priya Rao of Bangalore and Rekha of Madras— with a detailed account of what had sold through that month. 'The managers kept an exercise book record of daily sales which was compiled into a monthly report and posted to me at GK 1.'

The managers of the Bangalore and the Madras stores had been permitted to hand over the stitching of some of the garments to tailoring units in their own cities. While this made it easier to manage stock schedules it was also a cause of concern for Meena. She says:

> Priya would write to me and ask, can we also do shorts because my customers in Bangalore want them? And I would say, we have never done shorts so we cannot do them. Then she would say, but why can we not start them now? She would give her input and Kiran would send her recommendation but I was very possessive of our original Fabindia image and did not want it diluted.

There was some tension over these kinds of issues because the new teams were not bound by Fabindia tradition and could feel the pulse of a new, vibrant and young market. Fabric continued to be ordered from Delhi and kept in stock in the outstation stores to give to the tailors when required. This also meant that each of the shops had to rent additional storage facility.

The new stores initiated a ten-hour day and a seven-day week to accommodate working people. In the Koramangla store two shifts of staff were introduced to handle longer working hours. Women still comprised the bulk of Fabindia staff and housewives could not stretch their working hours. John Bissell had always maintained that women made the most committed and loyal workers. 'The best managers in this country are women,' he had once said to Monsoon. In fact John had many theories about why women worked better than men but essentially he respected them for their management skills, juggling different personalities and budgets in a household.

John decided to resign as managing director of Fabindia by October 1995. On 30 September 1995 he wrote a memo to the directors: '[I]t makes sense because I was planning to retire in March 1996—and illness makes 6 months earlier a good idea . . . I am tired and ready to go . . .' He said he would like to continue as Chairman of Fabindia and carried on discussing and communicating his thoughts through meetings and memos over the next couple of years. William says, 'He was sometimes encouraging, sometimes not. In the end he left it a lot to me, increasingly. He just did what he enjoyed doing.' He spent a lot of time at the Vasant Kunj store with Mala Malhotra, who was the store manager and Nilanjana Bose, one of the young merchandisers. Nilanjana remembers that John would come into the store with large computer printouts of the letters he had written to people and request her to email them for him. The Vasant Kunj store had a lift and John liked to sit on different shop floors watching business transactions and interacting with customers. Nilanjana remembers him advising a young customer who was soon leaving to study abroad. 'You must go,' said John, 'but come back here after your studies. There is heart in India.'

In 1997 the Bissell family sent out invitations to their family and friends around the world:

> John, Bim, William and Monsoon take pleasure in inviting you this autumn of '97 to a House Party at the 14th century Hill Fort of Kesroli.
>
> October 30 to November 10, 1997

As had happened eight years earlier at Ghanerao the Bissells decided to plan a celebration, this time in a recently restored fourteenth-century fort. Aman Nath and Francis Wacziac, reputed worldwide for their restoration of the Neemrana Fort-Palace, had just opened India's oldest heritage hotel 150 km from Delhi. The battlements of this fort rose 200 feet above the fields of a village in Rajasthan, bordered by the Aravalli Hills and other rocky outcrops. Charley Todd, a close friend and guest at the party, has written a moving tribute to this event in a note addressed to Bim:

> My account of the Kesroli experience is a tribute to one family's capacity for healing and to its genius for invention; and an acknowledgement that the power of this exceptional family's generosity is in their care for detail, in how they do things.

In the same note he says that he is touched by John's ability to celebrate life in the midst of severe disability.

What remains the same is the vital energy, a personal force which he exudes, and a quick wit and clear intelligence . . . the sometimes devilish humour is much in evidence. 'Is so and so coming,' I ask about a family friend whom I know John finds trying, 'I hope not,' he caustically replies.

Early in 1997 a young woman from Bombay was shopping in the GK-1 store in Delhi. While being introduced to John by a common acquaintance she asked why there was no Fabindia in Bombay. Shilpa remembers John hastily scribbling a reply on his note-pad. 'No money,' he wrote. On an impulse she said she would help with a Bombay store when Fabindia was ready to set up there. A year later William asked her if she was ready for her commitment because two properties had opened up for sale in Bombay with clear titles against cheque payments. He had been looking for such an opportunity for a long time and was keen to start the process. Kiran Chainani had located a block of four shops in Pali Hill in Bombay. Two shops were available and they were owned by a society of Parsis who were very particular about renovations. With a successful career in sales and marketing behind her and a six-month-old baby in the house, Shilpa Sharma joined Fabindia in Bombay. Ravi Kaimal was called in to do the interiors and Shilpa and Kiran did the spadework for setting up a retail establishment. After the two distinctive spaces they had worked with in Bangalore and Madras, these shops were 'soulless' says Kiran, but it was very essential for Fabindia to establish a presence in Bombay. It was decided that one shop would exclusively sell garments and the other would be the home store dealing with upholstery and durries. Space was limited and only four shutters could be accommodated in the home store. A shutter was a system of racks on which rolls of fabric could be suspended and displayed. Since only twelve to eighteen types of upholstery could be shown in the shop, a small warehouse was rented nearby to store the remaining fabric. The basement in the garments' store also served as the finance and accounts section, and Shilpa's office. Shilpa had spent one week in Delhi being inducted into the procedures and practices of a Fabindia store. She loved the product and totally identified with the company. Back in Bombay she recruited and trained staff. Since Fabindia did not encourage advertisements, Shilpa was given a small budget for a one-centimetre column in the local newspaper to publicize the store. She managed to fit in the words 'Fabindia is now in Bombay' with a phone number. Fabindia opened in Bombay in September 1998, but by then the thirty-eight-year-old company had changed forever. John Bissell did not get to see Fabindia Bombay.

John had a series of mini strokes in January 1998. Yet, according to Bim he continued his correspondence and typed out letters every day on his computer sitting in the veranda of his home. They were short, witty, sharp and incisive. John wrote about how good William was for Fabindia and how high the sales had been the previous year. He commented on the deterioration of values in Indian society and gave updates about his health. These notes were addressed to different members of his family in Connecticut, to his friends, to Terence Conran, Madhukar Khera and Meena Chowdhury. Here are some excerpts from his correspondence through the final months:

To his friends Mary and Tom Cox in Florida on 12 January 1998: 'Fabindia is doing very well thanks to William. We made 100,000 dollars last year after we paid our taxes my salary and other expenses ... There is lots of money in Delhi—some unfortunately unaccounted for ... Sales are good and parts of India are getting prosperous. . .'

To Sunita Narain and Anil Agarwal from the Centre of Science and Environment on 13 January 1998: 'Incompetence, corruption and feather bedding are great evils in India today.'

To Meena Chowdhury's son Aman in the US on 14 January 1998: 'I went to see your mother today and in spite of herself Fabindia seems to agree with her.'

To his sister Marie Prentice on 14 January 1998: 'I listen to tapes for my boredom—talking a little better, but walking not. I went a few days ago to my doc who was encouraging ...'

To his good friends Pixie and Art Schieffelin Powell on 15 January 1998: 'I really found a good vocation as I love being a merchant in India ... Almost 5 years ago ... I just keeled over with a major aneurism—I had been until then in very good health. It happened in CT; Bim looked after me and dragged me back from the pearly gates. I am happy now to have a full time nurse and enough to do. Sadly I get very dizzy when I stand and cannot talk worth very much or write but the computer which I am using lets me write so I am lucky and India is a very good place to be sick. I like it and will live here from now on.'

To his niece Nora Prentice on 24 January 1998: 'They [Meena and Morad] have been a terrific support to me in Fabindia since the beginning. Meena . . . runs everything and is a good friend.'

To Meena Chowdhury on 27 January 1998: 'Is our quality going down?'

To Lois Hager, whom he had taken on trips to Nepal and Kashmir thirty-eight years ago, on 28 January 1998: 'I am in good spirits and very well looked after . . .'

To Terence Conran on 29 January 1998: 'The figures from Fabindia are OK; they are in dollars for 1997. Sales; 50 million dollars . . .'

To his dear friend Adhar Mirchandani in Bombay on 3 February 1998: 'You sounded sad—come to Delhi—life is good, plenty of dinner parties. I picked a good line as handlooms make money; sales are up. There seems to be money in India . . .'

To Bim's uncle and his oldest partner, Gen. Krishan Sibal, on 8 February 1988: 'Thanks for all your help for years.'

To his brother-in-law in Connecticut, Milton De Vane, who had helped him start Fabindia Inc. in 1960, on 8 February 1998: 'I would not have started without you. I had a very good time and I hope I did some help. I also made a fine living. Thanks. Love, John.'

To his sister Marie on 21 February 1998: 'I go to Vasant Kunj at least three days a week—we work on Saturdays not like the 5 day week of the decadent west . . .'

To his architect friends Helene and Raj Rewal inviting them to accompany him to Pogi's farm in Sultanpur on 21 February 1998: 'I am going to Pogi and Ritu's farm Tuesday for supper and to spend the night—please come . . . Love John.'

That was his last documented correspondence. He seemed to have been saying goodbye to those who were not with him at the time.

On 2 March John suffered another massive brain bleed. Bim took him to NIMHANS and the doctors said he was not going to survive. William was in Kathmandu that evening exploring the possibility of opening a Fabindia store in Nepal. He took the morning flight to Delhi and carried his father back to their home in Friends Colony where Dr Naresh Trehan set up a life-support system in a van parked outside the house. A generator had to be installed to keep the electricity constant for the system. Dr Trehan explained to William that his father was brain dead and was being kept technically alive by support systems. John's heart was not beating on its own. There was no chance he would recover. He advised that it was best to stop the intravenous injections and let the heart come to rest. So they did. John Bissell passed away within the next few hours. It was 3 March 1998.

Talking about their father in 2009, John's children said:

> After all the maths and all the thinking, all I can say is that JLB was somebody who was extraordinary and I am extraordinarily fortunate to have had him for a father. I mean I got the lottery of the century. I didn't know it then because everybody's father is like that to them. After he went and after many years you go through all the grief about all the things you missed and all that you could have had. And then you come to the conclusion that the light has gone from being a yellow light to a white light. And every minute of every day you try to find that elsewhere. And you just realize that you are going to lead the rest of your life without that.

> William Bissell

My father and my brother are both sailors. My father had a little bit of money and he bought a beautiful but simple sailboat. His joy was in working on it, polishing it a little every day. But he also realized that he had a sense of how to sail. He loved to sail though he didn't quite know where the territory was and he told some people, come on board on a whim, on a dream. We will sail the seas and whatever comes our way we will do, but we'll keep it simple and we'll have a lot of fun on board. He was one of those captains that everyone trusted. And those on board did everything that needed to be done to make this little boat work. And in the process they changed a bit, added a bit to the boat and stopped at many little places and took this journey, and did some high-sea rolling as well. And they had a wonderful time. My brother never saw this as a small ship. He is the captain of a very big ship. And he took that small boat and hung it on the big ship somewhere as a reminder to him. And he is a great navigator as my father was. But he wanted to take bigger risks so he wanted a bigger ship. Some people may be there for the love of the seas but some people have to be there to know what to do if it springs a leak. Because they both realized that people's lives were riding on their decisions. And they both care about people. They have that fundamental feeling.

Monsoon Bissell

On 22 March 1998 the Fabindia store in the GK-1 market had an Open House in memory of John Bissell. It was his birthday and every item was marked down by 30 per cent. The proceeds of that sale went to the John Bissell Trust. Shaila Tyagi remembers 'that day the stores got cleaned out in Fabindia N-block, GK-1 market.' An era had come to an end.

Fabindia had undergone several changes in its corporate structure in the '90s led by the closure of its association with Habitat in 1992–93. This signalled the beginning of a transformation in the client base. In 1990 exports constituted 76 per cent of the total sales at Fabindia. But by 1994 when John Bissell celebrated a turnover of Rs 15 crore exports had already decreased to 65 per cent of the total sales. By the end of the financial year 1995–96 total sales had increased to more than Rs 17 crore and domestic sales had overtaken exports. The graph was clear; domestic sales accounted for 52.4 per cent and exports for 47.4 per cent of the total sales. Fabindia's second retail outlet at Vasant Kunj had opened in 1994 and the Bangalore store was being set up in 1996. By the time of John's death in 1998 Fabindia had opened its second outstation store in Madras and the turnover of the company that year stood at Rs 24 crore. By March 1999 the Bombay stores were up and running and Fabindia ended the decade with sales well over Rs 30 crore. Between 1994 and 1999, over a period of five years, Fabindia had doubled its revenue though its export markets shrank.

William Bissell had rightly gauged the direction of the next 'wave' and was poised to catch it at the right time. He began to strengthen the structure required to optimize the 'ride'. In 1999 William became the managing director of Fabindia. He needed to hire young professionals to form a new team that would direct the growth of Fabindia as a big retail player in India.

The Indian urban middle class was beginning to demonstrate a dramatic increase in its purchasing power. Profitability studies done at Fabindia in 1998–99 showed the growth trajectory of the four metro stores. Half of the total turnover of the company was from the stores in Delhi. The Bombay store at Pali Hill had already overtaken the Bangalore and Madras stores within six months of its opening. This is clearly indicated by the following figures of 1999: total Fabindia sales were approximately Rs 31 crore, of which GK-1 accounted for Rs 12.3 crore, Vasant Kunj Rs 2.85 crore, Bangalore Rs 1.57 crore, Madras Rs 1.33 crore and Bombay (in just six months) Rs 1.69 crore. Exports closed at Rs 11.71 crore that year.

Shilpa Sharma was pushing to open another store in Bombay

because she sensed that the two shops in Pali Hill were too small to justify the growing demand for Fabindia products in that city. Appreciating her business acumen William permitted her to locate another space in Bombay fairly close to Pali Hill. The new shop in Khar opened its doors in October 1999. That was the first property deal Shilpa Sharma had negotiated for Fabindia. Over the next ten years there would be many more. 'Just the faith they [Fabindia] reposed in my abilities gave me the strength to follow it through and do a great job,' says Shilpa. Within a year Fabindia Bombay (Pali Hill and Khar) was turning over approximately Rs 30 lakh a month.

The three stores outside Delhi were generating an increasing demand for products and styles different from those being supplied by Fabindia over the last forty years. The baton had passed on to William Bissell and he was seeking a plan to fulfil that demand while holding true to his father's mission. The evolution of Fabindia as a national retail brand, while preserving its focus on developing sustainable markets for rural artisans, is the story of the next decade.

·6·

THE TRANSITION YEARS
2000–05

Fabindia crossed into the new millennium with a turnover of Rs 30 crore, six stores, a management team of fifteen people and four directors. William Bissell has an analogy for this situation: Chugging along since 1976 in first gear with only one store in GK-1, Delhi, the car moved into second gear with the next five stores. Between 1994 and 1999 Fabindia had bought and opened retail outlets in Vasant Kunj, Delhi; Koramangla, Bangalore; Pali Hill and Khar in Bombay and Ilford House in Chennai. The car was now straining in second gear. 'I realized when I became the MD in 1999 that we had reached the top speed in second gear. We couldn't go any faster, with the engine saying change gear or slow down. I had a very vague idea about how to do it but I was very sure about what I wanted to do—growth in retail.'

If we analyse Fabindia's sale's figures from 1998 to 2001 we can appreciate the course of events. Their traditional revenue source, the export market, was slowing down while domestic sales were steadily increasing. In 1998 exports increased by only 2.9 per cent, while the annual growth in domestic sales was 24 per cent. In 1999 domestic sales grew by 30 per cent. And in 2000 Fabindia exports actually declined by 30 per cent, with a loss of Rs 25 lakh. 2001 was even worse with exports declining by a further 35 per cent, while domestic sales recorded a 24 per cent growth. By 2000-01 Fabindia's domestic sales had crossed Rs 31 crore while exports struggled to touch Rs 5 crore, not even 14 per cent of the total turnover.

Just five years earlier John Bissell had celebrated sales of Rs 15 crore with exports comprising 60 per cent of the revenue. However, over the last few years Fabindia had been unable to compete with the demand for the large volumes of standardized products required for the export market.

The road clearly led towards domestic retail. But 'Fabindia was built on export,' as William said to Kiran Chainani who had opened Fabindia's first stores outside Delhi. Kiran had also initiated a Fabindia joint venture in Italy with a cousin in 1999. Fabindia Spa had opened in a wonderful old fifteenth-century building in Rome, in collaboration with Sibilla, a distant cousin of the extended Bissell family. At a meeting in Fabindia on 22 September 2000 William reviewed the progress of the store in Rome. With monthly sales at Rs 10–12 lakh the store was just breaking even. In a note accompanying Fabindia Spa's first balance sheet in 2001 Sibilla wrote: 'To grow now we need to sell more, either to small shops or with a new (another) shop of our own.' But the model did not seem feasible. With an agreed mark-up of 50 per cent over the cost price, Fabindia products at the Italian outlet were far more expensive than those being exported to original wholesale buyers in the UK and Spain. Differentiated sales prices could create a conflict of interest detrimental to the Fabindia brand in Europe. A feasibility study for a store in Amsterdam indicated that the project was not cost-effective. But William wanted to develop the European market further for Fabindia products. He was convinced that that was one of the ways forward for stabilizing export growth.

Many of Fabindia's original clients were still part of their list. Between 1999 and 2000 Chandni Chowk, UK, imported over Rs 1 crore worth of merchandise. Then there were Heels, John Lewis and Indian Collection from the UK and the Conran Shop from the UK and France. Sales to Bijenkorf from the Netherlands had dropped, and been overtaken by a newer client, Aba-1. There were Authentics and Kokon in Germany, and India House and I & I in Italy. Zebayish (based in Australia) was still shopping at Fabindia for South Africa, and Gilbert Powrie for New Zealand. Australian buyers also included Ascraft, Calico and Ishka, and together with Zebayish, accounted for almost Rs 50 lakh of Fabindia's export sales. Inside from Hong Kong was relatively new and bought merchandise worth Rs 30 lakh from Fabindia in 2000.

To follow what happened to exports in the US we need to go back a little in history to Fabindia's original company in Connecticut. John Bissell had nurtured that company for over thirty years, personally building up the client list and developing new products till he fell seriously ill the year of Monsoon's graduation.

Fabindia Inc., set up in 1960, had seen some turbulent times after John's parents passed away in 1984. Through the years Bill and Elinor Bissell had continued to support John's work in India by handling the US company whenever the need arose. From September 1979 they were virtually on their own till Betty Capen joined and worked with the company for fifteen years. While visiting the US on a trip in 1990 Ravi Kaimal remembers John driving him up to a small, innocuous building and exclaiming, 'You are now looking at the worldwide headquarters of Fabindia Incorporated!' Betty Capen and her staff were proudly introduced as the 'Fab' ladies of Connecticut.

The business model at Fabindia Inc. had not changed much since it was incorporated in 1960. John would develop designs in India with the suppliers and send the samples to Canton. Betty visited buyers with those samples, attended textile fairs to showcase the products and booked orders. John had built up his client list over the years and the products had not changed much. There were the perennial upholstery fabrics and the bed and kitchen lines. Specifically fabricated for New England, the 'country plaid' look was very popular for what was loosely termed 'kitchen made ups' which included aprons, Jolly-Mollys (pairs of oven gloves joined at the base) and tablecloths. In the '70s Elinor Bissell had done quite well at the Canton Green Store with these products. But in the '90s the business had changed and large importers and retailers were finding their own suppliers in India. They were bringing in large quantities of stock and selling it to the stores in the US. But Fabindia Inc. had never really succeeded in matching stock to orders. US customers had sometimes waited for up to six months for merchandise while, on the other hand, unsold stock filled the warehouse.

In 1993 William turned his attention to Canton, the headquarters of Fabindia in the US. He and Bim spent five months in the US while John was recovering from his aneurism. That summer a young lady joined Fabindia Inc. 'She was passionate about India and what we did. So I said, let's start a store,' says William. He hoped to revive sales in the US through direct retail. In October 1993 Katherine Allen launched Fabindia Artisans in the same premises that had housed the Canton Green Store started by John's mother. Katherine pulled out fabric and bath and kitchen linen from old stock to display at the store. She added other accessories from friends' retail businesses. The shop ignited old memories with the Bissells and their friends and people dropped in regularly. It was great fun, reports Katherine, but the sales did not really take off. Seeking a more commercial location she moved the store to a 600 sq. ft space in a pedestrian shopping plaza a year later. It was a cute spot at the back of the West Hartford Centre and Katherine hoped to benefit from the footfalls at the plaza. But sales didn't pick up and it never became a viable business. In July 1996 Katherine wound up the shop and went back to college to earn a degree in Master of Sciences in Textiles from Philadelphia University.

Two years later when Betty Capen retired William and Madhukar convinced Katherine to rejoin as Manager, Fabindia

Inc. In 1998–99 Fabindia Inc. imported over Rs 75 lakh worth of merchandise from Fabindia Overseas. In 2000 this figure increased by 60 per cent, an encouraging sign that convinced the company to work on a plan to build exports.

At the twenty-third annual general meeting in August 2000 Monsoon Bissell was appointed a full-time director of Fabindia. The board now had five directors. There was Gen. Sibal, Madhukar Khera and Monsoon Bissell. William Bissell was the Managing Director and Meena Chowdhury was appointed the Executive Chairman. William was convinced that Fabindia could regain its advantage in the international market with a new and expanded range of handcrafted products. So the board finalized a two-point action plan. The idea was to develop new products to revive exports while continuing to push domestic sales through increasing Indian outlets.

A formal design team was set up to work on collections for export. William's long-term friend and colleague Sangeeta Sen would head the design group and focus on new designs for the export market. She had worked closely with him while developing products at Desert Artisans. They had also collaborated on the high-end Fabindia store in N-7, with handcrafted products sourced from different designers. The design group was shifted out of N-14/13, GK-1 to D12/4 Okhla, the warehouse built by Morad Chowdhury in 1992. From the beginning the building had been used for storing, packing and shipping merchandise exclusively for export. By moving in with the Export department, the group was meant to be able to monitor and supervise production and supplies more efficiently.

Katherine Allen worked with the design group to develop collections for the US market. Sangeeta Sen, Anurag Rana and Aloka Hiremath would work on different 'stories' every year, coordinating patterns and colours to make sets of kitchen linen and other stuff for Katherine. During 2000–03 she tried to resolve what she calls the 'backwater' problem by stocking larger quantities of inventory so that she could deliver merchandise on demand to her clients. One of Fabindia Inc.'s biggest issues had been their inability to keep to schedules due to late deliveries from India. But this plan entailed huge expenses as it was very difficult to estimate quantities and the logistics of transport and delivery were expensive in the US. Moreover to hold this increased inventory Fabindia Inc. had to rent sheds for storage. Working hard to facilitate sales, Katherine attended trade fairs around the US setting up stalls to display her Fabindia collections. But to cover infrastructural costs she was forced to maintain a certain minimum order and could not cater to smaller retail clients.

In 2003 Smita Mankad joined Fabindia as head of Exports in India. She had worked in a bank in Bombay dealing with export, finance and product development for corporate clients. Smita was given a mandate to clean up the Export department and take it out of the red. She first cleared backlogs of duty drawback applications that needed to be forwarded to the Government of India for recovery. This helped raise the bottom line. The old credit system had outlived its validity and outstandings were high. So Smita moved clients to advance payment or payment on delivery. It would take her two years to set up the recovery processes and clear debts.

To avoid the expense involved in holding large amounts of stock in the US and to circumvent extended delivery dates due to shipping delays, Smita negotiated a deal with United Parcel Company (UPS), the international courier company. Smaller packages could now be couriered to clients at a fraction of the cost entailed in renting warehouses and transporting merchandise within the US. At the other end Katherine worked hard on a new business plan. She would book orders, send the details to India and Fabindia would courier packages straight to the customers in the US. But orders were small and margins too low to justify the costs. Larger importers and wholesale buyers were dealing directly with producers in India. The experiment did not work. 'It was uphill all the way', reports Katherine. William Bissell says, 'Business was okay, but the highest sale we did there was about $750,000. I thought there was much more potential here [in India].'

Katherine managed to keep Fabindia Inc. afloat for another four years till William decided to shut the business in December 2004. Still holding 40 per cent of the shares of the Indian company Fabindia Inc. had passed on to both William and Monsoon after John died. It ceased to exist when Fabindia Overseas bought over the trademark brand 'Fabindia' from the US parent company in 2007. The shareholding corporate entity is now named JLB Canton Inc. after the founder John Bissell. Fabindia Inc. had fulfilled its role and passed on the mantle to the Indian company.

In October 2000, the shareholders of Fabindia Overseas passed a special resolution authorizing the company to make an offer to buy back a certain percentage of equity shares from those existing shareholders who wanted to exit. Since this was a closely held company, transfer of shares by the shareholders to a third party was not possible. The buy-back necessitated a valuation of the company so as to arrive at a fair share value. This would not only benefit those wishing to exit but also be value enhancing for those who preferred to retain ownership of their stock.

The price of each share worked out to many times its original value indicating the distance the company had travelled since John Bissell signed the first annual report of Fabindia Overseas Pvt. Ltd in 1977. Each share had multiplied into sixteen shares over four bonus issues, and each one of those sixteen shares was now valued at approximately Rs 61,981. So one Rs 5000 share bought in 1978 was now technically worth Rs 991,698. The company had returned incredible value to its shareholders over the past forty years.

Quoting from the Investor Document prepared by Fabindia in 2007:

Fabindia was incorporated in 1976 with two members who were also the first directors of the company. The capital was further subscribed by Fabindia Inc. in 1978, and other directors and their associates. Some members of management were also allotted a few shares for their commitment and loyalty at the time. With the same set of shareholders the company issued bonus shares by capitalization of reserves in 1981, 1984, 1987 and 1997. In this period the capital increased to Rs 80 lakh.

Some of Fabindia's original shareholders state that they had held on to their few shares for over twenty years like mementos. That they could translate into such a substantial monetary investment rather than a 'trophy' for emotional commitment had not struck them before. For them, it was a bonanza!

Intent on 'changing gears' at Fabindia William reverted to his favourite water analogy to visualize his future strategy. He says:

> Growth is like swimming in three different waters—a swimming pool, a river and an ocean. The pool allows a swimmer to swim in any direction. A river has to be crossed swimming diagonally along the current, or requires a small boat to get across to the opposite bank. An ocean definitely needs people to get together to build a boat to cross. Different sizes of business require different kinds of skills.

William knew the business was ready to move to another level and he had to find a person who understood how to scale operations. It was time to 'catch that wave' he had seen coming over the last few years. During 1995–99 reforms focused on trade liberalization, privatization and deregulation and helped push India's GDP growth rate to an average of 6.5 per cent. Economic analysts felt that domestic consumption was one of the key reasons for India's current rate of growth. William comments: 'That's when circumstances and Sunil Chainani came together to be a great combination for Fabindia.'

While working with Kiran to open stores in south India, William had met her husband Sunil Chainani in Bangalore. From 1980 to 1990 Sunil had worked with Britannia and then the parent company, Nabisco, with a three-year stint in London. Handling Britannia's International Division, he had been responsible for doubling the turnover twice in two successive years. The International Division was an independent profit centre and accounted for 25 per cent of the company's revenues. By 1990 Sunil was ready to take off on his own and began working as an independent management consultant. He started an export company and consulted with overseas investors wanting to enter the Indian market. Over the next two and a half years he successfully set up and managed an Indian company for an American entrepreneur. Finding a shortage of professionally skilled operations managers he also began teaching at a management institute in Bangalore. He taught courses on export and international business at business schools including his alma mater, the Indian Institute of Management, Ahmedabad.

In 2000-01 the concept of venture capital funds was still new in India. Private (or institutional) equity capital investments in early-stage high-potential growth companies had so far been limited to the biotechnology or IT industry. But Sunil had already helped a couple of friends to raise funds 'to set off an idea'. Flush with the success of this concept Sunil would tell people, 'You have a great idea, why not scale it up? Raise money for it and just do it!'

Sunil and William spent many evenings together during the years Fabindia was expanding its retail operations to Bangalore, Chennai and Bombay. They discussed the company's expansion plans. William was growing the home market conservatively, purchasing property and adding one store a year. He had already done feasibility studies for opening stores in cities like Ahmedabad, Pune, Kolkata, Gurgaon and Hyderabad. By 2000 the demand for Fabindia products had outgrown the existing stores in the four metros. Growth was inevitable, but before initiating further expansion he decided to rationalize operations in the head office in Delhi and focus on additions to the product range.

Since 1976 the Fabindia head office had functioned out of the same two-storied building in the N-block, GK-1 market where John Bissell had opened shop. All administrative operations were centred within N-14/13. The ground floor housed the original (now garments) store, and the first and second floors handled everything else at Fabindia—including administration, finance, William's office and the storeroom that received and distributed stock for all the stores. Charu Sharma says that so much happened within those walls that it was difficult to ascertain the actual expenses of the N-14 shop. Since the other five stores had opened, stock was being issued to all of them from this one 'godown' on the second floor. The profit and loss (P&L) account could not accurately differentiate between the expenses relating to the administrative operations of the entire company and those incurred solely within the shop on the ground floor. It was decided that the merchandise comprising the stock for the entire home market would be shifted to the export warehouse in Okhla D12/4. Also the head office would be transferred to an appropriate space as soon as one was located. William was cleaning up operations before setting 'sail'.

As we have seen earlier the story of Fabindia reflects and is a consequence of much of John Bissell's personal history. John started the business because he loved the product so much that he wanted to encourage the producers to make more of it so he could share it with the rest of the world. And so it was with his son. William developed an affinity to this ideology in his youth. Fabindia in the twenty-first century is a reflection of that vision and that commitment. The product timeline, post 2000, runs parallel to William Bissell's expansion plans and is an intrinsic part of Fabindia's incredible development story over the last decade.

William remembers the time when he would accompany his father to a much loved furniture shop in Delhi. Between the furniture that filled his home and the designers at the shop who were John's friends, it all left a deep impression on his mind. Walking in from a noisy market complex they would be ushered into a cool sanctuary smelling sweetly of wood and pipe smoke, where 'everybody walked quietly and spoke in measured and whispered tones.' In the 1980s Taaru was a revered name in the home furniture business in Delhi and most Fabindia customers would have, at that time, picked up furniture from the Taaru store. The furniture was made to survive generations of usage. 'It was like a rite of passage,' says William. 'Everybody I knew bought from Taaru. So when you walked into somebody's house which had Taaru furniture you were comfortable. You felt at home.' When William decided to set up his own home in 1997, therefore, he went to Taaru to buy his furniture. He ordered everything from there—his tables and chairs, his wall units and his bed—familiar shapes that had filled up his childhood and would one day become a part of his children's lives. William refers to his father's desk, bought from Taaru in 1964. Today the desk is with William, lined with a patina from the past, marked by portions of John's history, and an indispensable part of the Bissell household.

As William prepared for the future Taaru was closing down. The family had decided to retire from the business after a good innings that had lasted forty years. William found the idea of living without that 'institution', as he called it, untenable. So he decided that Fabindia would reproduce the same line of furniture and keep the craft alive. Jodhpur was becoming a furniture hub with producers churning out mass assembled units for export. With his new team of young and enthusiastic designers William developed a range of furniture with production units in Jodhpur, Jaipur and Punjab. The wood they worked with was mango and sheesham (Indian rosewood). But there were obstacles at the

beginning. It was difficult to get just a few pieces made because
the manufacturers were exporting large quantities and would not
deliver smaller orders in time. Smaller manufacturers were
unreliable and would take shortcuts, using unseasoned wood that
warped and got damaged by termites creating a whole bunch of
unhappy clients. Eventually William located a reliable
manufacturer in Ludhiana. The company was called Fishers and
their product designer, Heinz, worked on the same functional,
clean lines that William wanted. Along with the furniture Fabindia
also started a selection of hard goods which included trays,
mirrors, picture frames and lighting. Visible in the Fabindia
stores since 2000, the clean dark lines of furniture have acquired
a brand equity reminiscent of their Taaru roots.

In 2000, a few years after setting up his home, William married
Anjali Kapoor. By this time Fabindia's product categories included
garments, soft furnishings, handwoven durries, handloom and
handcrafted textiles, linen, furniture, hard goods and lighting.
This was the product line that would support the business
through the initial growth years between 2000 and 2003.

In 2001 Shilpa Sharma, manager of the Mumbai store, was
asked to locate retail property in Pune. She found a 6000 sq. ft
space on the ground floor of a commercial building on Sassoon
Road. A loan was taken from the Saraswat Bank, located next
door to the Pali Hill store, to buy the property. Simultaneously
a building was taken by Fabindia on a lease-buy arrangement in
Gurgaon which would allow them to purchase one floor a year.
William wanted to open a large store in the fast-developing
national capital region (NCR). In November 2001 the board
sanctioned loans to help fund these two new properties, and both
stores opened before the end of the year. So far the pattern being
followed was the same for all stores that had opened after GK-1.
The properties were owned by the company and large enough to
accommodate the full range of Fabindia products. They were all
in the metros or close enough to take the spill-over resident or

office populations, such as the ones in Pune and Gurgaon and they were opened at a comfortable pace, viz., one a year. 'In those days we had the luxury of spending six months to set up stores,' says Shilpa Sharma.

Based on the 2000–01 balance sheet William made a presentation to the board which seems to be the first step towards looking at growth in a far more 'organized' way. William had done his homework. He had been working on a business plan for the company with his old colleague Mala Malhotra. He also enlisted the help of Maggy King, an old friend and supporter of the Bissell family. Maggy had worked in India as head of the bank, BNP Paribas, and understood finances. Together they finalized a plan that would take Fabindia to Rs 100 crore in five years.

It was 2002, and these figures would become the springboard for the ambitious plans that were to follow. Fabindia sales had recorded a turnover of Rs 36 crore. Net profit that year was Rs 2.2 crore. Reserves stood at Rs 17.18 crore and the dividend payout was Rs 14 lakh.

The objectives outlined in the plan aimed at capitalizing on Fabindia's brand equity and infrastructure to expand retail trade within India and abroad. Since the independence of the company was a priority, its shareholding needed to be consolidated to retain control and enhance value. Management participation was seen to be crucial for long-term commitment to the company and its ideology. To achieve these objectives the plan laid down some key action points: to conserve resources by giving lower dividends, to follow a path of expedient expansion in key locations, to initiate a buy-back policy for retired members and those wanting to exit, to institute a proper Employees Stock Option Plan (ESOP), and to upgrade operations through technology leading to better coordination, controls and transparency in the company.

Sunil Chainani remembers the call he received from William sometime in early 2001. William said, 'You were talking about raising money to upscale the business. Well, now I am ready. Do

234 / The Fabric of Our Lives

you have the time to help me?' By 2002 Sunil was signed on as a consultant to develop a growth strategy for Fabindia. In 2003 he was appointed a director on the Fabindia board. Over the next six years Sunil would set Fabindia on a course that would change the history of the company.

William knew that Sunil Chainani could be that catalyst for the growth required in Fabindia. He says:

> Sunil came on board in 2002 to consult with us on strategies for growth. He had experience with large companies and brought a lot of corporate learning with him. Fabindia was not run like a corporate. We needed to learn how to think, organize, implement and execute in scale. Sunil brought that DNA with him.

Soon after joining Sunil Chainani set up meetings with several venture capital companies to look for funds for Fabindia on the basis of that business plan. But there were no takers. Sunil says:

> Fabindia's P&L had declined a bit, also the 'dot com' bubble had just burst. Funds had lost money and so became conservative. Nobody was willing to touch Fabindia at that time. One of them said, 'Come back to us after you have a hockey stick for the P&L.'

The result was that Sunil decided to 'get behind the numbers' and discover ways to improve the business and accelerate growth without external investors in the initial stages. He calculated that the company could get to a Rs 100 crore turnover in less than five years. What was required was a need to take hard business decisions keeping the long-term perspective of the company in mind. Sunil initiated sound corporate practices by asking difficult questions that older team players did not like hearing—'thinking with the head rather than with the heart and evaluating strategies in terms of the bottom line.' Focusing on the growing market in India, Sunil chartered a new course for Fabindia.

William and Sunil discussed the new strategy with the management team at Fabindia. Those present were Charu Sharma, Shilpa Sharma, Priya Rao, Anisa Puri and Mala Malhotra. Charu recalls the meeting (as quoted in the Harvard Business Case Study, July 2007):

> William walked in and said that we were going to be a [Rs] 1 billion company in four years. I just went blank. We were a nice little company doing good business and suddenly we had to go for planned growth. We weren't sure where it was going to come from.

On 8 April 2002 William presented the Fabindia Vision Plan to the members of the board mapping the company's objective for the next five to seven years. This presentation is reminiscent of the case so eloquently put forward by John Bissell to his family and friends on the porch of the old Canton house in August 1960. John was then appealing for investment to start a company. Forty-two years later William was echoing a similar sentiment. These are his words:

> Fabindia is a unique organization. It has retained its original ethos and purpose for the marketing of traditional crafts, maintaining rural employment, and showing a strong commitment to environmental conservation while becoming a major force in the Indian retail market and maintaining a sound financial footing. It has a brand identity and a reputation for integrity which are unequalled. In short the 'Fabindia formula' developed over the last forty years remains highly successful. The objective is to grow the business according to the 'Fabindia formula'; safeguarding the core values of the company while ensuring that it has the means to continue to operate successfully in the future global business environment.

Then he outlined the development plan. The idea was to expand rapidly, opening stores aggressively in new cities and consolidating their position in the metros. Both Shilpa (Bombay) and Priya (Bangalore) had felt the pulse of their markets and knew Fabindia was ready to travel. The company planned to open two more stores in Bombay and Kolkata, and enter the market in sixteen more non-metro cities over a period of four years. This time around stores would be rented, not purchased. As Sunil stated emphatically, 'Business is not property valued, but brand or P&L valued.' In addition the focus would be on finding properties 'with character', that would become destinations, as had happened with Koramangla (Bangalore) and Ilford House (Chennai). The intent was to maintain the 'look and feel of Fabindia' while building a national brand. As he says: 'We pick our store locations carefully and choose buildings to create a unique consumer experience.'

In November 2002 the Fabindia board approved of the plan. The original business plan was split into two phases and looked at first achieving higher profitability levels for better valuation of the company, so that it could proceed to the second part. The expected growth in turnover would be monitored carefully to translate into increased profits. This would address the issues raised by the investors and develop confidence in the proposed utilization of funds to achieve projected returns. Thereafter Fabindia would be in a better state to commence equity restructuring and to find an investor.

Targets were reset and so were the requirements for capital. Sunil was confident that Fabindia would be able to invest the necessary funds through 'debt' finance. And so Vision Plan 1 was born. Its objective was to carry the company from sales of Rs 3 crore to 8 crore in a month by a clever allocation of cash flow reserves, bank borrowings against stock and unsecured loans from supportive friends. Finally launched in 2003 it looked forward to a completion time of four years.

Before going further it is important to understand William's perspective on vision plans. According to him:

A Vision Plan is like an orchestra. You write the music and then you have a conductor who makes sure all the different instruments come in at the right time. It's like a very complex choreographed performance where money is spent at the right time. You plan it all and try to do it in the correct sequence. It is a resource allocation tool which tells you when you need resources for different stages of growth, so growth becomes effortless.

In August 2002 the company head office shifted out of their first home in GK-1 to a house in a residential colony in Panchshila Park. After eight months it moved to its new home at B-26, Okhla in 2003. The basement and ground floor in Okhla were rented and renovated in 2003 and every year one more floor was added till Fabindia had occupied 60,000 ft by 2007.

Meanwhile in GK-1, the original store had spread over the ground floor and the basement of both N-14 and N-13 as well as the first floor of N-14 vacated by the office. Since the central warehouse had now also shifted to Okhla, N-14 was holding stock only for its own shop and for the home stores across the park in N-5 and N-7. For ten years stock had been ordered and distributed to all the stores from N-14. But by 2000 Fabindia ran seven stores and stock management had become a problem. In 1990 the company had bought Rs 5 lakh worth of stock; in 2000 more than Rs 1 crore of stock was purchased. Increasing sales led to large volumes of inventory and Fabindia urgently required professional management systems. The shift to Okhla was aimed at rationalizing these procedures.

Meena Chowdhury had been handling merchandise for almost forty years. First it was just for export. Then domestic retail started and Meena looked after stock for all the stores in the GK-1 market. Then she had to order for the outstation stores as they opened one after the other. By the end of 2001 there were ten different stores to coordinate and another three were added the next year. When the office moved to Okhla in 2003 Meena requested to be relieved from day-to-day work and said that she would prefer to come to Fabindia only two to three times a week to mentor the team. She had started winding down and closing the loops. Riten Mazumdar was still receiving annual pay cheques from Fabindia for products carrying his designs. John Bissell had contracted to pay Riten a royalty on orders placed rather than for products sold, and Fabindia was continuing the practice. In 2002 Meena wrote to Riten saying that Fabindia would release one last flat payment to take care of the few designs that still remained in the inventory. Thereafter Riten's account with Fabindia closed. Maqbool and Nihal, the two printers who had printed most of Riten's designs, still hold samples of his work in anticipation of a revival. There were very few Riten products left in Fabindia when Meena Chowdhury formally resigned in 2005. Meena had spent forty years of her life with Fabindia, and seen the company grow from a turnover of one million rupees to almost a thousand million rupees.

Through the expansion, as management structures were reorganized and more jobs created, Fabindia tried to upgrade incumbent staff by instituting training programmes at different levels. 'Greater responsibilities and designations, more specific jobs were first offered to Fab staff,' says Charu. The company also focused on recruiting professionals who could be empowered to take independent decisions. It brought senior managers on board like Anita Thapar Kathpalia who had studied management at IIM, Ahmedabad, and had worked for many years in the service industry. There was Elizabeth Nanda who had specialized in Industrial Relations and Human Resources from XLRI, Jamshedpur, and joined Fabindia after twenty years of experience in different sectors. Jashwant Purohit was a specialist in Organics, Dilpreet Singh was a senior chartered accountant, as was

K. Prakash. Damini Narain was an interior designer who had also worked with a lifestyle retailer in Hong Kong. Along with the older, experienced managers at Fabindia consisting of Charu Sharma, Anjana Batra, Mala Malhotra, and Priya Rao, among others, Fabindia was witnessing a 'sea change in staff culture', says Sunil Chainani. This was a team who would be relied upon to add value to corporate strategy and lead the company into planned growth.

To enhance staff participation in the growth process the Vision Plans linked bonus to productivity in an inverted hierarchical pyramid. The more senior a person was in the team, the greater the productivity variable constituent. Therefore, the junior-most workers had the largest percentage of fixed salary in their final pay package. The twenty-five executives comprising the management team at Fabindia in 2003 were allotted shares under an ESOP with the quantity per individual being decided by responsibility and length of service. These measures were taken to consolidate the team and ensure commitment to the Plan. At this point each original Rs 5000 share was divided into 50 x Rs 100 shares, to accommodate the ESOP.

Shilpa Sharma was one of the new crop of professionals who was cut out to be an entrepreneur. The Vision Plans provided her with a goal. She feels 'that what was so wonderful about working at Fabindia was that I had the freedom to use new ideas and concepts.' She joined Fabindia as the Bombay store manager in 1998. In 2002 she was appointed General Manager New Projects. By 2005 she was in her new designation as Manager Operations & Business Development, West. In 2006 she became the All-India Market Head. By the time she moved on to become Head Product Development and Buying in April 2008, Shilpa had been responsible for opening forty-nine stores out of the eighty-seven that were added between 2002–08. 'There was never a dull moment in my life!' she says.

The Kolkata store was the first one lined up in the rapid

expansion plan. At Hindustan Park, there was a hundred-year old building owned by a lady whose husband had been a litterateur. The place had a feel and an ambience that qualified its position as the next Fabindia destination store after Ilford House. It was a large shop occupying 4500 sq. ft in the ground floor of the building, and offered Fabindia's entire range of products. It was set up in a record time of one month and opened in October 2002. Hyderabad followed in 2003 with 4800 sq. ft of space, another 'full' Fabindia store. By now Shilpa had learnt the routine and was confident about entering new cities and locating properties for stores. There was a further list of cities in line for the next two years. These had been selected on the basis of data on their economic viability as upcoming industrial hubs or as satellite towns for corporate centres. The following is an illustrative example of Fabindia's entry into a new city.

Through a friend, Shilpa found a contact in Chandigarh, one of the first cities in Fabindia's unravelling expansion plans. The contact led her to a couple of reliable estate agents. Shilpa travelled to Chandigarh and conducted a recce of the commercial areas with the agents after which she prepared an assessment report on the market scenario: the presence of other competitive brands and rents and sizes of properties. There were other factors to be considered also. Should a property be selected in a successful commercial area like Sector 22, where it would benefit from spill-over footfalls from other retail stores and cafés? Rents were disproportionately higher for such properties and the chances of finding a suitable available size were low. How did that weigh against a reasonably upper-income but quieter area close to the residential sector, example Sector 9, where rents were lower and there was the possibility of acquiring more floor space in the next year if required? Sometimes Shilpa would show photographs of the spaces in question to William and sometimes he would accompany her to close a deal. But most often she presented the assessment note and they went ahead. In this case, 3000 sq. ft was rented in Sector 9. The shop in Chandigarh became another 'full' store occupying the basement (for storage) and first floor. It opened in 2003 with Diltaj as the store manager. The first stock of merchandise for the stores was always decided taking into account the floor area and the number of shelves that were installed. Since Fabindia has continued with the 'clothes on shelves' format, the numbers of shelves determine to some extent, the quantity of items that can be displayed at one time.

2003–04 turned out to be a pivotal year. The pace of expansion increased rapidly with Sunil Chainani on board.

A decision was taken to set up outlets in shopping malls, then a novel concept in India. Multiplexes and malls were being built across the country at a rapid pace catering to the increasing per capita incomes of middle-class families. Mall stores would introduce the Fabindia product to a new customer—the working person who had little time to spare and therefore preferred to shop for everything in one place. And Fabindia would also benefit from the advantage of increased footfalls of customers who were not familiar with the brand. So they opened a small store in the Spencers Mall across the road from Ilford House in Chennai. Within a space of approximately 700 sq. ft the shop sold only garments—women's wear, men's wear and garment accessories. It did very well, and according to Shilpa, 'Spencer's was a catalyst for drawing more traffic into Ilford House', which was located on a somewhat obscure road. The only problem was that retail space in malls was always at a premium and rentals were charged for double the space acquired. That often meant longer gestation periods for profitability. The store at a mall in Mulund, Bombay, lost money in its first year but after two years it was doing so well that Fabindia invested in another floor right above it and built an internal staircase to connect the two. In 2009 the Mulund store was among the top twenty in the country with a monthly turnover of Rs 50 lakh.

The Kala Ghoda store in Colaba, opposite the Jahangir Art

Gallery in South Bombay, is one of Fabindia's most beautiful outlets. It occupies 12,000 sq. ft in a heritage building owned by a Parsi family for about a hundred years. It took two years of intensive restoration and renovation, authorized by the Bombay Heritage Committee, to uncover the aesthetics and style of the original structure. The initial project cost doubled from Rs 76 lakh to Rs 1.46 crore as the architect stripped off the false ceilings, the linoleum-covered wooden staircase and the cement-encrusted pillars to discover teak-wood rafters, cast-iron Corinthian pillars and an original terracotta tile floor. Shilpa remembers the challenges involved in optimizing display space within different levels of floor and ceiling to be able to justify the project cost. 'The density of shelving had to be high to get a return on the whole investment.' The mezzanine floor, unusable for product displays, now houses a popular café. As a destination store it is Fabindia's *pièce de résistance*, and jostles with Delhi's flagship store in GK-1 as the top revenue earner in the stable. It is one of those landmarks in Mumbai of which you'll hear people say, 'Meet you in Fabindia.'

After the Colaba store opened in October 2004 Shilpa moved across the country opening another six stores between 2004 and 2005. There were one more in Kolkata and Bangalore each, another in west Delhi in Rajouri Gardens and one each in Indore, Jaipur and Ahmedabad.

Sunil Chainani says the company took a call on exports in 2004 and decided to try a new business model. The plan was to move into international markets 'where the Fabindia brand was known'. So Fabindia set up a partnership company in Dubai to open a store for the large population of Asians who were residents in the Emirates. Monsoon Bissell moved to Dubai for six months to set up the store. Opened in 2004, the Dubai store brought in over Rs 2.5 crore of revenue in 2008.

By the end of the financial year 2004–05 the figures were substantial. Fabindia sales had recorded a turnover of Rs 87.61

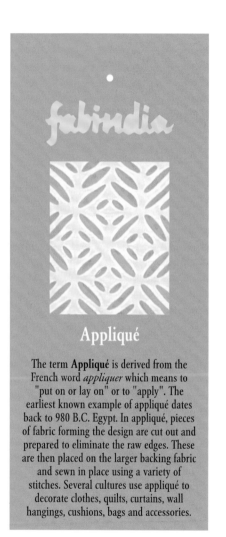

Appliqué

The term **Appliqué** is derived from the French word *appliquer* which means to "put on or lay on" or to "apply". The earliest known example of appliqué dates back to 980 B.C. Egypt. In appliqué, pieces of fabric forming the design are cut out and prepared to eliminate the raw edges. These are then placed on the larger backing fabric and sewn in place using a variety of stitches. Several cultures use appliqué to decorate clothes, quilts, curtains, wall hangings, cushions, bags and accessories.

Chanderi

Chanderi, a small town situated on the flanks of the Vindhyachal, has been a well known centre for beautiful woven saris. Chanderi fabric renowned for its very fine gossamer quality, placement of motifs and design intricacy, has been the chosen fabric for saris produced for the royalty. The fabric's unique qualities result from the traditional method of sizing and hand weaving developed over the centuries.

Craftmark tags certify the authenticity of handmade Indian products while describing the craft processes used.

FABINDIA'S 3 CATEGORIES OF FOOD PRODUCTS

 Products displaying our **Green logo** are 'Fully Certified' Organic. All processes, from growing to preparing to packing have been done according to National and International standards, verified by accredited agencies.

 Products displaying our **Blue logo** are 'In Conversion'. This means that the farmer is using purely organic techniques, and has registered and is complying with set standards. Farmland must be managed Organically for about 3 years before it can be fully certified.

 Products displaying our Yellow logo are 'Natural'. This category contains products produced by small farmers who use purely Organic techniques, but who have decided to not yet register for certification. It also includes some processed foods, which do not contain any synthetic preservatives, colours, flavours or additives.

Poster demystifying the stages of organic certification for Fabindia food products.

Dyeing yarn at the Naugaon Artisans Handicrafts Ltd, a community-owned company. Amroha, 2009.

Selecting products to send to a Fabindia store. Deccan Crafts & Weavers Ltd.

To enable artisans to participate in the wealth creation process, Fabindia restructured its supply base into seventeen community-owned companies. These are located across India and have artisans as shareholders and directors.

Tailoring unit at Saptrangi Crafts Ltd. SRC based in Ahmedabad, 2009.

Shareholders at the second annual general meeting, Delhi Artisans Ltd.

© Pradeep Dasgupta

© Pradeep Dasgupta

Sample interior layouts with Fabindia furniture and products.

Sample layouts
with Fabindia
furniture and
products.

Fabindia interior layouts.

Children's furniture at Fabindia.

Fabindia's flagship store at N-14, GK-1. Delhi, 2010.

crore. Net profit was Rs 5.61 crore. Reserves stood at Rs 27.76 crore and dividend payout was Rs 1.08 crore.

Sales increased by 27 per cent in 2004 and by 40 per cent in 2005. By mid-2005 monthly sales were averaging Rs 8 crore. The first Vision Plan had been achieved in two years instead of four as planned. Fabindia had twenty stores in eleven Indian cities, and one each in Rome and Dubai.

As the stores grew so did the product line. For twenty years Fabindia had only one store in India. The product line had originally been developed for the export market, but by the time the second and third stores opened in 1996 domestic sales had overtaken exports—with the home market constituting 52.4 per cent of total sales, and exports 47.6 per cent. Sometimes leading this growth, sometimes following it, the Fabindia product line grew, adapted, morphed and regenerated itself dramatically through the years. At the beginning merchandise sent to the stores in Bangalore, Madras and Bombay was entirely a reflection of what sold in Delhi. Things changed. Just as the main product categories were developed originally by John and later by William, so too can the young managers of these stores be credited with being a large part of the process and development of the garment product line after 1996.

Beyond the natural extension of the product range lay the decision taken by the company to stay within the parameters of perceived Fabindia lifestyle options. Sunil Chainani says:

> We had a fantastic brand, unbelievable growth and very loyal customers. We could have expanded with a whole lot of new products which would not necessarily have fit in with the old Fabindia image, but may have worked because of the customer base.

These could have included commodity type, mass volume T-shirts, easily produced from large production vendors. That would have been much easier on the supply chain and on quality control than dealing with thousands of artisan suppliers spread across India. 'But we chose not to do that. We opted to stay with hand-processed products.' Looking at new products, the company thought about what the Fabindia customer might want that would fit the image and add value to the Fabindia lifestyle. There was no doubt that anything new would have to be derived from environmentally and socially conscious sourcing. William had already committed himself to that concept many years ago.

In 2000–01 William had met a Dutchman in Delhi called Hay Soiree. He was married to an Indian doctor and William and Hay liked each other instantly. Hay was a specialist in organics and was interested in India's long history in the scientific uses of its biodiversity. And William too had developed an interest in organic farming since his years in the US.

While in college he had worked for a couple of summers with Gordon Ridgeway, an organic farmer. Gordon and William would set off in the very early mornings in an old pick-up truck to collect sap from the maple trees in the forest. In end-March the nights would still be freezing and there would be snow on the ground. The warm days would have started the 'life force' moving in the maple trees working hard to produce the young shoots for the new year. The sap would drip into pails hung overnight on the trees. The man and the boy went from tree to tree emptying the pails into a large tank at the back of the pick-up truck, driving through forest trails where the sun slanted in. Then the sap was carried down the hill to the sap house where it was distilled over hours of wood fire, while Gordon talked to William about the balance of nature and how important it was to understand man's natural affinity to the land and its products. William loved it. 'We'd have moments of exquisite beauty . . . it was so meditative . . . There you understood what organic is about and why it is important. Working the land you get an affinity for it.' In India, the Bissells' good friend John Singh was already experimenting with organic farming on his land in Jaipur and felt passionately about living a

natural lifestyle. William returned to India knowing that one day
he would become a part of this movement. So it was only a
matter of time when Fabindia's existing network of rural artisans
would include India's agricultural workers in the production line.

The time presented itself in 2002 when the company decided
to invest in organics. Hay came on board and he brought in a
'young, great guy who really loved organics'. Jaswant Purohit
joined the company as head of Organics, and with Hay Soiree as
consultant organics were introduced into Fabindia. They began
with coffee and honey and finally presented a full range of food
items in the stores by 2004. Jaswant has been quoted in the
Harvard Business Case Study, 2007, as saying:

> Our customers are drawn predominantly by our ready-to-
> eat items, such as dry fruit, cereals, and pickles. The good
> news is that once they try the product, they tend to
> become repeat buyers. The bad news is that since the
> supply chain can be shaky, they tend to get upset with us
> when the product is out of stock.

In 2004 William requested Mr Agarwal of Muradnagar to start
producing organic pasta for Fabindia. Mr Agarwal, credited with
consistently supplying some of Fabindia's best-sellers since 1972,
(Goa light and heavy fabric, the Shaila and Rajput bedcovers,
Satnapalli bed sheets, Cutwork fabric and since 1986 Fabindia's
famous Jacquard towels) had remained its most reliable and
successful supplier. Agarwal had no idea what pasta was but he
agreed to give it a try. After some research he imported a pasta
machine from Italy. Fabindia had been buying organic wheat and
sugar from agriculturists who had certified organic products. So
Agarwal picked up the initial lot of raw ingredients from the
Fabindia store, put his youngest son in charge of the project and
rolled out his first batch of pasta in 2005. The procedure was
complicated. The production unit had to build a special facility
for storage. Wheat had to lie above the ground on a layer of

wooden planks placed at some distance from one another. This would guarantee air circulation and keep the cereal from rotting. Also the water used in production had to be 'organically' clean, so a bore-well was dug specifically for this purpose. Agarwal employed a chain of women to clean the floors of the unit several times a day to fulfil the stringent conditions of hygiene that were required. Today, after years of trial and error, the Agarwal unit is also packing for other Fabindia vendors who have started producing organic food. At the beginning it incurred losses, but has been making profits since 2007. Agarwal is now producing pasta in different shapes and flavours, and his whole family has developed a taste for organic whole wheat and pasta!

Since 2004 Fabindia has added many other products to their range but Organics still accounts for a small percentage of the revenue. Even though the average Fabindia customer is aware of the harmful effects of pesticides and chemical fertilizers, the Indian market is not ready to shift to the relatively more expensive organic products for their household needs. As Sunil says, 'This is not going to be our biggest line of business but it is an important addition.'

Till 2003–04 the garment product flow continued largely as it had for years with expanded and specialized teams. The Product Design Group (PDG) worked with the suppliers (increasingly referred to as vendors) with colour palettes and designs to help develop different products. Suppliers would then prepare samples of those products and return them to the PDG for approval. Once they were satisfied the PDG presented the new designs to the selection committee which basically consisted of William Bissell and Charu Sharma. This stringent process was necessary to maintain what has been identified as the 'Fabindia look'. Charu says: 'No new product will go to the stores till it has passed through us. Ultimately nothing should detract from the essential Fabindia "look". Any mistake today with the volume of products we are doing would be a disaster!'

Approved and selected products were then passed back to the suppliers to fabricate. The Production department had merchandisers who ensured the consistency of the items while in production. These merchandisers were the contact point for the stores managers who ordered stock on a weekly basis. So they kept track of orders, quality, quantities, schedules and delivery. Stores would be sent small quantities of the new products for trial sales along with their regular orders. These were called Direct Purchases because they were outside the regular product line which constituted the 'bread and butter' of the business.

When Kiran Chainani asked Priya Rao to become store manager in Koramangla, Bangalore, in 1996 she told her that she had better familiarize herself with the distinct 'Fabindia look' that was an integral part of the Fabindia store. The interesting thing is that most people who have joined the company and worked with it for any length of time have internalized the Fabindia ethic so completely that they have now become a part of that 'look'. So what comprises the Fabindia 'look'?

The intrinsic value of a Fabindia product comes from a belief that the company is developing unique handmade products and thus providing employment to thousands of rural artisans whose livelihood depend on the market for these goods. This ideology and confidence in the authenticity of the product had to be passed on to the new Fabindia staff who were being recruited during the rapid growth of the company.

In 1998 there were ten categories of business. These were divided into two main sub-categories, Garments and Home. Garments was made up of Indian and Western women's wear, men's wear, kids' wear and garment accessories. Home included bed and bath linen, table linen, floor coverings and upholstery. The Fabindia 'look' also extended to the display format in the store. When a store opened, three or four people would come from Delhi and spend a week initiating staff into the Fabindia way of displaying and selling merchandise. 'How not to do things' was as important as 'How to do things'. For instance, there was only one way to fold and stack towels in Fabindia. These were the handloom pile towels with cheerful stripes and solid colours from Mr Agarwal in Muradnagar. The folding was done in such a way that the edges did not show and the stripe was visible at the fold. Then they had to be stacked with the stripe towel interspersed with the solid colour towel, one on one, so that the contrast showed. The Jacquard reversible's on the other hand had to be folded and stacked so that alternate sides could be seen. Then there was the method of sizing stock from top to bottom. Large towels on the top shelf, medium on the middle, then hand towels and face towels and last of all, on the bottom shelf the bath mats. 'God help you if you do not have five shelves!' says Shilpa.

There were teething problems at the beginning. The old established 'order' in Delhi clashed with the enthusiasm and new ideas of the younger staff in the 'outstation stores' as mentioned before. Once Bangalore received a shipment of twelve Jahangirpuri bedcovers of the same colour at the end of the month. Priya tried to suggest that the Koramangala store was a small one and that they would not be able to sell more than two to three bedcovers of one colour at a time. She was told, 'That's how it is—orders have to be in these quantities, because weavers produce a certain yardage in one weaving cycle and we have to accommodate them.'

Then there is a story from Bombay when a particular shipment of fabric did not match the swatch from which a customer had ordered upholstery fabric. So Shilpa sent it back to Delhi with a note about the production fault. She received a call from Meena Chowdhury asking her if there was no possibility of her selling that fabric in Bombay because Fabindia in principle did not return merchandise to the suppliers. Shilpa says that even though she respected Meena hugely, she often felt the need to sit down while receiving her calls! The result of that conversation was that Shilpa was sent off to the production units in Naugaon to see for herself how the weavers worked and lived. She returned from Naugaon a changed person. She says:

> I was surprised that the white looks like it does. I didn't know a warp from a weft! To me it was a huge learning and I understood the Fabindia philosophy. To provide a platform for the weavers and artisans we have to be on their side.

This level of training has now become an integral part of Fabindia's business plan.

Between 2000 and 2007 the central warehouse was the hub of all merchandise orders and deliveries between the suppliers and the stores. Orders were sent by email and on the phone, sometimes up to two or three months in advance.

Store managers based outside Delhi slowly started initiating processes that they felt would affect the top line. Store timings were the first to change. Delhi had maintained a strict six-day week, between 10 a.m. to 6 p.m. from 1976. The girls in Bangalore and Bombay had their stores open all seven days between 10 a.m. and 7.30 p.m. to cater to working people. Then local fabrication of garments began. The choice of size, style and colour between the cities varied and, as the managers discovered, fabrication rates were much lower in all the other metros compared to Delhi. Soon all three stores were handling 40 per cent of their own job work with tailors in their own cities. The fabric was still ordered and shipped out of Delhi by Charu Sharma and the warehouse teams but production had become decentralized to some extent. This independence allowed the girls to decide kurta lengths, colours and fabrics to suit their clientele. In the absence of a specific mandate, as long as the 'Fab look' was maintained and the top line increased, the girls managed to recreate products for their shop shelves. They converted dupattas to kurtas, left-over fabric to lamp shades and even towels to towel slippers!

Geographical diversity and climate variations also determined product styles. Since Fabindia sales were growing phenomenally in Bombay (50 per cent growth, year on year), the best-sellers became significant for understanding the new markets. To accommodate the tropical heat Bombay clients bought thin upholstery fabric to be used without lining. Nabha light and Madhulika were two light-weight fabrics that did well there. Durries were not popular and constituted less than 5 per cent of Home sales in Bombay. People living in small flats in a warm climate preferred bare floors. Madhukar's large woollen durries stopped being ordered for the Bombay stores and went off the shelves. Towels were big sellers but the heavy Jacquard ones would not dry in the monsoons. Thinner ones were required which were very absorbent and dried fast. Soon light-weight khadi 'gamchas' started being developed in Naugaon and Bijnor.

Shilpa says it took years to get Fabindia to lose its Delhi-centric product orientation. Seasons in Delhi do not keep pace with the rest of India. As Delhi is celebrating spring in March and has just moved out of woollens into crisp khadi, Bombay is into summer and will not buy khadi now till the winter. In the heat of June, Delhi wants to wear whites; but the monsoon has already hit Bombay and light shades get dirty very quickly in the rain. Delhi is a conservative city and the men like to wear greys, olive greens, deep blues and brown; but Bombay hosts the Bollywood culture and men like their shirts in slim-fitting styles and bright colours like orange and purple. To deal with these differences the Bangalore and Bombay stores ordered fabric in brighter colours and fabricated men's shirts for their clients. The woollen Nehru jacket, Fabindia's signature product, collected dust on Bombay shelves, 'It took them six months to sell six jackets in Bombay, Bangalore and Chennai'. So the Bombay store started styling lighter fabric into jackets with the same cut.

Till 2005 the PDG's focus was designing collections for the international market because that had been a priority for the company right till the first Vision Plan. But the domestic market was growing so rapidly that the company moved on to consolidating resources to deal with expansion within India. In 2005 the Fabindia Export department was downsized and the D 12/4 warehouse was sold. Fabindia Overseas however continued to export to its franchisee stores and to its wholesale overseas clients.

In 2004 William Bissell set up an organization to represent weavers, producers, wholesalers and shops selling fabric. It was a lobby group aimed at influencing government policy that was threatening to levy sales tax and VAT on handloom cotton yardage. This would impact all those working in the industry by raising prices and affecting the trade in handloom fabric. The legislation would hit Fabindia seriously since 90 per cent of its basic fabric was still handloom.

The All India Artisans and Craft Workers Welfare Association (AIACA) was instituted in 2005 with senior members from the textile and fashion world. There was Laila Tyabji from the craft organization, Dastkar; Pritam Singh from Anokhi; Ritu Kumar; Madhukar Khera and Fabindia. This became an advocacy body for a consortium of crafts groups and instituted the Craftmark, a trademark certifying authentic handmade products. Craftmark now funds research and consumer awareness programmes and publishes a catalogue showcasing new craft products from the member groups.

·7·

THE RETAIL STORY
2005-10

Focused on the growth of domestic retail, Fabindia had launched Vision Plan I in 2003. It aimed to increase monthly sales from Rs 2 crore to Rs 8 crore within a period of four years. But incredibly, by mid-2005 the target had been achieved. Coming out of Vision Plan I two years earlier than anticipated, Fabindia geared itself up for the next step in the growth plan. Vision Plan II was initiated in 2005 with the objective of carrying the company from the current monthly turnover of Rs 8 crore to Rs 20 crore. The project timeline again forecast a four-year period for Fabindia's yearly sales to cross Rs 240 crore.

William Bissell wrote to the board:

> This plan will attempt to create a brand made up of distinct businesses whose common features are that these products are handmade, environmentally sound, largely produced in rural areas and at fair wages and remuneration. In its entirety Fabindia will represent an 'alternative' model based on the principles of partnership, profit sharing, economic development of rural areas, resource conservation and shareholder value.

Broken into its constituents the plan aimed at company growth through expansion and consolidation. Expansion translated into opening more stores as well as enhancing the product line with new selections of seasonal and high-end products. Simultaneously, the plan suggested converting the company into a number of business hubs spun out from a core which offered logistics, planning and financial support. The hubs would be the growth centres within Fabindia, each independent and linked to the other in a matrix of naturally sustainable profit rather than in a hierarchy of authority and regulation. Markets and products were defined as hubs. Markets were divided into four regions each with its own manager—North and East, West and Central, South and International. Market heads would identify new cities to open stores.

To ensure a continuous supply William envisaged strengthening the supply chain. Suppliers and staff were seen as the 'multipliers' of these businesses; and because their commitment was essential, they would be linked in to different profit-sharing arrangements. Thus, suppliers would become shareholders and staff remuneration would be linked to productivity through a transparent financial system. Each support service would become a fully operative system divided into its subsidiaries. The support or core systems were Finance, Human Resource, Communications, Design, Business Development, Logistics and Technology. Each of these would be handled by professional teams. The plan looked forward to a comprehensive restructuring of the company creating 'multiple growth centres with strong institutional support.'

2005 was a significant year for Fabindia. The Fabindia website, www.fabindia.com, was launched. Smita Mankad and Shilpa Sharma had worked on the online shopping website, also called the B2C (business to consumer) module, uploading the product range and linking with domestic and international courier companies. It would serve the international market and also develop domestic business.

In addition, work had started on software that would connect the stores directly to the central warehouse so that orders and delivery could be streamlined through the system. The B2B (business to business) programme would be a forecasting tool to project future growth. Fabindia was expecting a 20–35 per cent growth per year over the next few years, so it looked for profitability ratios that would attract external investors.

As it turned out, the second Vision Plan coincided with the highest GDP growth India had ever seen till then. During 1999–2000 and 2004–05, the BJP-led NDA government under Atal Behari Vajpayee continued to push economic reforms introduced by Manmohan Singh in the early '90s. The average growth rate stayed well above 7.5 per cent between 2003 and 2005 and, under the Congress-led NDA government thereafter, averaged an all-time high of 9.2 per cent between 2005–06 and 2007–08. Fabindia's sales increased by over 40 per cent every year and the second Vision Plan target was achieved in another record two years. Fabindia would close the financial year 2006–07 with a record turnover of Rs 200 crore.

During 2005–07, another thirty-six retail outlets were added. There was Priya Rao opening stores in the south; Shilpa Sharma was adding markets in the west, and Dilpreet Singh was in charge of new projects in the north and east of India. Five of Fabindia's most beautiful stores were opened during these years.

Pondicherry was identified as a destination store for European visitors to the French quarter in the city. It was felt that Fabindia must 'have a presence' in Pondicherry and Shilpa located an old, beautiful house on the Rue de Suffren. Fabindia opened the shop in the ground floor in April 2005. The store remains 'a must see, must do for tourists visiting Pondicherry'. The Cochin property belongs to a well-known Kerala family. Says Shilpa, 'The house is fifty years old and its beauty lies in its wood work, tiled roofs, wide verandas and terraces. The view from the first floor is breathtaking.' This store opened in June 2005 and turned in sales well over Rs 4 crore in 2008. The Fabindia Mysore store is housed in a regal building which is over a hundred years old. It has double-height ceilings and wooden beams; due to excellent cross-ventilation the store has not had to install air conditioning.

Trivandrum also has a lovely store. This traditional Kerala-style house had earlier belonged to a famous south Indian film actor, and the seventy-five-year old property was in pristine condition. Two alabaster lions dating to the eighteenth century flank one of the entrances and there is an intricately carved inner courtyard. This Fabindia store is a commercial success story because Trivandrum's population consists of affluent spice families, rubber plantation owners and tourists on their way to the famous Kovalam resort by the sea. The first Goa store opened only in 2007 after Shilpa had identified the perfect property fitting the 'lazy, old world charm' idea the company had of Fabindia in Goa. The pretty bungalow is situated at the end of a lane leading to the river in the capital city of Panjim, and 'it was a dream come true', says Shilpa. She continues:

> The joy of every Fabindia store is that it lends itself to the character of the location it is set up in. There are nuances in all these properties that give the city away—the handmade tiles in Goa, the historical calligraphy embedded in the walls of Kolkata's Hindustan Park, the carving on the Corinthian columns in Jeroo, Mumbai. You walk into a property and you know what a Fabindia could do there. It is so 'Fabindia' to do that.

In all the varied locations, the different formats and the changing settings, it is the merchandise and the way the staff in the stores conducts themselves that identifies the Fabindia brand, says Shilpa. By 2010 Fabindia had opened two more outlets in Goa, but the Panjim store remains one of its top twenty.

In 2005 a group of developers setting up an eco-resort in the Nankun mountains in China contacted Fabindia for cotton fabric to decorate the interiors of their building. Their interior designer was a lady who had worked in Delhi and was familiar with the brand. The developers were so excited when they saw the product that they opened a franchisee Fabindia store in

Guangzhou, the closest city to their resort and just two hours from the Hong Kong border. It was a small home store selling silk upholstery, bed and table linen and garment accessories.

Through these years rigorous and continuous sales analyses identified return on capital per square foot of usage, and store formats were rationalized for optimum product sale. It became quite clear that garments gave the best sales-to-space ratio and upholstery the least. In place of one furniture unit five garment racks could be placed. In durries the 9" x 12" sizes went off the market soon after the first Vision Plan since their sale did not justify the space they occupied. Furniture suffered the same space constraints. Displaying furniture meant utilizing 50 per cent floor space to sell a product that was contributing only 10 per cent of Fabindia's annual sales. Yet, working within the economics that only optimized sales per sq. ft of space would be detrimental to the Fabindia brand. A compromise had to be sought.

Store formats were re-conceptualized several times during the planning process. The company tried to find a size-to-format ratio that would optimize the sale of Fabindia's complete range of products. There were four basic formats: the Mini Garment store which could be 1200–1800 sq. ft the Compressed Full store, between 1500–3500 sq. ft; the Full store, between 8000–15000 sq. ft and the Home Store, a large space between 30,000–50,000 sq. ft. There would also be Bodycare kiosks, requiring 100 sq. ft that would be set up within Fabindia stores. These were independent open shelf units that could be set up anywhere in the store to display organic products.

Sometimes the market determined the type of store required and it surprised the company. For example, Fabindia had decided to open a 'concept store' in Dehradun. The space rented was small and the company designed walk-through areas like in a furnished home, with racks and shelves of garments on the sides. The idea was to end up in a 'drawing room' where the client could order products through catalogues and swatches placed there. But the demand for Fabindia products was very high and clients would not agree to wait weeks for all their requirements. Therefore a compressed full store soon replaced the concept store. In Delhi's upscale Khan Market, Fabindia started a high-end fashion outlet with designer wear. Most of the Khan Market traditional stores have been replaced by international brands that have made the real estate one of the most expensive in India. So the company decided to offer only an exclusive range at the upscale retail destination. But regular clients would have none of it and demanded their familiar Fabindia products. They were 'shocked' at the high prices and 'disappointed' that the classic signature collections were not available. From the day it was converted to a full store the sales have been excellent. Opened in 2005, it now returns the fifth highest turnover of all the stores.

Charu says, 'Till 2003–04 by and large new products came in as and when designed, as an insert . . .' It was only after 2004 that production was organized for the seasons. It had a lot to do with the stores opening in Bombay, Bangalore and Kolkata. 'They demanded summer clothes earlier, and wanted new and lighter fabrics, more colour and better styling.' Fabindia had earlier provided perennial products which sold through the year except for woollen durries that were displayed in winter. And in the early years, it had not really focused on delivery dates for the home market. The few vendors who used to provide Nehru jackets to the Delhi store would deliver them in September and others would say 'production in two months, and that would be fine with us.'

Now there were stores all over India and seasons had to be taken into account. Also during festive seasons Indians do not wear white but want colour. That had to be factored in too. So products had to be developed and improved all the time. On 6 August 2005 William informed his store managers about developments in the product line:

There are a lot of new products . . . Collections have been co-ordinated so that the table linen even co-ordinates with the pottery. In upholstery there is a new collection of tightly woven fabrics from the south . . . In towels we have finally cracked the absorbency problem (no more water-proof towels!) which is a great breakthrough.

It was at this time that the concept of seasonal collections began. In 2004 Fabindia design teams went to Lucknow to organize vendors to supply chikan work. Chikan is embroidery on white power-loom cloth. Being white it required minimal handling. So they had to find vendors who would buy the fabric, get it embroidered and stitched and then washed and packed in plastic. Chikan changed the production cycle at Fabindia and helped organize the unorganized sector. Vendors offered to set up production units to provide the finished product, starting from the fabric to the stitched, packed garment. This became what is known as a 'direct purchase' item. Earlier fabrics were purchased from weavers or artisan groups and handed out to job workers to be fabricated. Now vendors could make presentations of finished products to Fabindia for selection.

Handloom fabric could not keep pace with the increased demand from the expanding Fabindia market. The use of power-loom textiles was justified by adding at least one aspect of hand-craft to the power-loom base of that product. So for example, chikan embroidery was the craft component of a product based on power-loom fabric. At this point, an important decision was taken. Anita Thapar Kathpalia, as quoted in the Harvard Business Case Study, 2007, says:

One could say that we did 'compromise' somewhat when we decided to use mill-woven cloth for some of our handblock-printed home furnishings, but we did so because the supply of mill-made fabric was more reliable and available in larger volumes than the hand-woven equivalent.

In that case, we ensured that the link to craft is maintained by using mill-made fabric only where it acts as a base for a handicraft such as block-printing or embroidery.

Then linen came into the collections. Linen is a fibre that grows in Bengal and though the fabric looks textured it is a power-loom product. Linen was brought in to make good Western formal wear like trousers and skirts. Customers had been demanding formal wear for a while but Fabindia had rejected the concept of power-loom trousers so far. Then they found they were 'losing out on that market' and so linen was introduced. Linen could not be embellished so no 'craft component' was added. By 2009 power-loom products constituted 1–2 per cent of Fabindia's turnover.

Chanderi fabric was another product added at this stage. Desert Artisans, William Bissell's original artisan's company set up in Jodhpur in 1990, had branched out to Jaipur and later to Bhuj, to develop products with craft groups. They had now set up a unit in Chanderi in Madhya Pradesh and were working with artisans there to develop different weaves for garment fabric. Chanderi weavers had traditionally only woven saris; and since the market was shrinking for their product they were in trouble. Their looms were set up only for saris. They had to be persuaded to weave plain fabric without borders that could be used to make garments. Charu explains that since traditional sari weavers were paid for their time they preferred to weave intricate designs that would take longer and therefore pay better. They needed training to learn to weave up to 10,000 m of plain fabric.

These products helped to set production and delivery targets for the seasons. Chikan work had to be in the stores in summer and needed six to eight months of lead time, so work had to start in June–July of 2005 to be in the stores next February. From 2005 consolidated collections began to be prepared for specific seasons including the festivals, while perennial products continued to be fabricated throughout the year.

Perennials are the 'bread and butter' of Fabindia. Even though the 'kurta' could have once been regarded as a perennial Fabindia product, today there is a difference in perspective. Within the category of kurtas the white khadi, the Satnapalli, the Surbhi and the Malhotra prints are the perennials but the Lucknow kurta is a seasonal product.

A range of Personal Care products was also launched in the Fabindia stores in February 2006. These were natural products without colours, preservatives or flavours, and the range included body and hair care. It was an extension of the partnership developed with artisans in rural communities. Fabindia did path-breaking work in this area, encouraging farmers to grow organic products and helping them with their documentation and certificates.

By 2006 Fabindia products had extended to sixteen categories. These were women's wear, Indian and Western men's wear, kids' wear, garments accessories, bed and kitchen linen, table linen, upholstery and curtains, fabric and floor coverings, furniture, hard woods and lighting, organic food and body care.

Today, garments constitute almost 70 per cent of the turnover of the company, fabricated from a wide variety of material from all over India. 66 per cent of this is woven cotton fabric sourced from Naugaon in Uttar Pradesh and Mangalgiri in Andhra Pradesh. 21 per cent is printed cotton fabric which is first woven and then printed in Sanganer and Bagru in Rajasthan, and Bhuj and Baroda in Gujarat. There is kalamkari from Machalipatnam in Andhra Pradesh, and Bagh from Madhya Pradesh. 8 per cent of Fabindia garments are made from silk supplied from Bhagalpur in Bihar, Champa in Chhattisgarh, Bhandara in Maharashtra and Murshidabad in West Bengal. And there is ikat, the traditional dyed fabric from Orissa and Andhra Pradesh. Chanderi is a recent addition to this list along with linen and wool blends from the hills of Kumaon. Fabrics for the Home collections are now also being sourced from Kannur in Kerala and Karur in Tamil Nadu.

The organic food range consists of everyday items such as grains, cereals, pulses, sweeteners, spices and herbs as well as processed food like tea, jams, preserves, pastas, pickles, seasoning, granola and dried fruits. The brand Fabindia Organics sells 50 per cent certified organic and 50 per cent wholly natural products.

In October 2006 the company convened an important meeting in Dungarpur, Rajasthan. The whole management team went down for three days to discuss the future strategy of the company. William remembers that a spectacular monsoon had just ended and the mood was upbeat. 'What was exciting was that at the end of VP II we were confident that we could do it. We had managed to achieve the growth targets earlier [than planned]. We were feeling good!' So they 'hammered out all the issues' at the Dungarpur Conference 'at the edge of the lake' and came up with Vision Plan III.

Vision Plan III was ambitious, bold and radical. Its aim was three-fold. To create 100,000 sustainable jobs in rural India, strengthen the Fabindia brand in India and the international market, and improve the profitability and capital equity of the company. The plan envisaged an increase of average monthly turnover from Rs 20 crore (in 2007–08) to Rs 60 crore (in 2011–12). It was presented to the company along with the budget requirements in 2007 and looked towards mobilizing approximately Rs 245 crore for upgradation and expansion of the company over the next five years.

The plan had arisen from the deep commitment and shared ideology of the Fabindia board to the following five premises:

a) that the mandate of the company is to make profits while providing employment and creating a market for good craft products from rural artisans;

b) that the Fabindia brand continues to derive its strength from the handloom and handicraft industry and therefore must secure the supply chain to ensure continuation;

c) that people are motivated by long-term maximization of

profit in an atmosphere of free enterprise and personal choice;

d) that centralized large operations are inimical to sustained growth since they create inflexible hierarchies that hinder creative action; and

e) that utilization of new technologies can increase the efficiency of systems by optimizing costs in time and resource management.

The steady increase in Fabindia revenues corresponded with the annual GDP growth rate of the Indian economy. The Congress-led UPA government under Prime Minister Manmohan Singh managed to push reforms despite being stymied by the Left parties. And the economy responded by generating a high growth in the services and manufacturing sectors. All economic reports point to a dramatic increase in the spending power of the urban middle class estimated to be over 150 million people. The National Sample Survey (NSS) data showed that for urban India as a whole the purchasing power had expanded four times between the mid-'80s and today; in Gujarat, five times; Chandigarh, four times; Andhra Pradesh and Karnataka over four times; and Kerala almost five times. So it was pretty clear where the new Fabindia shoppers were coming from.

The Vision Plan III document spelt out a detailed process, which was:

to create and retail unique products which come from a vertically integrated business in which all manufacturing and product developments are controlled by product specialists. Our objective is to achieve this within a corporate structure which minimizes hierarchies and accelerates decision making by introducing automatic approval pathways.

The plan incorporated all activities from the creation of the product to its final purchase in a Fabindia store within four verticals that were 'activity and role specific'. These were the Production Selection Committee, Supplier Regions, Global Support Practices and Markets Regions. They were linked and operated through software that integrated database management with financial productivity and optimized incentives. In its ideal manifestation the structure allotted points for rewards and penalties for every activity within the process thereby minimizing management intervention and control. The only variable, and perhaps the most important, was the sourcing and modification of the craft and its identification as a Fabindia product. At the core of this lay the most significant paradigm shift affected by Fabindia.

Supplier regions corresponded to geographical areas that had concentrations of production units supplying products to Fabindia. There were almost 40,000 artisans and crafts persons working in these regions. These included weavers, dyers, printers, embroiderers, embellishers, leather workers, fabricators of clothing or furniture, farmers and manufactures of organic products. Fabindia identified seventeen such supplier region areas around India and drew each into a corporate entity with the artisans in that region invited to become shareholders. Thus, seventeen community-owned companies or Supplier Region Companies (SRCs) were formed. Initially 17,000 artisans opted to become shareholders in their respective companies. It was difficult to get artisans to buy into the idea since they had little knowledge of corporate structures and Fabindia had to spend quite a bit of time and energy setting up these companies. But the effort has paid off and becoming equity partners in these companies has given artisans a sense of ownership.

The concept of the community-owned company was born out of William's initial attempts to run an artisan's cooperative in Bhadrajun in 1989. That had materialized into Desert Artisans Handicrafts Pvt. Ltd based in Jodhpur. DAH was the first successful experiment with artisan partnership and equity and

William had not given up this ideal of artisans being co-opted to manage their businesses. Instead of cooperatives, the SRCs were public limited companies with artisan shareholders and common systems to streamline production and delivery processes. This model turned the concept of social entrepreneurship on its head. Artisan-owned companies would learn to compete in a market that guaranteed a steady revenue stream as long as they produced quality products that Fabindia would buy. If this plan succeeded the company would achieve two fundamental objectives. Fabindia's supply chain would be assured and the artisans would be empowered to control their means of livelihood. In an interview to *Business Today* on 10 August 2008 William said: 'SRCs create value for member artisans in three ways: they give the craftspeople sustainable jobs, an investment opportunity and appreciation in the value of their shares.'

The role of the SRCs was very clearly defined—to develop products with the product specialists, install processes for quality control, make payments to the artisans for their products, manage a warehouse for holding stock in anticipation of orders from Fabindia, purchase raw material in bulk and therefore at competitive prices and finance projects that would lead to product enhancement. They were also expected to identify new artisans (and crafts) within the region and draw them into the supply chain. Funding for the SRC would come from Fabindia in the form of equity investment, from artisan shareholders and from bank loans partially guaranteed by Fabindia.

To provide affordable working capital for the SRCs, a joint investment fund was created which was a partnership between Fabindia and a national bank. The idea was to offer loans to these rural companies with Fabindia as the guarantor. The model was secure since Fabindia was committed to buying everything produced by the SRCs. In late 2006 this was incorporated as a 100 per cent owned subsidiary of Fabindia under the name of Artisans Micro Finance Pvt. Ltd (AMFPL). It is a non-banking finance company whose prime purpose is to act as an investment vehicle for Fabindia. It is a promoter and incubator for the seventeen SRCs—to set up the companies, recruit and train the teams, locate warehouses, put the IT systems and processes in place, and link the artisans and suppliers of that geography into the SRC. 49 per cent of the equity of each SRC is currently held by AMFPL, 26 per cent by the artisans, 10 per cent by the employees, and 15 per cent by external investors which are usually social venture capital funds.

Smita Mankad, the MD of AMFPL who is busy stabilizing operations of these seventeen SRCs, has remarked in an interview with *Business Today* on 10 August 2008 that though these companies only supply to Fabindia at the moment, 'they will also be allowed to deal with other buyers in the domestic and export markets in the future. Fabindia also envisions diluting its shareholding in these SRCs as they mature, allowing the artisan shareholders to increasingly take care of their business.'

Professional product specialists and designers were appointed to work with the SRCs to develop new products and maintain quality control. They needed to be familiar with processes and techniques required to create, produce or fabricate items that could be added to the inventory after approval from the Product Selection Committee at Fabindia. Ideally their remuneration would be calculated as a percentage of the sale of their specific products in the stores. Each designer was the head of the product category that was her specialization. In 2009-10 there were eleven specialists in charge of the different product categories: Women's wear, Indian and Western; Men's wear; Garment accessories; Teens and Children's wear; Home textiles; Furniture and home hard goods; Personal care; Organics; Jewellery; and Garment fabric.

Vision Plan III defined market regions by revenue responsibilities. When the sales and purchases (at cost) of a particular region crossed a certain threshold, a market region could be created. These could technically be cities, states or nations. The Market Region Head served on the boards of all the SRCs in the region and was also a member of the Product Selection Committee. She handled all the stores in the region and coordinated the activities of the SRCs including their investments and debt. She was also responsible for exploring new markets and setting up new stores, hiring store staff and maintaining the market region warehouse. As with the professional product designers, the market region budgets were calculated as a percentage of sales through the stores in that region.

Today Fabindia has many designated market regions around India, each with its own warehouse and distribution centre.

The final vertical in the structure was the global support practices. This comprised a common pool of services including Finance, Technology and Software, HR and Training, Communications, Legal, and Programme and Strategy Implementation. These services were available to all the businesses and were charged on the basis of time sheets or a schedule of fees as determined by the service. The stores had an expense budget for services against a calculated percentage of their annual sales.

The work flow was comprehensively integrated into a computerised B2B programme, so that any activity set off a chain of actions in a designated path leading either to the source or to sale. These actions were also covered by formulae that controlled sales and cost ratios within predetermined margins so as to maintain optimum efficiency.

Within the system, every unit of sale was referred to as a Stock keeping Unit (SKU). An SKU is a product item. To illustrate the definition let's take a simple men's khadi kurta. The product category 'khadi kurta' could constitute several SKUs broken down to specific colour, size, length and type of collar. So a blue khadi, size 42", long kurta, with full sleeves and a Chinese collar is one SKU. A similar kurta in another size would be a second SKU and so on. Each variable in a product makes for an SKU because it is a specific sale item on the invoice. Each SKU is also linked to the status of the item—perennial, festive, seasonal, essential, artisan and classic.

In 2009–10 Fabindia was carrying 200,000 SKUs in its system. According to Charu Sharma, 'Fabindia's strength is the variety offered. More then fifty different fabrics are made into *x* different styles, in different colours. Limited designs do not work for today's client. The new client needs variety on the shelf.'

Now we shall illustrate the work flow. We'll start with a weaver who is also a shareholder in his regional SRC. He weaves some yardage and shows it to the SRC. The SRC calls in the designers. They like the fabric and decide to develop it further. They work with the weaver for a couple of weeks and develop some more samples. These are shown by the designers to the Product Selection Committee at the next meeting. The fabric is then approved and the cost price finalized. The quantity of fabric to be produced the first time is pre-determined by the software based on a minimum stock requirement ratio, and an order is given to the weaver to make the product. The weaver produces the requisite amount of fabric in a month and brings it in to the SRC, which enters the fabric into the system after designating an SKU number for the item. The SKU is now a part of the Fabindia range of products online. The fabric is stored in the SRC warehouse. New SKUs are flagged in the system and if a store manager likes it, she places an order on the B2B. The order goes to the SRC and that quantity of fabric (SKU) is transferred out of the system and the SRC invoices the store for it. The fabric is transported from the SRC warehouse to the market region warehouse that is responsible for that store. The SKU (fabric) is transferred in to the market region warehouse and held there till it goes to the store. In the meantime the SRC has replenished the same quantity of that fabric from the weaver as was sold to the store to maintain the 'minimum stock level' at the SRC warehouse. The cycle is complete.

In 2006 in anticipation of the next stage of planned growth, William Bissell had prepared an investor document with details of the company's financial statements. The company decided to try again to raise some private equity. 'When we were looking for a valuation in 2002–03 that started at Rs 100 crore, nobody was willing . . . four and a half years later we got a valuation of Rs 600 crore. It was a much higher valuation,' says William.

In 2006–07 Fabindia sales had recorded a turnover of Rs 188.45 crore. The net profit was Rs 12.05 crore. Reserves stood at Rs 43.79 crore and dividend payout was Rs 1.92 crore.

Chart A: Sales Explode...

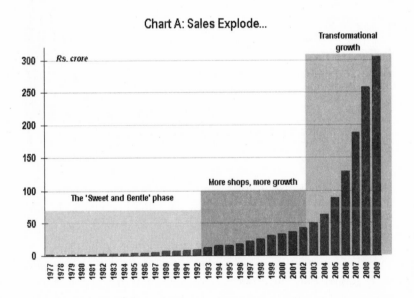

Fabindia's growth rate had been spectacular between 2004 and 2007. For the year ending 31 March 2004, on sales of Rs 63.14 crore, its profit before depreciation, interest and taxes (PBDIT) was Rs 7.95 crore, and profit after taxes (PAT) was Rs 3.34 crore. A year later, sales had risen to Rs 88.57 crore; PBDIT to Rs 12.26 crore and PAT to Rs 5.66 crore. By 31 March 2006 sales had shot up by 46 per cent to Rs 129.39 crore; PBDIT to Rs 18.46 crore and PAT to Rs 7.81 crore. The growth continued. For the year ending 31 March 2007 sales had risen to Rs 188.59 crore; PBDIT to Rs 27.21 crore and PAT to a bit over Rs 12 crore.

Chart B: As Do Profits...

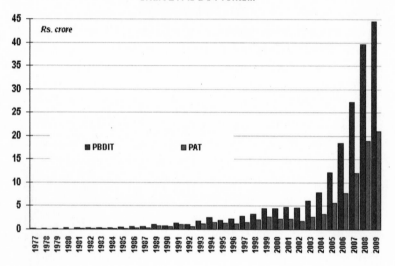

James Wolfensohn, former president of the World Bank, had visited India many times as head of the bank between 1995 and 2005. After retiring, he set up a private investment firm, Wolfensohn & Company LLC, in 2006 and was interested in investing in significant developing countries. Not only would such investments be economically viable but if done within a context of social responsibility, would enjoy wider support and greater accountability. WCP Mauritius Holdings, a company promoted by Wolfensohn & Company LLC, took a modest stake in Fabindia in 2006. In an interview to Anil Padmanabhan, Wolfensohn says he made this investment because he liked the company. 'I think the founder and the management of Fabindia are wonderful people. Secondly, the philosophy of Fabindia is something I believe in very much—which is to sponsor manufacturing and distribution in a parallel way.' (*Mint*, 24 April 2007.)

In 2006 Fabindia increased its authorized share capital to Rs 2.5 crore and allotted shares to several members of the board as well as to the Fabindia Employee Welfare Trust. Shares were also allotted to WCP Mauritius Holdings, and in April 2007 Sanjiv Kapur was appointed director on the board as a nominee director of the investing company.

The board had undergone some major changes. Meena Chowdhury had resigned as chairman of the company when she retired in 2005. Lt Gen. Sibal who had been a director of Fabindia for thirty years also retired. Vijai Kapoor, William Bissell's father-in-law, was now a director and so was Sean Sovak, a friend who had co-founded a private equity business in India. Charu Sharma was invited to join the board in 2006. William continued as managing director, and Madhukar Khera and Monsoon Bissell as directors. Sunil Chainani was part of the executive board along with William and Charu.

By 2007 Fabindia was in transition to Vision Plan III. To move forward the company would use its own reserves for the first phase of the plan. The projected total sales figure for 2007–08 was Rs 240 crore. But Fabindia closed the year much ahead with Rs 257 crore and a profit after tax of almost Rs 20 crore. In the annual report of 2007–08 William announced to his shareholders:

[The company] put in place the infrastructure for growth planned during the five years of VP III. We managed this transition while achieving a sales growth of 37 per cent and a growth in profitability of 57 per cent. I would compare this to rebuilding a ship while cruising at full speed ... [This year] Fabindia opened 27 stores in 21 cities; of these 14 stores were in cities in which Fabindia did not have a prior presence—Agra, Bhopal, Candolim, Faridabad, Jalandhar, Jamshedpur, Kanpur, Ludhiana. Mohali, Nasik, Panchkula, Surat, Trivandrum and Vizag.

The other stores consolidated our presence in Ahmedabad, Bangalore, Chennai, Delhi, Gurgaon, Jaipur and Kolkata. On March 31, 2008, the count stood at 84 stores in 37 cities.

In August 2007 the company had signed a franchise agreement with one of the Gulf's prominent businesses—the Al Jazira Group—based in Bahrain. The Group opened three Fabindia stores in Bahrain and one in Qatar.

Fabindia was in top gear. SRCs and MRWs (Market Region Warehouses) were being set up around the country. The central warehouse, a centralized hub for servicing the eighty-five stores, was being dispersed into seventeen different businesses buying and distributing their own products. IT systems were being designed to regulate the whole Fabindia business and the Finance department was being restructured. It was imperative that everyone pulled in the same direction. Smita Mankad comments: 'The business chain is so interdependent that one glitch impacts everyone down the line.'

Products were redefined in 2007 and a new line of garments was introduced. Independent designers were requested to present collections specifically designed for the high-end market. The idea was to create long-term relationships with designers on a royalty basis. Riten Mazumdar and Fabindia had maintained a long association based on royalty paid for his designs over a decade ago. Today Anjali Kalia is one of the designers whose styles have incorporated the Fabindia 'look' successfully enough to retail at stores at prices double that of the mainline collections. These styles are fabricated in quantities of 1500–2000 pieces at a time, in different colours and sizes, and distributed mainly in the flagship stores. In 2009 Fabindia was working with thirty to forty such designers on different products—accessories such as scarves, stoles and bags, as well as home products like lamps.

Charu says, 'There is more competition today in handloom and cotton garments so the company has included high-end products as well.' These collections brought about the first major shift in the Fabindia store display format. Expensive and restricted clothes cannot lie folded in shelves one on top of the other. Designer wear has to be displayed on hangers, with the styles and sizes immediately visible to the customer, so it is 'not pulled out and piled up on the table in original Fabindia fashion.'

A small selection of handloom cotton saris had been selling in Fabindia since 2002. Shilpa Sharma focused on expanding the range and revived classic designs and prints in 2007-08. Three distinct ranges of saris were introduced—the classic, the traditional and the contemporary—along with a selection of semi-stitched sari blouses. This led Shilpa to introduce jewellery as a new product category in Fabindia as a natural accessory to the sari.

In April 2007 a Capital Expense Committee (Capex) was set up to approve and sign off on all capital expenses undertaken during the expansion plan. Shilpa pitched for her new product with a well-researched presentation. The project was approved in December 2007 and the Fabindia jewellery collection was launched in August 2008.

Laila Tyabji developed some jewellery for this collection with Dastkar craft groups—'lovely designs which were high-value items.' In the meantime Shilpa sourced jewellery across the country working on different 'looks' for different consumers. There was Anasuya which was expensive and made from gold-washed silver and semi-precious stones; Ananya, a middle-level range in silver; and Amina for young people who wanted to wear 'fun stuff'. Specially designed modules were fabricated for product displays on shop floors. Launched in 2008, jewellery was an instant success and within the next year it was turning over revenues of Rs 80 lakh a month. In 2009-10 it is expected to cross sales worth Rs 12 crore.

While Fabindia was fast tracking through Vision Plan III in 2008, the worst financial crisis since the Great Depression hit the banking world in the US and the markets crashed. A deep and widening recession spread through the Western world and its ripples impacted domestic economies in every country. India's rapid economic growth, pushed by the technology and service industries during the past decade, slowed down. The Indian stock markets reflected the doom in the international markets; but partly protected by a regulated financial sector and a conservative attitude to savings and investments, the Indian market did not crash. Shares fell and players in the stock market lost wealth. Consumers stopped spending money on inessential commodities. And Fabindia's growth rate declined. This would affect revenues the next year and the consequences would spiral down the supply chain to the SRCs.

In the 2008–09 annual report of the company William stated clearly that 'It's been a tough year.' The directors and management of Fabindia initiated a cost-cutting programme by voluntarily cutting their own salaries by 5–25 per cent. More stringent criteria were introduced for approving new projects and operating budgets were trimmed, 'even if that meant that we would have to reduce our rate of growth in sales for the year.' William went on to say: 'We took a conscious decision that we would sacrifice a year of rapid growth to focus on improving our profitability.'

In 2008–09 Fabindia reported a growth rate of 18 per cent with sales of over Rs 304 crore and Rs 21 crore profits after tax.

In pursuit of a continued interest in establishing a strong presence in the international market Fabindia completed a new transaction in January 2009 and acquired a 25 per cent stake in East Limited, a UK-based retail brand. Originally called Anokhi, the company was started in 1970 to market clothing made from hand-block printed textiles that were produced in Jaipur. The UK company had started its wholesale trading in Indian garments with two shops in London. In 1994 it was renamed East in recognition of the broadening of its supplier base to include China. By 2009 the company had grown to seventy-two retail outlets in the UK, and Anokhi in Jaipur was still one of its suppliers. Fabindia merchandise would retail at those stores.

John Singh was one of Anokhi's initial investors and he and his wife Faith had handled production for the business from Jaipur, exporting textiles and clothing out of India to the company in the UK. John and Faith started their own Anokhi shop in Jaipur in 1971, and were good friends of the Bissells. All the years John was developing his business at Fabindia he was very certain he would not sell shirts fabricated from hand-printed textiles in direct competition with Anokhi. It is one of those interesting twists of fate that John Bissell's son William has now invested in that company. 'I had huge respect for the brand,' says William.

On 20 August 2009 Fabindia launched the first East store in Delhi's N Block, GK-1 market. Another three stores opened soon after in Saket, Delhi, Pali Hill, Mumbai and Koramangla, Bangalore.

Fabindia had invested in East in January 2009, when it was having a tough time in terms of sales and profits. The Fabindia board had great faith in East's management team, and it was given a free run in handling the operations. This resulted in a remarkable turnaround in the fortunes of the company in an increasingly tough UK market, still suffering from slowdown. 'A loss-making company has turned in significant profits and has wiped out all the accumulated losses in the balance sheet,' says Sunil Chainani.

In the meantime the SRCs completed two years of business and Smita Mankad prepared their annual reports. Each SRC was now a public limited company. An Indian banking partner was supporting them with working capital loans. Fabindia's entire range of merchandise was being purchased from these seventeen community-owned companies based around India. After two years of operation, their P&L statements were beginning to show profits and the companies had started trading shares. Some artisans who had initially bought shares at Rs 100 were were now trading these at Rs 200 to Rs 300. The Jaipur SRC, Desert Artisans Handicrafts, had done well, with their shares trading at

Rs 500. Artisans were now able to buy or sell as many shares as they wanted depending upon their availability. The Rajasthan SRCs began experimenting with daily share trading. This was to enable the artisan to treat his share as an asset and to appreciate the value of equity participation. Smita says that fourteen of the seventeen SRCs have earned profits in 2009–10.

These community-owned companies have a clear mandate. Once they have stabilized and are bringing in steady revenue they are allowed to explore new markets with different products. Sourcing and developing new products is one of their primary roles. They can also upgrade facilities in their production centres and move up the supply chain. Some SRCs have already started competing with each other by offering a better price to Fabindia for the same product.

One of their missions is the role they are to finally play in their communities. William's vision is that the SRCs will become catalysts in community development projects in the region and, with support from Fabindia, will implement programmes on health, education and infrastructure. To be empowered enough to get to that stage they have to be self-sustaining and compete as equals in the open market.

Shaila Tyagi is the CEO of her SRC, Dilli Karigari Limited, working out of Okhla, Delhi. She has been associated with Fabindia for sixteen years. 'What a joy ride I've had!' she says. She was an employee of Fabindia during 1994–2007. During those years she worked in every department in Fabindia. She started work on the shop floor in N-14, GK1, folding clothes and placing them back in the shelves. She graduated to the cash counter and then spent eight years in the Finance section. She says she did not know how to load a stapler when she joined Fabindia. At Finance she got to know all the suppliers while handling their payments. After that she worked on cleaning up the inventory. Her next job was to start the Rajouri Garden store and then the Khan Market shop. In 2002 when the central warehouse started she was deputed to manage it. She said the central warehouse floor was as large as a football field. Every day she would have the floor washed to keep it clean for the stock that would arrive from the suppliers. Like in a post office the stock would be separated into separate piles for the different stores and then dispatched to stores against orders. That was where she learned supply chain management. She was directly in touch with suppliers who brought in the product. Product management got computerized and so did the store requests. Supplier payments got rationalized as well. As Fabindia opened new stores orders increased and so did production. One of the weavers, Milind Sar, a weaver who used to bring 500m of khadi in six months, is now supplying 5000 m a month. Large quantities meant that Fabindia could negotiate for better rates per metre of fabric. 'Earlier a weaver would bring two "*thaans*" (bales) on his back to Fabindia, now he drives in an Armada,' says Shaila, referring to Muhammad Yasim from Usha Textiles in Naugaon. In 2007, when Vision Plan III began to take effect,the central warehouse was converted to an SRC and Dilli Karigari Limited was incorporated. Shaila Tyagi opted to become the managing director and left her job at Fabindia. Her salary is now coming out of the budget and profits of the SRC.

The SRC's 2008–09 annual report defines the role of the company:

> Essentially a garment producing SRC, the company provides support to SRCs in Amroha, Bijnor, Chanderi, Jaipur, Jodhpur, Mumbai and Kerala, [which] in turn are helping the weavers of remote areas situated in these locations. The company purchases handloom fabrics and issues it to the tailors to convert into a finished product; products are then supplied to Fabindia.

There are two artisans on the Board of the SRC, and 850 artisan shareholders. In the first year Dilli Karigari Ltd did Rs 4 crore of business. In 2008–09 the turnover was Rs 63 crore. Profit after tax was Rs 90 lakh. The company had borrowed Rs 10 crore from Axis Bank for working capital requirements the first year. Shaila hypothecated stock to the bank against the loan and they are paying interest on it. She is confident the SRC will repay the loan eventually. Since she is dealing with suppliers and fabricators, she has to negotiate rates with both sets of vendors. She purchased stock to the value of Rs 46 crore. Most of that fabric was made into garments by the same tailoring units that used to work for Fabindia. Quality control is very important and a specialist has been hired to advise the SRCs because Fabindia cannot compromise its reputation with bad quality. Shaila knows that garments contribute 70 per cent of Fabindia's total revenue.

Shaila's largest buyer is the N-14, GK-1 store in Delhi. Almost 8 per cent of Fabindia's total yearly turnover comes from this flagship property. Radhika Diesh is the manager of that store. She gets 80 per cent of her stock from Dilli Karigari Ltd. The rest is from SRCs in Mumbai and Kolkata. In 2007 the average monthly sale in the shop was Rs 1.75 crore. In 2008 the average increased to Rs 1.85 crore. Garments account for a major percentage of its revenue. Within the garment category women's Indian wear is the 'hottest selling product'. The volumes are so large that N-14 receives stock thrice a week. Eighty packets of garments arrive every week; each packet holds between 150–200 garments. So the store gets approximately 16,000 new garments every week. This stock is manually transferred into the stockroom, each garment being counted and checked for size before being signed in to the register. Every day at least 1000 garments are signed out to be taken down to the store to sell.

The shop inventory is the value of the stock that can be purchased in a particular year by that shop. It is a percentage of the average monthly sale of the store. In B2B terms, it is the 'wallet' and shops with large turnovers like N-14 are permitted to hold three months' stock in house. Since all transactions are carried out through the B2B programme the wallet decreases by the value of the order placed by the store to the SRC. As the product sells and is invoiced by the store the wallet opens up and more stock can be ordered. In 2009 Radhika Diesh could hold Rs 1.5 crore x 3 (months) worth of inventory at any point of time. However she would only order against half that value so that her wallet was always kept open for contingency sales. Those could be triggered by the weather for example. An unprecedented cold wave would have customers flocking in for woollens. Radhika managed to cash in on such situations by ordering woollens from the SRC against her balance account.

Radhika and her team have narrowed down their products to the top fifteen best-selling fabrics and styles in all categories through monthly sales' analysis. But demand varies by the month in a store like N-14. Colours and styles are determined by the seasons and sometimes sizes as well. Customers tend to wear slimmer fitted shirts in the summer months. There is a ratio of size to sale in every style. Some styles sell more medium and some more of the smaller sizes. So this has to be calculated before the order is placed. N-14 places orders for its seasonal styles three months in advance because of the large volumes that are required. An order sent to Dilli Karigari for 10,000 white shirts just one month before they are to be displayed would mean that Shaila would not be able to fulfil the demand. So summer whites are ordered in January for April and winter jackets in August for October. On the other hand perennial items only need a month's lead time. Therefore, coordination has to be perfected between the store and the SRC.

Now we come to the order process flow through the month for the next month's stock (for perennial items). Between the first and the fifth an Excel sheet is prepared by the store for the demand order as per sale as per ratio. This describes only 70 per cent of the next month's order. This is emailed to Dilli Karigari. By the twentieth of the month, Shaila (from the SRC) returns the sheet with available products highlighted as per the order. She also mentions alternatives for products that are not currently in stock at her SRC. On the twenty-first, Radhika places her final order on the B2B as per her demand and the availability of the products in the SRC. Her wallet closes to the extent of the value of her order. This order is serviced by Shaila and the products are sent by Dilli Karigari to the market region warehouse to be transferred to N-14 by the first of the following month. This is still only 70 per cent of the month's requirements.

In the meantime, by the fifteenth of the month Radhika sells some proportion of the month's stock and calculates how much more will be required to get through the month. She now uses the balance 30 per cent of her 'wallet' to place the 'back up' order on the B2B after checking that the products are in stock with Dilli Karigari. This order is a much smaller one and is received by the store on the twenty-fifth to place in the shop for the last few days of the month. Some months when sales are low the back-up order is not required because there is still sufficient stock.

The shop's annual expense budget is based on the previous year's sales with a certain percentage increase. All expenses including the rent, administration and infrastructure costs and stock purchases have to be accounted for within the budget. Each store has to be an economically viable and profitable business at the end of the financial year. Staff members are linked to this profitability in varying ratios for their bonus and other incentive-based schemes. It is a precisely calibrated system and requires intense commitment to the numbers that steer it.

The store at N-14, GK-I market has maintained its position as the highest revenue earner of all the retail outlets in the country. In 2009–10 its annual sales exceeded Rs 20 crore. Aware of the fact that she is managing Fabindia's oldest store Radhika Deish talks about Fabindia customers who have been buying from N-14, GK-1 for over thirty years.

They already know what they want to buy. Most times it is to replace a Fabindia product that has worn out with repeated wearing. They just walk in, put out their hand and pull out a garment from the shelf like they are reaching into their own cupboards.

She says that regular (older) customers want their familiar products to be displayed exactly in the same place as they always were so they do not have to waste time looking for them. Those items are the perennials of the business. But the newer clients are younger, trendier and they like embellishments and different styles. They are interested in the designer wear that is hanging on the racks, the 'direct purchase' items and the new product categories that have been developed. These clients are driving the market and the phenomenal sales at Fabindia. It is they who are responsible for Fabindia being cited as one of the best-known national retail brands associated with India.

Fabindia is a brand that is bigger than the company that has produced it.

It has achieved this status without any advertising in all these last fifty years. That is an unbelievable achievement in this age of obsessive media publicity. In the '70s the Fabindia 'look' became a cult that promoted Indian hand-spun and hand-woven fabric among the elite in Delhi. Over the last decade Fabindia has defined an Indian sensibility and become a lifestyle option for the urban middle class in India.

This remarkable growth has no precedence in the retail industry in India. Fabindia has set standards for hand-crafted quality products that are being emulated by other brands in the market today. The creation of community-owned companies to secure the supply chain for the vast quantities of products required by Fabindia is being cited in management schools as a dynamic new model of social entrepreneurship. The company's bottom line has continued to grow as have share values in the artisan companies, creating wealth for both buyer and producer, as equal participants in the process. The fifty-year-old company has kept its commitment to its shareholders, its employees, its customers and its suppliers alike.

Many years ago John Bissell had said: 'In addition to making profits our aims are constant development of new handwoven products, a fair, equitable and helpful relationship with our producers and the maintenance of quality upon which our reputation rests.'

In 2007 when Fabindia was featured as a case study at the Harvard Business School, William Bissell stated:

> We are promoting an alternative vision for the future. It is collaborative (with the suppliers) in the true sense of the word; it is participatory (with the customers that share our views); and the products have an intrinsic value proposition as opposed to imposed value ... I believe that the only way to alleviate rural poverty is to generate sustainable employment, and the only way to do that is if we run our business in a profitable manner. It seems contradictory that we pursue both a social goal and profit, but I believe that is the only way to do it.

This commitment is the Fabindia phenomenon.

This year, 2010, the company celebrates its fiftieth anniversary. A quick glance at the timeline throws up some significant facts.

One Fabindia share bought in 1977 for Rs 5000 is equal to Rs 1.6 crore today.

In 1961, after its first year as a Delhi-based export company, Fabindia Inc. had Rs 40,000 worth of sales. Fabindia has pulled into its fiftieth anniversary year with a turnover close to Rs 350 crore.

In 1960 Fabindia Inc. kept one fabric in stock, Delhi Handspun Cotton (DHC), which the company purchased from the Cottage Industries Emporium.

In 2010 Fabindia has a product line of 200,000 SKUs made by

approximately 40,000 artisans who are organized into seventeen community-owned companies in which about 50 per cent of them are shareholders.

In 1960, the year Fabindia Inc. was incorporated, there were three people working in the company. In 2010 there are 850 employees on the rolls.

In 1976 Fabindia Overseas Ltd opened its first store in Delhi. Today Fabindia sells its merchandise in 120 stores in India and worldwide.

From 1960 to 2010 has been an incredible journey with many stories to tell along the way. This is just one of them.

Acknowledgements

It has taken me over two years to research and write the story of Fabindia. Following the thread of John Bissell's life against the background of the revival of craft in India has been one the most fulfilling experiences of my professional life. Some of the characters spanning the story had passed away before I touched that history, two more were lost along the way, others are hanging on by that same thread. It is crucial to have it all said now before it loses its authenticity. That is what I have tried to do.

There are two important facts I need to share about this project. The first is that my primary research material has consisted of over 1000 letters written by John Bissell to his parents during 1948–84 sharing details of his personal and work life that would have been lost otherwise. Correspondingly, copies of John's father, Bill's letters to his son were also found with Marie, John's sister. Efficiently preserved by the family this personal archive was generously handed over to me for reference. The second is that all the people I have interviewed for this book have not only told their Fabindia stories with candour but have remembered details with remarkable clarity, corroborating each other and the facts unwittingly.

All the data for this history has been collected from one or more of the following sources: photographs, letters, cards and notes from the family; official correspondence—memos, telegrams, emails, invoices; Power Point presentations and films; Fabindia annual reports; administrative journals; salary registers, sales' reports; suppliers' invoices, buyers' briefs; financial statements; fabric sample files; promotional posters and press reviews. The seventy interviewees include craftspersons, buyers, members of the Bissell family and friends and Fabindia staff, past and present. I have met the extended Bissell family in Connecticut, visited their beautiful homes and seen the varied commercial spaces occupied by Fabindia Inc. over the years. In India my research has involved travelling to crafts' villages, production units, suppliers' homes and factories, to buying agents, family friends, Fabindia offices and stores.

I have many people to acknowledge and thank for their support to this project. But there are four who helped pull me through with their unfaltering trust in my ability to write this story. They are William and Bim Bissell, Madhukar Khera and Prableen Sabhaney. And there is Meena Chowdhury who, after months of persuasion, really got the book started with her precise, chronological narration. I would like to thank Marie and Tim Prentice, Nora Prentice, Erica and Hector Prudhomme, Margaret and Milton DeVane, J.S. Cox, Katie Reynolds, Betty Anne Cox and Lois Hager for their time and affection. And to Katherine Allen for introducing me to Fabindia Inc. in more ways than one.

The Fabindia story has been stitched together with the help of many people who have given me access to their memories and therefore their lives. I would like to thank Adhar Mirchandani, Amita Prashar Gupta, Amrita Verma, Barbara Schieffelin Powell, Bim Bissell, Bir Singh, Bob and Blaikie Worth, Charles Puttkammer, Charu Sharma, Faith Singh, Har Krishan Sibal, Joe Lelyveld, Kalyan and Anita Paul, Kiran Chainani, Laila Tyabji,

Lakshmi Jain, Madhu Mathur, Madhukar Khera, Meena Chowdhury, Meena Sharma, Minnie Boga, Monsoon Bissell, Naugaon suppliers (Golden Handlooms, Maulana Textiles, Mehboob Textiles, Nishad Handlooms, Raja Textiles, Shabana Handloom, S.K. Handlooms, Usha Textiles), Neela Sontakay, Nilanjana Bose, Oktay Yenal, Patwant Singh, Pogi Menon, Prakash Tripathi, Priscilla Conran, Priya Rao, Radhika Diesh, Rahul Gupta, Raj Kathuria, Ram Avtar Agarwal, Ravi Kaimal, Saurabh Mehta, Shaila Tyagi, Saveen Sharma, Sandhya Sakhuja, Shilpa Sharma, Smita Mankad, Sudarshan Madhok, Sunil Chainani, Suraiya Hassan, Townsend and Felicity Swayze, Tara Sahney, V.R. Prasada and William Bissell.

Special thanks to Monsoon Bissell who shared a daughter's legacy with me.

I would like to record my appreciation to Anita Duggal who dug out forgotten Fabindia files from dusty cartons and patiently set up my interviews around India. And thanks to my friends Alpana Khare and Sunil Gupta for their help with the cover and photo inserts, and to Laila Tyabji for unconsciously fulfilling her role as one of the icons in my life.

Thanks also to Ranjana Sengupta for her support and to Debasri Rakshit for editing my book and teaching me track changes. I promise not to be a first-time author next time!

My husband, Omkar Goswami, worked hard on this project on my behalf, demystifying figures and turning Fabindia's fifty annual reports into five-feet-long ready 'reckoners' for quick comprehension. He also wrote me a 'guide' to India's economic and political history between 1960 and 2010 from which I have quoted liberally. His support has helped me realize a long-awaited promise to myself to write a book.

At the end of it all I thank my parents Prem and Swaranjit for having shown me the way.